STEPPING INTO THE RIVER:
AN AMERICAN PSYCHOLOGIST IN MOTHER INDIA

Marc Nemiroff

ISBN: 151222345X
ISBN 13: 9781512223453

DEDICATION

To Mother India:

May you step into your River
Of purification
And protect your women of poverty
In their strength and dignity,
And their children,
With their resilience, vitality, and intelligence.

They are your great, untapped resource.

Protect them.
Aid them.

And may you be healed.

Jai Hind!

Introduction

Part One

Part Five

Part Six

Epilogue

AUTHOR'S NOTE

Stepping Into the River: An American Psychologist in Mother India is a work of non-fiction that describes several of my life experiences. However, the names and other identifying characteristics of all individuals and organizations mentioned in the book are purely fictitious. The only exceptions are my colleague in India, Asha Dutia; her husband, Gopal Dutia; my wife, Linda (Lin) Nemiroff; my brother, Ronald (Ron) Nemiroff; and my son, Gabriel Nemiroff, each of whom has graciously allowed me to use his or her real name. For these reasons, any similarities between the fictitious names and characteristics used in this book, as described above, and any real people and organizations are strictly coincidental.

INTRODUCTION

MARIGOLD LEAVES AND CORRUGATED TIN

In one of the unearthly 12th century CE Hindu temples near Hassan in the state of Karnataka, saffron-robed priests stood on ladders to reach the head of a twice-life-size statue of Shiva. They were bathing it in milk, pouring from pitchers and watching it cascade down the beautifully smooth bronze head and torso, down the legs and out sluices at the bottom. I didn't move. I doubt that I could have. I don't even know if I was breathing. After the milk, the priests applied a paste to Lord Shiva's forehead, neck and upper torso, and wrists. A slight breeze moved the hair on my arms, as I noticed a black pillar covered with pink, red, yellow, and green powder in the afternoon light of the temple interior.

Twelve pilgrims, in black robes, walking from holy site to holy site throughout Karnataka, noticed me and scowled. I was standing alone. The men were in a group. There were a random handful of other people walking around the interior of the temple in the musky air redolent of fresh and decaying flower petals, split coconut offerings, and incense.

Transfixed by the statue and the ritual, I stood completely still. Although I of course didn't understand it, somehow I felt it. After the paste was applied, the residual milk on the floor was washed through the sluices with water. Then the two priests climbed back up the ladder, each with a large earthenware red dish full of individual saffron and orange marigold petals. They let the marigold petals fall from the top of the statue's head all the way down the body and to the temple floor. The petals gently but swiftly slid off most of the statue, coursing down the smooth milk-soaked bronze, but they stuck wherever paste had been applied.

Within minutes, the milk-gleaming Lord Shiva was wearing a marigold orange and saffron crown, necklace, and bracelets, in full shimmering glory. I started to cry and at the same time one of the pilgrims, the primary scowler, started walking toward me with great purpose, followed by one of his fellow pilgrims. As he came close to me, his scowl, really his determination to speak, yielded. He said something urgent to me that I didn't understand. His follower friend translated, referring to reincarnation: "He says to tell you that you've been here before." After the translation, the "scowler" smiled and called all the others in his group over and wanted to talk about their pilgrimage. How had I been here before?

An image that had stayed with me from my wife's and my first trip to India was of the hutments filled with the people of Delhi, living in structures held together with ropes, glue, and hope. Again I was most struck by these towns-within-cities, and the people who created that intense density. There, I saw for the first time the ramshackle, make-do, crowded collection of corrugated tin sheets, plastic sheeting, shreds of plastic tablecloths, bamboo poles, hanging laundry still faded after washing, glass shards, rats at the beginning of their night patrol, and people, more people than imaginable on such a small amount of land, all constituting a hutment, a mini-city, a slum. It was an inhuman human-scaled anthill of living and inanimate refuse, society's discards.

We had travelled the typical tourist route around northern India, filled with the splendor of Mughal buildings including the Taj Mahal, dust, brown smiling spitting camels with red crepe paper flowers on their noses, traffic, the smells of dung, tar, sandalwood and tree leaves, paved roads morphing into sand, women working wearing colors to match the heat in intensity: turquoise, vermilion, purple. Many evenings, after all the palaces, the lotus-perfumed gardens by candlelight, the sight and the feel of the crush of people, the temples, mosques, and Sikh temple community *gurdwaras*, my wife and I would enter our hotel or guesthouse room and I would start to cry, overwhelmed.

India is often experienced as an affront or an assault on all senses, including the sixth sense. Others find the sometimes insinuating, sometimes immediately visceral sensual experience somehow just "right." I loved having my eyes confront colors too intense to stare at, my ears hear the beating of drums and banging of gongs in temples while simultaneously smelling floral offerings and dog urine, my skin feel the heat of the skin of people all around me as the Hindu priest unveiled the statue of the temple god after lighting incense and waving a curved candelabra, and my mouth overstimulated by the hot spices, cool yoghurt, and those highly sweet balls of fried dough, *gulabjamuns* in their sticky sweet syrup.

The wish to offer myself in some way, to try to do some small thing, to try to be helpful, felt imperative. To consider attempting to make some difference on even just a handful of 1.3 billion people, seventy percent of who live in horrifying conditions was and is madness. I also felt a religious obligation. As a practicing Jew, we are taught that each of us has a responsibility to try to "repair the world" (*Tikkun Olam*), and I was going to find a way to do that where my heart wanted me to be. My own sense of quivering immediacy, however, extended beyond this and I did not know why.

When out and alone, perhaps in the middle of a field, I was repeatedly overcome, with a stray tear coming out of one eye; I was simply overflowing. In the Hindu temples I felt at ease. I didn't understand why then, and more than a decade and eleven trips later I still don't. Now I don't care about understanding. I just know that it hurts to leave.

PART ONE

INTRODUCING MYSELF: A BAD BEGINNING SAVED: 2004

Resolved not to let more time go by, dreading a return without having acted on my conviction to try to make some difference, I acted quickly when we returned home. I was determined to network a connection on my own because I didn't want to associate with any umbrella organization. I don't do rules well and there were more than enough of them at home. I was aware that I would need to put myself under an Indian professional's formal supervision, and this is what I did, after finding the right person to make the right match. Within three weeks of returning home, I had my Indian contact, after undergoing a vetting process in the Washington DC area, my home. I offered a ten-year commitment as long as I could afford it; was healthy; might be useful; and wouldn't be a burden to anyone.

The person whose name I was given was Mrs. Asha Dutia, Marriage and Family Therapist, a cosmopolitan Mumbaikar

(Bombayite) who received her graduate education at The University of Oregon. My home contact had been her mentor. He had gotten in touch with her and asked her if she would undertake this project of working *pro bono* with this American clinical psychologist.

I had become a "project." I don't think Mrs. Dutia was looking for a project, nor a volunteer, nor was she then involved in any ongoing social action projects. But, as I understand it, her mentor had asked her to take me on and so she consented. Since she is not a person to undertake something she doesn't want to do, I truly don't think she was unwilling. Just...surprised?

Since I knew that her mentor had been in contact with Mrs. Dutia about me, I took this to mean that we had been informally introduced. Therefore, I e-mailed her using the most common American salutation, "Hi, Asha." I also signed it with my first name only. In response, I received a return e-mail with the formal salutation, "Dear Dr. Nemiroff." In the opening paragraph she properly introduced herself. The second paragraph, however, went something like this: "It is most appropriate when addressing someone you don't know to begin with 'Dear Mrs. Dutia' rather than 'Hi, Asha.' It is expected that you wait to be invited to use someone's first name.'" Her e-mail was signed, "Regards." I culturally misread "Regards" as part of the cultural upbraiding, when in fact it is the standard Indian ending to any e-mail.

Decidedly and embarrassingly, an inauspicious beginning.

But only a beginning. This cross-cultural gaffe would be forgiven as I expressed my apologies for my inappropriateness in my return e-mail. Indians are quick to forgive honest mistakes by foreigners. My correspondence was duly offered in proper form and the reply I received was signed "Regards, Asha."

From the formality of the earliest e-mails Mrs. Dutia, now Asha to me, and I — now "Marc" to her, evolved an increasingly engaged and warm correspondence. I had thoughts that the e-mails of those first eight months before we met each other would in themselves make an interesting book detailing the mutual orbiting of two strangers from two very different cultures. Alas, my computer had a brain hemorrhage and destroyed them.

Eight months of e-mail: could we work together? Could this Indian, American-trained Marriage and Family Therapist, and this American-trained psychoanalytically-oriented psychologist, find a common meeting ground and some projects to undertake for a first-year trial? We wrote at length of our philosophies of being with people, of where our common interests might lie, of what sorts of venues might be appropriate as formal psychotherapy of any stripe did not seem appropriate.

I think our first point of true meeting was our fierce joint concern for social justice.

PAST LIVES

Who were Asha and I? Where had we come from?

Asha is from a Rajasthani aristocratic family, with multiple siblings in several parts of India, none in Mumbai. Her interests have been ethnographic and focused on post-traumatic stress disorders in the people of Southeast Asia and Africa, suffering in poverty and living in war zones.

Asha grew up in a sophisticated, highly educated family and has, although she might not like my saying so, a quietly regal air about her. Patrician and iconoclastic, proper and sly, serious and witty. Her thinking is free-range but always grounded. She is a proud Indian and benignly chauvinistic: intensely proud of her culture, her country, her people. Always impeccable, whether sitting cross-legged in jeans with a whiskey in one hand, or dressed elegantly for an evening out. She maintains a consistent just-rightness, even when a bit anxiously attempting to get on to a Bombay Commuter Railway carriage right before it starts to move, or worrying whether I'm going to be able to make the leap onto the now-moving train.

She lives with her husband Gopal in the only flat in a block long building in downtown Bombay filled with businesses. He had an important career with UNICEF and has also been a force in the creation and organizing of international film festivals in Bombay, a friend of the great director Satyajit Ray and host to Louis Malle. He has a reputation within the world of serious Indian film criticism. Current film critics speak of him with reverence, his friends with deeply knowing affection.

The entry to their building is wedged between a vegetarian restaurant-cum-hotel and a large storefront public medical library. The wide staircase leading up to the lift is dark, the wood once well carved now decayed. Such an interior suggests an abandoned building. However, it houses perhaps thirty businesses on the three stories above street level. Asha and Gopal live on the top floor. The lift is required, as these stairs don't go all the way to the third floor but shift from a full-sized staircase to a bare wooden slat ladder to go from the second level to the third. The lift boy (a man, but men in service positions are referred to as "boy" preceded by a descriptor: the "lift boy" who runs the elevator, the "room boy" who cleans the hotel room, the "house boy" who serves the family he lives with) has therefore made himself an essential part of the building. As an American, the use of the term "boy," referring to an adult, has racial and discriminatory implications, hard to overcome.

Asha adores her city. While clear-eyed about all of Mumbai's problems, she is besotted with it and would choose nowhere else to live. When I am with her as we make our way around this enormous city, I can feel her become filled with her city and feel alive.

Bombay is her oxygen. Asha's curiosity is unending. She opens every window for learning that she can find (and cares about). She is interested in art, politics, dance, film, philosophy, literature, music, food, Indian culture, other cultures, and is currently a student of Vedanta (an Indian philosophy of Unity, as opposed to the more typically Western Dualism). She is also exceptionally discerning, hears every word, and is quick to call me on something she disagrees with. She also is quick to change her mind if my response makes sense to her.

I was born in Brooklyn. Brooklyn is technically part of New York City thanks to an election in the late 1890s, but to a Brooklynite there is Brooklyn and then there is New York: that which is not Brooklyn. My paternal grandparents were immigrants from Russia, actually the Ukraine, although they insisted they were Russian and did not speak Ukrainian. My mother's parents were alternately Austro-Hungarian, Polish, Ukrainian, and, finally, Polish. They never moved. The national boundaries around them did. All four of my grandparents emigrated to parts of New York between 1900 and 1910 to escape the oppression of Jews. My maternal grandfather was a tailor, his wife stayed home raising eight children. My father's father worked as a jewelry salesman; my grandmother cleaned houses and gradually became a Licensed Practical Nurse.

My father's parents, the "Russians," are the grandparents with whom I most identify and who were the most benign. They were interested in art, literature (particularly Russian literature), music (primarily Russian music but always Beethoven as well), and, especially, politics. They joined the American Communist Party, which at the time had nothing whatever to do with Russia and everything to do with American civil rights and social justice. They did not talk with me about any "glories" of Soviet Russia. I know that Stalin appalled them and that they were profoundly heartbroken by the clear failure of the promise of early Russian utopianism. Instead, they spoke of the human rights violations during the McCarthy era, and that it was a heinous crime to keep people from achieving their potential through economic and labor abuse.

They cared most deeply about social injustice, wherever it might be found, and since they were Americans, their concern was the failure of equal opportunities at home. Racial bigotry and economic exploitation mattered most. And so they taught me about the treatment of African-Americans in the south and of the inequity amidst American workers in American factories, living in American slums, employed by wealthy white men. A few years before she died, my grandmother with her cardiac condition was in the streets picketing the Republican National Convention.

HINDU AND JEW

As far as we know, Hinduism is the longest continuously active religion and culture in the world. Judaism is about two thousand years younger and is the second oldest continuing culture in the world. Asha and I share our pride in our backgrounds and often talk and compare how each of our traditions might understand a life circumstance. The longest-running discussion to date concerns the different understandings of what is the proper thing to do based on a famous Talmud scenario: Two men are walking in the desert and one man has brought enough water for one person to be able to survive the walk. The other man neglected to bring any. What is the man with the water to do? According to the Talmud, the protection of the sanctity of one's life is the greatest good. The man who possesses the water should not share it but should drink it so that he can survive. The taking of one's own life is impermissible. If he were to share his water, both men would die. For Asha, the two men should share the water and die together in friendship. She is, I believe, a bit appalled at the Jewish viewpoint and sees it as cruel. After many talks about this, we looked at the different beliefs that underlie each point of view. The Jew lives in the present. To take one's own life is an offense to God who gave that life in the first place; it is only God's to take back. For the Hindu, this life, ending for both men in the desert, is one of many in a series of lives, thus the emphasis on dying together in friendship and the dharmic addition of a good deed to the man who offered to share his water and thereby die. Asha and I will never come to agreement on this and it is an excellent example of two exceptionally different cultures at work.

WHERE TO START?

Asha and I had been introduced. We had made e-mail contact and I had been graciously forgiven for my overstepping the bounds of Indian propriety. I had been taught my first lesson in a cross-cultural partnership. Actually this globe hopping was unilateral; I was the one who did the hopping and needed to cross cultures. I learned from my e-mail error that I must begin from the Indian perspective. Later I realized that it was my responsibility to submerge myself in the Indian perspective. India had to be the home culture; this is where we would do our work. This Westerner was entering what I feel is the world's the most interesting and complex Eastern culture. I would come to learn when and how to leave America behind. But first, Asha and I needed to get acquainted via e-mail and a few photographs.

We "talked" for months about what we might do together, what was there in our professional background that could serve as meeting ground? Where could we begin, and begin to see if this voluntary alliance for me and perhaps imposed alliance for Asha might be viable and enduring. As I write, we have just completed the eighth of my promised ten years. I don't think we understood what we had somehow accomplished in the first year... a little over three weeks of work plus days of travel time, a month away from my office and my patients...until we were putting together the second year.

We decided to start with two projects: providing mental health services to abandoned elderly blind residents of The Institution for the Blind Elderly in the Maharashtrian countryside, and working with street children in a program designed for them in the heart of lower Bombay. Both of these settings met our joint requirement that whatever we ended up doing, it would be in the interest of the poor, the disadvantaged, the dispossessed, the discarded. The major part of all our work together over these eight years has focused on such victims of social injustice.

THE INSTITUTION FOR THE
BLIND ELDERLY: 2005

The Institution, unaffiliated with any larger organization, was first built many years ago when its town was a British hill station northwest of the city, past Matharan, an elevated and green place of refuge from the more southern Bombay city heat.

We took a train north from Bombay for hours, and then a taxi to the Institution. An orange and white metal art-deco gate, touched up by periodic repainting, marked it. The building stood in a dusty flat area, all its straight lines softened by stucco, with white outside walls and orange trim. Residents parked themselves on grey graveled stone benches in front. They sat alone, facing away from each other, three to a bench. Inside was a large, cool, dark and dark-colored entryway stretching the length of the building, occasionally visited by a stray cow or a group of dogs. The wild pigs stayed outside. The workrooms were placed on the ground floor: weaving, knitting, embroidery, chair caning, paper bag- and candle-making sections. The looms, made of strong wood decades before, provided a rhythmic smack-thunk throughout the compound. The men, some partially sighted, walked around in silence. The partially sighted men helped the completely blind ones. Downstairs housed the administrative offices as well. Staff maintained institutional hierarchy through the existence of separate bathrooms for themselves and penalties for residents who crossed the "elimination boundary."

The dormitories, each housing about thirty men, smelled stale, with walls of pale yellow flaked and peeling paint. Each man had an iron bed, a small dresser and a trunk. The following year, three women became residents in their own area of the building. The kitchen, also upstairs, necessarily highly institutional but with fresher paint, offered rather good food from a cadre of Nepalese cooks. Resident conversation confined itself to complaints about the food, small and large personal grudges, and resentment about wages. Men with grievances that run too deep need something trivial to cavil about.

Perhaps the most shameful thing that can happen to an Indian is to be abandoned by his family. The families of most of these men had summarily dropped them off at the Institution. These families either could not, or would not, take care of them any longer. The men carried a shame so deep that it was nearly impossible to talk about. These men, some of whom had lived and worked next to each other for ten, fifteen, twenty years, knew little of each other. Some didn't know if the man in the neighboring bed had any living family, if he had been married, had children, grandchildren, or what he used to do before coming to the this institution. Most of the men were born sighted and became blind as adults. Many were from rural agrarian areas and were illiterate. Some were from urban areas and had a college education. Several were relatively fluent in English. When filling out their initial papers, and asked whom to list for notification of death, many of these men said, simply, "Nobody."

The residents were, as Asha and I saw it, living in a state of psychological institutionalization. They passively followed the convenient rules, mostly did what they were told, offered no original ideas, did not talk to one another, and shuffled from place to place in a manner resembling psychiatric patients who had been hospitalized for years. They enjoyed complaining about administrative staff but only to themselves. The residents interacted minimally with the staff and almost not at all with each other. They shuffled to morning prayers, Hindu, Muslim, Sikh, and Buddhist (and Jewish, in Hebrew, when I joined them), shuffled to their work stations, shuffled to morning tea, shuffled back to their work stations, shuffled to lunch, then back to their work stations, back for afternoon tea, back to their work stations, back to their dreary dining hall for dinner, then shuffled back to the benches where they faced away from each other. At day's end, they shuffled off to their dormitories. Sixty-two men, living together for decades, knew almost nothing of each other. This increased their black isolation. Occasionally they would take a walk aided by their canes several hundred yards to a local store for crackers. Smoking, liquor, and homosexual behavior were all forbidden.

A few of the men had visitors; most never did. The majority were illiterate agrarian people, without book learning but not without wisdom. They had philosophical opinions although they would never call them that nor know what the term meant. They had a perspective on life as understood by someone who had been disposed of. They had stories of their Lives Before Blindness. But they didn't tell them. In the implicit agreement to hide their individual personal shame with silence, they prevented the creation of a community that might prove healing.

Asha and I were given a surface carte blanche: "Do what you want." However, we needed to provide some kind of report so the Administrator of the Institution did not feel excluded. Her interest was in maintaining the appropriate care of the residents' physical welfare. Their psychological care was not really of interest, yet. She had little curiosity about this but needed to be assured that we knew that she was In Charge. To be fair, without her willingness to accommodate us, nothing would have happened and so, whatever her motives, the men were given the opportunity to be exposed to mental health intervention focusing on their isolation, shame, and community-building.

NOW WHAT? OR, "PUT UP OR SHUT UP"

What were Asha and I actually going to do? I remembered my intensive training in a psychiatric hospital, years before, and therefore my experience of psychological institutionalization. I also relied on my training in treating groups. I had been taught about groups through the psychoanalytic work of British psychoanalyst Wilfred Bion. In this approach, a group is approached as a whole and the group consultant speaks to the group as a whole, refers to the group as a whole, and does not deal with individuals. "There are no innocent bystanders in a group" is the mantra. This was our first endeavor. I felt like this was a test. I think Asha more reasonably felt that this was simply a beginning: we would see how it went. We agreed to try this approach.

We decided to work in groups. It made sense given sixty-two residents and one week. We saw five groups of twelve or thirteen residents in ninety-minute sessions every day, with fifteen minute breaks in-between, and brief breaks for morning and afternoon tea and lunch. For much of the time, we sat on a large frayed carpet placed outside under trees, helping to get the men out of their dingy interior. They couldn't see but they could certainly smell the difference between institutional disinfectant and clean fresh leaves.

We selected as our theme the happy and sad aspects of life, hoping that this would give the residents some reason to sit down and talk. Experience is a balanced circle of good and bad and we gently and slowly asked the men to talk about their life experiences. They were a bit confused at first. Who *were* these people who wanted to know about them? We described ourselves, Asha, I, and the residents, as creating our own village for the coming week, meeting daily under the tree to talk. Gradually they started to tell their stories. Some men were willing to speak fairly freely, especially those who had been educated. This was initially in order to show off the fact of their educations. Most of the men were illiterate and from agricultural backgrounds. Almost all of the men relished being away from their workstations. All but a small handful had been sighted until mid-adulthood, when either disease or job-related accidents took away their sight. Only two had been born blind. Most had wives and children. All but the blind-from-birth had held down jobs either in their villages, in the fields, or in cities. I think the most important point is that almost all of these men had been productive members of society, capable of supporting a family and proud of it. They had been stripped of that ability: Insult Number One. They had become an increasing burden on their families: Insult Number Two. They had become an unbearable burden on their families: Insult Number Three. They had become unwanted, Insult Number Four, and then, the most appalling of all, they were abandoned, the Final Insult. No wonder they didn't want to talk to each other. The conundrum is that their common shame is what kept them apart. Our task was to try, as humbly and gently as possible, to make a dent in this and break the emotional and personally isolating deadlock.

Asha and I made clear efforts not to treat these broken souls as objects to be herded. After prayers, and breakfast, we announced to the entire population of the Institution that these groups would be happening and who had been assigned to which group. We stated clearly that participation would be voluntary. We asked the staff not to force anyone to participate. We said where the groups would be held and that announcements would be made regarding which group was meeting when. They were to get themselves to the meeting space under the tree, a real novelty. Sixty of the sixty-two men attended their groups throughout the week.

The men approached each group in lines: a partially sighted person was at the head with six or so men behind him, hand on shoulder down the line. The sighted men helped seat the fully blind men and then took their own seats on the carpet. (This is where I began to learn to sit cross-legged on the ground for long periods of time.) Asha and I explained that we were, for the week, creating our own village, and that since Asha and I were strangers, we would like to learn about everyone else just as they said they wanted to learn about us. India runs on hierarchies, and homes calcify hierarchies into something immutable. Asha and I were going to be different. We sat on the same level as the men; we would take our turn (if asked) answering the same questions we asked the men.

THE CONTEXT IS MY TEACHER

S o we began. The American kept referring to the group-as-a-whole, following his Western theory of group consultation. The American was most appropriately shot down within ten minutes. "Why do you keep calling us 'the group? We are each people." And so one outspoken man taught me a critical lesson. In thinking of the group as a whole, like the Westerner I am, we ended up working against our own purpose: to help the residents understand each other as individuals. Unintentionally embarrassed, I acquired a teacher: one man representing the group, who had spoken up to me. The hierarchy could begin to be broken. Quite simply, we were all people.

I learned another Indian lesson: I had the obligation to respond to the group differently. This ever-changing responsiveness to the context, stemming from one discarded but wise man's comment, is still my mantra. I used it then; I use it in all the work Asha and I do; and I use it at home. "It is my responsibility to respond to the context. It is *not* my responsibility, nor is it appropriate, to change it." The context is prime; I must work within it, account for it, understand it, alter my own views based on it. The context is my teacher.

The men took pleasure in their relief from the disinfected dankness of the confines of the Institution building and, under the trees, they were willing to talk from the beginning. Not, however, about their pre-Institution lives. They liked the idea of their group becoming its own, albeit short-lived, village and that those of us, all of us, in each group would get to know something about each other. The content of what was shareable was only complaints about the rules of the Institution. The matter of their discontent was the only joining point that they could find. The tea was cold. The food wasn't good enough. Meat should or should not be served (according to each man's religious tradition and level of observance). The Institution did not sufficiently police for theft of personal items. They also joined each other in their curiosity about the American psychologist whose English sounded unlike any Indian's English, and about America in general.

My foreignness began to become an asset, although it required our working in two languages: English and Hindi. Asha served as translator. It became clear after awhile that we really needed a translator for a third language: Marathi, the official language of the State of Maharashtra. Although a Mumbaikar for years, Asha doesn't speak Marathi and so we all needed a translator. India must be the mother referred to in the phrase "necessity is the mother of invention." Problems like this occur all the time and are somehow always solved. A junior staff "boy" linked himself up with us without our asking and we were set.

"What is it like in America?"

MN: "What would you like to know about?"

"How do they treat blind people?"

MN: "How do you mean?"

"Do blind people get put away in places like this? Do their families put them out? Are there many blind people? What do they do for money? Do you have any American currency on you?"

AD: "I don't think currency is what you're interested in?"
"Are Americans kind to the blind?"

I described my experience of the blind in my country and, most intriguingly, the use of seeing-eye dogs that allowed blind people to live independently. Asha and I chose to stay with the unusual (for the men), the use of seeing-eye dogs because we felt that this was a safe beginning. The men ever so slowly started to express their sense of damage, of outrage at how they had been treated, of feeling outcast. But this was the first group session and we didn't want to push. The turtle had let his head just a bit out of his shell. We didn't want him to go back into hiding.

The dogs of the Institution helped us out as they went racing through the middle of the group barking and chasing a wild pig, while a nearby wandering cow decided that the shade was just right in the middle of the group. We therefore had a circle of blind residents, Asha, me, a cow in the center, a pig running through, and a pack of five dogs chasing after it. It was easy to talk about another use for dogs in America. I'm still grateful for that wayward pig. He kept Asha and me from moving too quickly into painful feelings with men we had just met. For all I know, this may have been a daily ritual that the pig thoroughly enjoyed.

The day of groups went on, and by the second day the men were changing groups, attending multiple groups, wandering into and out of groups, but usually landing in one group and contributing. It took me awhile to realize that to my well-ordered fifty-minute-hour-every-patient-arriving-on-time-and-leaving-on-time-with-the-next-patient-waiting sensibility, the arrangement of moveable group members, cows, pigs, and barking dogs, was not the chaos it appeared to be. When I reviewed each day after dinner, I realized that all the men who agreed to participate had indeed participated and that the men were getting something from the groups—membership open—or else they would not have kept coming every day and talking.

At the end of the second day one of the residents, a blind musician, short and compact with wavy grizzled grey hair and a crude wooden flute, offered a traditional folksong, along with another resident singing as he played under the trees. The flutist finished and offered his translation "How good it is to have a friend. You don't have to see to know you have a friend. You can feel it in your heart."

The men began telling their stories after two days of our getting to know each other. These blind intimate strangers respectfully listened to each other and always looked, without seeing, in the direction of the speaker.

A tall, slim, seventy-two year old man in Institution-issue khakis began: "I had a wife and two children and supported them with my job. My eyesight started to get bad; I started to see two of everything. Then there were days when everything seemed very dark and other days when they were fine. I couldn't work at that job anymore so I tried selling fruit that earned less money but at least my children could eat. People started cheating me out of the right amount of change because they knew I couldn't see. I had to stop work and become a burden to my family. My wife said she would get another job and we would be all right but she wasn't making enough money and she was getting angry with me. I was so ashamed... (he began to cry) that I wasn't really a man because I couldn't feed my family. Then she told me that I couldn't stay there anymore; I was too much to care for because I didn't earn any money and I needed someone to take me to doctors. So she told me I had to leave right away. I had nowhere to go. She brought me here (sobbing) and left me. That was fifteen years ago and nobody has been to visit me. I will die here and no one will know."

A charming black-shirted man with a lilting smile, fifty years old, and wearing sunglasses, spontaneously took a turn. "I was a taxi driver and we lived in a small house just one room but we had enough to eat and my children never were hungry. They would get angry with me because sometimes all we could afford was dal every night but at least they ate. Some of the other families didn't have enough but we did. We never had any extra. One day I was driving my cab and I just stopped seeing. I knew where I was so I pulled the cab over to the side. It made the other taxi drivers angry. I thought it would just go away but it didn't. I kept not seeing. It never came back. I've been here eight years and I still can't see. I wear the sunglasses because maybe if I do start to see, the sun will hurt my eyes and I want to be ready. My family visits me two times a year, after *Diwali* (the festival of lights) and *Holi* (the festival of colors)." My children, there are two of them, both boys, are big now because I can put my hand on their heads and that way I know."

I heard the looms slam-thunking in the background and wondered how much of this naked sorrow could I bear.

A sixty-five year old man had put on a coat and tie for the occasion of this particular session. He stood up, at attention: "I was in the Army. Then I got out and got married. I loved my wife and she loved me. We had three children, all girls. I became a Christian and followed what Jesus taught. I tried to be kind and not hurt anyone. I had a job. Something blew up at the factory and a piece of steel went into my face and hurt both my eyes. They couldn't save my eyes. They could keep them in me but they wouldn't ever work again. My wife became angry with me." He started to shake. "She hit me. Can you imagine a wife beating her own husband?" By now he was sobbing and ashamed. He asked for a tissue which another man gave him. I needed one, too. "And then my daughters started hitting me and laughing at me and I couldn't catch them and fell over and they laughed at me. Didn't Jesus teach people not to act like that? Why do people act like that? I had nowhere to go. My brother didn't want me in his home in the village. I had nowhere to go so I came here. I don't know how long I'm here but it's a long time no one has been to see me." Two men, sensing his depletion, got up and gently helped him sit down. This man died within the year. I don't know the cause of death; he was not among the oldest of the residents. I wondered, perhaps a broken heart can be lethal.

One morning after prayers, the Administrator called me. "Dr. Marc, would you please spend some time with Mr. Oke. He's become violent again. Someone must have done something, that's the only time he reacts like this." I found Mr. Oke, in disheveled blue scrubs, yelling in English to the air, clutching his arms, scratching at himself. He had just assaulted another resident who had quipped about Mr. Oke not understanding some administrative directive. As he sensed my presence, long before I was close enough to speak to him, he became quieter. By the time I reached him he was rocking back and forth, rubbing his head, arching his neck, and mumbling quietly to himself in a mixture of Hindi, Marathi, and English. Mr. Oke was an educated man. He had a volatile temper that usually was set off when he felt that he wasn't treated with respect. He had idiosyncratic ideas about the gods, the grass, the sun, and his shoes. He perceived and misperceived others as treating him badly. I asked myself, what in the world does this Western stranger have to offer this man? And just what kind of task had I taken on in general?

I asked Mr. Oke's permission to stand next to him. He tentatively tried to find my hand to hold. As he could only approximate its location based on where my voice came from, I offered it to him. Same-gender handholding or other physical signs of respect and affection are common in India. It is cross-gender touching that has been traditionally unacceptable. I then put my arm around his shoulder and asked if he wanted to take a walk and talk about what had happened. "Oh I don't deserve your time; you're an important man."

"You deserve time because you're very upset, and…I'm not so important. I'm just a person."

"But you're a doctor." He kept his head down, as if ashamed of himself.

"Doctors are just people like everyone else." We walked, alternately holding hands or with arms on each other's shoulder. "Dr. Marc, I went to college."

"I wondered if you had, because you speak like an educated person when you're not too bothered by the others."

"They bother me because they treat me like I'm stupid."

"You get very bothered when you don't feel respected."

"Yes they talk to me like they talk to an animal I'm not an animal but they sometimes act like animals they can't even take care of a toilet I understand why no one comes to visit them but I don't know why my brother or his children don't come to visit me never have they come to see me and I have been here sitting at that front table answering the phone for many years and they never call and my brother didn't go to college and I did but no one comes to see me."

"And all you're asking for is to be respected. It's not so much to ask, is it?"

"No. You are a smart man smarter than me."

"I don't know if I'm smarter than you. I'm just not upset now and you are, because you don't feel respected by the people here."

We started to walk back to the main building and Mr. Oke told me of going to college and his compensations for his failing eyesight while studying. He spoke of special lights and magnifying lenses and expressed his deserved pride that he had finished college. He had found a job in an office but he couldn't function there. The lighting levels were too low and so he was let go. He was placed in his older brother's care but his volatility was too much for the family to manage. Thus he ended up in the Institution many years ago.

Mr. Oke came to his group session later that day. He was still somewhat agitated but much more in control of himself. He asked where I was sitting on the large rug under the large tree. I spoke and he came over, sat down next to me and held my hand. When he started to become more upset, he leaned against me, shoulder to shoulder. I felt like a friend had joined me. When it was time for the group to end its session, he spoke to me softly: "Thank you. I like you."

The men revealed further abuse and indignities, sorrows and grievances, as well as simple kindnesses. The less literate men spoke of their agricultural upbringing and some of what they endured. They spoke frequently, as almost everyone did, in metaphors. One man, in his eighties and quite angry, burst out: "Do you think it's right for a mother goat to make her kid mount her? And to do it over and over? This is WRONG. I say this again. This is WRONG. A baby (animal) belongs on the ground on all fours." Thus we learned of this man's forced incest with his mother, and he gradually shed quiet angry tears.

Over our days at the Institution, every resident, to a man, told his story. They treated each other with respect, always listening to each other, patting an upset member on the back, and somehow knowing when to comfort and when to keep distance. The always faced the person speaking despite the fact that they could not see the speaker and he could not see them. Day by day, they increasingly started to walk and talk to each other.

While we were at the Institution, my wife and I lived within the compound in a small, semi-detached cottage that had been made up for us. We were in the difficult position of showing gratitude for the trouble the staff had taken while living in these quarters filled with dirty floors and dusty furniture that housed various unknown insect species. The mattress smelled of mildew; mildew and mold decorated the walls in splotches; every breath we took was of mildew. We were clearly not going to win The Battle of the Mildew and the Mold. Out of the rotting bathroom window we could watch the peregrinations of the wild pig and its canine pursuers. I had wondered then whether the dogs would have somehow been disappointed had they ever actually caught the pig. The game would no longer be afoot.

On our last day, the men touched Asha's and my feet and moved their hands in the *Namaste* gesture to their foreheads to show their respect for us. And we, to their shock, touched their feet and, putting our hands in theirs, brought them to our own foreheads to express our respect for these men, their humility and their willingness to let us, and therefore each other, into their lives.

The home had planned an unorthodox act of respect and kindness to me. The original schedule had us present on Republic Day, January 26. This and Independence Day, August 15, are the two most important secular holidays in India. On January 26, 1935, the Indian Constitution officially replaced the Governance of India Act by Great Britain, an important step toward ultimate independence.

There are celebrations throughout India with a panoply of pageantry centered in the hours long parade in Delhi that begins with jet planes flying over, dropping saffron, white and green flower petals over the immense audience. I had attended this parade several years earlier. Bands play, military equipment is rolled out on display, each state has its own float, regiments of soldiers in dress uniforms march decorously. A regiment of caparisoned elephants and then a flyover of Indian jets in formation cap all this.

The Institution was planning its own modest celebration, beginning with the ceremonial raising of the saffron, white, and green Indian flag with its chakra wheel in its center. It is a great honor to raise the flag. It is reserved for Indian dignitaries, and Indian

VIPs. After all, Republic Day is India celebrating its recognition of itself. It is barely tied, in my experience, to the British any longer. Republic Day is India proudly stating, "I am India and I celebrate myself." Independence Day has more to do with marking freedom from Britain. Republic Day is thoroughly Indian.

The Administrator of the Institution had decided to offer me the honor of raising the flag, as a gesture of gratitude and an act of true generosity. They needed to acquire special permission from authorities. Permission granted, I would have raised the flag, quite humbled by the honor. Unfortunately, because of a change in schedule, we had to leave one day early and so this never happened. Still, the sheer loveliness of the gesture remains as if it did.

⟞⟝

From the former British hill station, we headed south by van to Bombay itself, where we would spend the rest of our time. Once within Bombay city limits, which extend for many miles, it took three hours to make our way to our home for the next two weeks, the Colaba Family Association International Guest House in southernmost Mumbai.

BOMBAY: "NOT IN KANSAS ANYMORE."

Bombay (Mumbai), 2005. A grey sprawl from street level, crawling with people: hawking vendors, shoeshine men, knock-off clothing laid out on a blanket on the footpath alongside sunglasses, sandals, motorcycle helmets, shoes, pirated CDs which may or may not have a CD within the knock-off jewel cases. Clothing jostles handicrafts that abut the sugar cane juice machine clanging loudly next to the lemonade maker who stands next to the master of luscious-smelling street food, unfortunately best left to the locals' and not Westerners' stomachs. All the sellers speak at once, either to each other, their neighbor on the street for years, or to passersby. The footpath is constructed of gracefully designed dark pink and grey curved bricks that do not stay in place. They are replaced every year and continue not to stay in place. Thus is work created.

The sky is unnoticeable because it is essential to look down at the jutting bricks, unpredictable holes in the street, broken cement, or mere slant of the footpath that separates the vendors on the street side and the proper stores on the inner side. It is often hard to find a particular store while negotiating the perils of the footpath and the lively hubbub of the hawkers. The emotion of the entire scene lies somewhere between animation and desperation. Add to this the occasional large, sari-clad, intimidating eunuch dancing for you on the corner and not letting you pass until you pay him something, and the flavor of the Bombay street scene becomes clear. The footpath teems with people: children in school uniforms, businessmen, college students, chai carriers, delivery men, shoppers, people on the way to or from work, everyday people going about their everyday business.

I usually experience the streets of Bombay as controlled madness that is somehow comforting, at least to this person who grew up navigating himself through the streets of Brooklyn and Manhattan.

The Bombay roads belong to the cars, buses, bicycles, and motorcycles. The red and green of traffic signals occasionally mean something, more often they do not. It is necessary to look in all directions, not only because of the possible unfamiliarity with the British system of left-is-right and right-is-left, but because a bike, motorcycle, or an occasional cabbie may decide that driving against traffic is somehow a more efficient way to get somewhere. Honking is *de rigeur* and seems not to signify "hurry up," but rather stands as a simple if noisy reminder that there is a vehicle behind.

Does this sound like a madhouse? Yes. But despite the dangers of even crossing a street, the vitality of this apparent mayhem has always been intoxicating to me. Strategizing how to get from one side of the street to the other, or how to run the gauntlet through the mass of hawkers is a bracing challenge, albeit at times a tiring one.

From a low rooftop, the city is ever so slightly less noisy. The chaos can seem choreographed and the sky is at last visible. Seagulls gracefully float over the skyscape of this peninsular city. Grey stone nineteenth century British Gothic style university buildings, mosques, large hotels, and new multi-story apartment complexes jut upward. Doing the arithmetic, adding the scene below with the scene above, I feel a sense of completeness. I love the vibrancy of the streets of Bombay, as I love its skyscape on those occasions when I can see it.

Bombay, therefore, is less a city than a person, a Being with a heart and a soul, full of good and evil, kindness and cruelty, charity and venality, saints and sinners. It lives, and it lives most fully. It is not a city filled with sites readymade for tourists' cameras; in fact sightseers, if they stop by at all, usually stay for only a day or two. The many things that make Bombay addictive, appalling, and appealing do not make it into guidebooks.

The most interesting aspect of this wondrous horrible indelible impossible city is that beating heart, right beneath those broken bricks on the footpath. To be in Bombay is to be a participant; the city demands it. It will never be a place that can only be observed. Its pulse will fill you and only diminish if you want it to. This is likely why every year, exhausted as I may be from nearly a month's grueling work, I am near tears at the thought of leaving.

THE COLABA FAMILY
ASSOCIATION GUEST HOUSE:
2005

I n Bombay, there are two types of places to stay, the deluxe hotels
that provide respite from the onslaught of the streets or hostel-
style accommodations. In other words, to hell with the budget or
watch every rupee. And then there are just a few anomalies, reasonably priced but rather basic hotels.

The Colaba Family Association Guest House, my wife Lin's
and my home every year that I've worked in India, manages to be
both startlingly basic and curiously endearing. The building is
slightly separated from its neighbor. Most rooms open on to an
outside hall overlooking a grey airshaft. The rooms are spartan.
Two narrow plank beds with three-inch mattresses of a certain
age. One flat lumpen pillow on each bed, of an even older certain
age. Most rooms have flaking paint on the walls, the effect of the

salt air of the Arabian Sea that closely surrounds the far southern Colaba district of sprawling modern Bombay. The curtains may be compatible with the yellow walls or they may be something like purple. There are two armoires, each with a safety lock compartment that may or may not have a working lock and may or may not have a matching key. The armoires themselves do have keys and working locks most of the time. The lighting is low, the product of two dim wall fixtures, one light over a table that serves as a desk, and two painfully harsh fluorescent reading lights, one over each bed. The bathroom has one fifty-watt bulb. It also has a narrow shelf by the unglassed louvered window (to keep the pigeons out), a sink that may or may not be sufficiently secured to the wall, and a shower with a quarter-inch high lip guaranteed to create a wet post-shower floor. The shower also contains a bucket and pitcher for a "bath" that creates a somewhat drier post-shower floor and guarantees sore knees. The Colaba Family Association Guest House does its best. But because of a chronic water shortage, it cannot guarantee twenty-four hour hot water. On some mornings, it cannot guarantee any water at all. This is usually short-lived.

On our first working visit, after our first look at the room where we would be living in this initially heart-sinking environment for almost a month, the Colaba Family Association Guest House began to work its magic. The room was, despite its worn and mismatched furnishings, quite clean. We discovered that the linens were changed and the floors washed daily. Fresh—worn but clean—towels were provided daily. The bathroom was inside our room, to our relief. The room boy and floor sweeping/mopping woman worked hard to maintain a well-kept space for guests. (It is still hard to refer to grown men as "boys." It has become more natural saying the words when in India, but the social implications are discomforting to my American ears.) Staff can be found every-where, all the time.

The Colaba Family Association Guest House has employees of many years' standing who look after its guests. They know very quickly who is in which room. They are concerned should you miss breakfast or dinner, included in the $75.00 daily rate, and will perhaps knock on your door to be sure you are all right. If you appear ill, someone will ask after you and see if there is any-thing he can do for you. There are people working twenty-four hours a day. Gradually, the discomforts become background and the attentiveness overtakes it. The Colaba Guest House begins to feel like home even though it is nothing like home. During the infamous attack on Bombay, when the Taj Mahal Palace Hotel (three blocks away), Chatrapati Shivaji Terminus (CST) train station, also known by its British colonial name of Victoria Terminus (VT), and other landmarks in this vicinity were held hostage by terrorists, the desk staff of the Colaba Family Association Guest House took it upon themselves to locate every person staying there to be sure they were safe, and offered to contact family anywhere in the world. Indian warmth and sense of duty trumps any luxuri-ous bed in an impersonal large hotel.

THE APARTMENT:
BROOKLYN, 1947

*B*rooklyn: the Madison section between Flatbush and East Midwood. The brick-faced, wood-framed apartment house sat in an endless line of six-story apartment houses separated from each other by no more than several feet of treeless concrete. Brown brick, yellow brick, red brick, pale brick, randomly repeating colors in randomly repeating apartment houses, perfectly aligned just so many feet from the curb. Placing the fire escapes on the sides and backs made an endless clean row of brick and window, brick and window, brick and window facing the street.

This apartment house made of dark red brick had been built twenty years before, in 1927. It had a concrete "backyard" intended for children to play. No tree grew out of this backyard's concrete, and children didn't play there.

The lobby shut out any outside light and was especially gloomy in late October when Brooklyn, and even New York, has the most beautiful late afternoon golden light.

The door to the apartment was locked. It was mid-afternoon and no one was home. The outside of the front door of the sixth floor two-bedroom apartment was painted dark brown streaked with ochre, like light brown highlights in a brunette's hair. Inside, the small entrance area, closed-in and dark, was perhaps a three-foot square.

It opened onto a small area intended as foyer. Forced to function as a formal dining room, it contained a wooden oval table that had been sanded and smoothed and painted a high glossy black. The chairs were also wooden and high glossy black. This dining area was pushed as close to the rear wall of the foyer as possible for there to be sufficient passage from the rest of the apartment to the front door, the way out. This area also contained the coat closet.

The inside of the closet was sardine-tin packed with jackets and coats suitable for all seasons and types of weather. The top shelf had empty boxes, gift-wrap, tissue paper, ribbons in shoeboxes, and one baby book with photographs. The closet floor was home to galoshes and a tool kit. Everything in the closet was ordered. The jackets and coats hung by season and owner. The gift materials were carefully stacked on the right side of the top shelf, the baby book on the left. It wasn't used much. The galoshes stood on the right side of the floor, easy to get to. The toolbox was not so important. The super could always be called when needed.

This makeshift but formal dining area, lit by a single 120-watt bulb in a modest fixture of the period, faced the living room. The living room was large, nothing "make-do" about it. It was perhaps twenty feet long and twelve feet wide. A twelve-inch television in a blonde wood cabinet was its centerpiece. It only looked like what it really was when the cabinet doors were opened. Two narrow windows precisely framed it.

The draperies, a source of great pride, were considered stylish: a repeated abstract design of black lines angularly crossing a grouping of three red-orange shapes on a bright white background. They hung against dark green walls, creating an opaque light, and matched the deep red-orange linear design of the scratchy club chair nearest them. Next to the chair was an ash wood low bookcase, of angular design and precisely placed to fall exactly on the middle of its long wall. The bookcase, like the television cabinet, was not what it seemed. It had been designed as a kneehole desk but was pushed against the wall so that it would look only like a bookcase. It had two bookshelves. In the middle of the first bookshelf a Zenith radio sat, perfectly placed in the center of the shelf. The radio had books on either side of it, as did the space below, nearer the floor. The books on those shelves were carefully arranged by vertically matched height and, if possible, by color. A tall book on the upper shelf had an equally tall book beneath. The books created a horizontal double wave: high to low and back to high. The contents of the books were irrelevant to their placement.

On the top of the not-a-desk bookcase stood a carefully placed tall ochre curved vase, exactly in the middle of the desk by length and width. Dried pussy willows filled it, the soft parts matching the ashen color of the wood. If a stem of the pussy willows fell out of place, it found itself repositioned by the next morning so it always looked the same.

Along the opposite wall sat a long, curving, deep green sofa, also made of scratchy upholstery, flanked by blonde wood coffee tables with matching nondescript lamps. The floor was covered with a tightly woven deep taupe carpet. It was soft to walk on but the nap was so tight there was never any evidence of a shoe or footprint. Although several magazines came to the apartment every week, only one was allowed out at a time and it had to be placed on the table to the right of the sofa. The other magazines were kept in the table drawer.

The living room, for its time, was seen as very fashionable. The room was used for a good deal of entertaining. However, it always seemed empty and it would be returned to its precision by the next morning as if nothing had occurred and no one had been there.

Pink glossy walls dominated the small kitchen and a grey Formica table was squeezed against the wall so only three sides were accessible. The dishes were always put away; the dish drainer always empty; and the refrigerator stocked with food for no more than two days' worth of meals. Two apples. Two pears. One can of fruit cocktail. One quart of milk. One loaf of bread. One stick of butter. Six eggs. One package of chicken breasts. The refrigerator's interior looked like a strange community of distant cousins, each in its own neighborhood because the various foods had their specific places on their particular shelves but somehow related. The narrow kitchen window opened onto a five-foot distance to the opposite apartment's kitchen window. This made for little light, a windowed wall of dark brown brick, but the borrowing of an egg was easy, as it could be hand-delivered across the outdoor narrow divide.

Through the kitchen was the parents' tiny bedroom. A double bed slammed up against the far wall, two windows that let in some light, and a combination dresser/desk/bookcase. A very few personal items lay on the dresser surface: a watch, some keys, and one small bottle of perfume. The drawers had carefully folded underwear and shirts and blouses. The desk, however, opened onto disorder. The ledger pads with overworked entries were not in a neat stack; the pencils had teeth marks, and the detritus of sloughed-off eraser rubbings collected at the bottom. The small pads for doing sums all had blank top pages but the indentations from previous arithmetic calculations were deep. The open bank statements, freed from their still present envelopes, had circled entries in different colors. Opening the desk made the air vibrate.

The windows in this room were the only ones that misted over on winter mornings. These were the windows that were good for making finger drawings in the moisture.

The bathroom was down a long hallway. It had an apple green tiled floor, green porcelain toilet with black seat, green sink, and a frosted glass window placed high above the green bathtub. No one could see what went on in there.

The baby's room was almost as large as the living room, sharing a wall with the parents' roomless room. Why did the parents choose their tiny room and give the baby such a big one? This was the brightest room. The two back windows faced the rear of the building. The fire escape was attached to the left window and obscured the light. The parallel window was the one place where the afternoon light, unobstructed by any neighboring building, draperies, or fire escape, could freely enter. It collected in that one corner of the room. In time, that collection of sunlight would become a haven, often a threatened haven. The third window faced a neighboring building. It was easy to look into various apartments but people rarely did that. It was as if there were invisible curtains on all those windows and an unwritten agreement that nobody looked into anyone else's place.

The baby's crib was placed near the middle of the room, for some reason on the diagonal. It could not be seen by neighbors, should they have chosen to look. The walls were a light chocolate brown and the floor was covered with a maroon carpet. There was a baby blanket folded on a blue-pillowed daybed, to be placed on the carpet when the baby was taken out to play. A few small clutch toys lay nearby. The wooden crib had narrow wooden slats. Next to it a changing table showed some of the same agitated attempted organization as the ledgers and bank statements hidden in the desk drawer. Cloth diapers, too many stainless steel safety pins glinting in the available light, powder, diaper pail, were all present and ready for immediate use, but otherwise conspicuous precision was quietly askew. Despite the appropriate appurtenances, this was a baby's room that did not seem a baby's room. The air was different in this room, its stillness disquieting.

MUMBAI 2005
THE STREET SPEAKS

Namaste!

Noon on a weekday and my footpaths appear clear except for the millions of people walking on the grey concrete and the hawking vendors in their black slacks and khaki or white shirts. Doesn't look like a residential neighborhood. However, by seven tonight, I will be filled with people living in their street homes. Having a street home is not the same as being homeless.

Look! Over there. Do you see the tree with the ash-colored bark that somehow freed itself of the concrete and is flourishing? In the crotch of that tree stands a postcard of Lakshmi, Hindu goddess of prosperity, all pink and indigo and gold. The postcard tells you that the space between the tree and the wall is a family's home. You enter it by stepping up on the curb and being asked in.

By the wall, do you see? A small pile of greying white-and-blue bedding, and brown and navy clothing. This family's belongings will stay here until tonight. Then the family will reassemble its scattered self. Children will come home; their parents will return from their jobs. One of the parents will cook a meager dinner of rice and brown, red, or yellow lentils—*dal*, perhaps with some *chapatti* bread picked up for a few extra rupees. The rest of the family will unroll the bedding, assemble their tin plates, and they will all have dinner. They may eat with their fingers as many Indians do. It brings them closer to the food. The children will try to do their homework, using the single light bulb that has been diverted from the public electricity supply in the knots of black wire overhead. The light bulb hides behind the wall during the day to hide the illegal tapping of power that users should pay for. The wife's mother-in-law will supervise everything, commenting only with her eyes. Five people live in the small space between Lakshmi and the wall. I feel the warmth of their poor bodies as they lie down for the night. They have been here for eight years, a long time without being forced to leave by the police only to find another tree and another wall.

A few steps down, also on the bare brick and fading white-washed wall, stands a single metal bed. At one time paint made it look white. It takes up very little footpath space and is left alone during the day. The bedding is rolled up, as are cooking equipment and clothing, and placed underneath. Nobody will bother it.

Seven people live here. The bed is not intended for comfort. It is for space. A mother and father sleep on it, hunched together, and because they are elevated there is space underneath for their two daughters. Their five-year-old son is in a sleeping bag at the foot of the bed. Their fourteen-year-old nephew sleeps a foot closer to the curb. He keeps the family's money in his pillow at night and hides it during the day. I won't tell you where. The family's street space is respected, as are its belongings. Its money may not be, and therefore must be watched, carried, or hidden.

Across the street. Do you see? Next to the portico of that building. Another seven people lie huddled. Two brothers and a sister, their widowed mother, her sister from the village and her sister's two adolescent daughters. The mother has taken them into her home to live with her and her own children. Both women work, sweeping and emptying wastebaskets. The older girls have small jobs after school. The family has placed a fragile, painter's tape blue tarpaulin above them, supported by two poles leaning against the wall behind and two poles gerryrigged into the sewer openings in front so that they will stand. Their home remains open on three sides, but is protected from above and by the wall behind.

This family has lived on me for ten years. They have fended off police threats of removal and "renovation" and "demolition," which are actually demands for bribes to permit them to stay. Bribe demands come reliably intermittently. "Rupees 14,000, please." (US $310.00) "Or move." The two women, people of dignity, to keep their home will prostitute themselves until they have Rs. 14,000 to give to the policemen. But only until then. The police will leave them alone. Until the next time. I wish I could open up and swallow the police who prey on these women, on all my families, and let them live out this life underground.

If you walk farther down, you will see one of my families that is lucky enough to have a blue canvas tent that they don't have to take down every night. They have also tapped into the public electricity wires running overhead and so they have a lamp and TV. The tent is eight feet by six feet and six people live here. Bedding, clothing, and kitchen equipment share the space. On one of the bedrolls is a copy of the *Gita*, so someone living there is able to read. The parents in this space make sure their two children are at school everyday. A canvas bag of basmati rice is elevated on the pile of clothing—off the ground and away from the rats and insects. This family has the comfort of knowing that everyone will at least have enough rice for dinner. They worry whether enough rupees can be earned each day for everyone to have enough lentils, for the children to have enough protein and the parents to have the strength to work. The tent can be closed at night so the rats are thwarted in their quest for food or babies' toes.

On my other side…look over those cars…tilts a tarpaulin and bamboo and back wall structure like so many others. The father has a space on the pavement for his shoeshine box. Each day's, rations depend on how many shoeshines he can cajole from passersby. He has to pay the local gangsters what they will demand monthly to keep his space on my footpath. Tonight he came home without having shined enough shoes. He is desperate and feels less a man because he cannot feed his children. As he enters the living space, his son is playing the radio loudly. SMACK! The father slaps his son. "Lower the radio; I can't stand it." His son, being a child of the streets, understands that it is his father's despair striking him.

As all my children come home, they help their mothers with chores. They wash pots, prepare what food there is. Sometimes, not often, there is enough for a full meal for everyone. They change their clothes if they have a change of clothes. Otherwise they wear their school uniforms until bedtime. Their chores are finished and it is still light.

My children then gather in groups and walk down my footpath to find their friends. Their brown eyes sparkle and white teeth smile as the boys start a pick-up game of cricket in a small, empty, sand and broken glass lot, and the girls dance to the soundtrack of the latest Bollywood film playing on a small black radio. They sing dance bat run and yell until the light starts to fade. Then they happily go to their homes.

They might pass the nook in the street where two buildings join at an angle. In this nook of mine lives thirteen-year-old Manjula. She hasn't the energy to join the other children. Manjula is preternaturally beautiful. She is rape bait but she hasn't been raped. She lives with both of her parents. Her mother works long hours cleaning houses, three a day if she can manage it.

Manjula is with her alcoholic father without her mother's protection in the early evening. His friends like to hurt her. They hold her down, pull up her school uniform and slash her buttocks with a razor blade until she screams. They enjoy her screaming. When she screams they get excited and laugh and grab their own crotches. They don't sexually touch her. Her screams are pleasure enough for them. They slash her beautiful face. Just one deep slash. Just one long scream. That is enough. They are satisfied. Manjula's mother comes home each night never knowing if this has happened yet again. What no one knows but I, the eternal street, is that thirteen-year-old Manjula will be dead in five months.

These are my families.
These are my children.

I celebrate them.
Sometimes I mourn them.

They are mine
And I bear witness for them.

They are too easily overlooked.

Sometimes all they leave is a postcard in a tree.

THE "SAINT" OF THE FOOTPATH

Near these street children in east Bombay and providing a haven is "*Friends of the Footpath.*" This is a before- and after-school program sponsored by a civic organization that provides a safe place for the children until they must return to their street homes. They receive tutoring from a regular rotation of sources as well as a modest but protein-rich meal provided by The Times of India.

The building is a large former church, taken over by the civic organization. It was built in the mid-nineteenth century of light grey stone and dark wood, with a wide central former nave and a small area for preparing food. Nothing more. There are remnants of stained glass, a stone tile and linoleum floor, the smell of faded sanctity, along with overhead fans that unaccountably keep Friends of the Footpath reasonably cool in the oppressive Bombay heat. A cast-off building to shelter the children of India's cast-off families every day after school.

The children sometimes stop by Friends of the Footpath in the morning, but almost always are there on school afternoons, dressed in their tattered uniforms. This place provides safety, the possibility of quiet or at least more quiet than they will find on the street, nutrition, and nurturing from its director, Manoj. The children refer to Manoj as "Sir," Hindi for "head" (the body part), as well as the accepted term of authority that he has earned. To attend "Friends of the Footpath," Manoj insists that all children attend school, for education is the only way out of poverty in a society that does not want its poor to rise from their penury.

Sir rules with a stern tongue and severity of tone that belie his love for all his children. The children respect him and love him and accept his discipline. He knows each of the perhaps one hundred youngsters who gather each school day. He will sometimes administer old-style, British-derived Indian-style discipline such as a smack on the palm or a swat on the bottom. Older boys who misbehave kneel on the floor with their hands above their heads for a period of time.

Asha and I wondered if these forms of discipline were abusive. After watching Manoj with the children and their responses to him after discipline, we decided that it was not. These ministrations were done with love. Manoj was truly trying to teach the children how to behave so they could make a good impression in the world outside, a world that looks down on them and doesn't want them. He wanted them to pass muster so they might overcome being societal discards. The children seemed to understand as they took their punishment with a look of respect and love for Sir. They repeatedly came up to him to show him their homework or some project or just to stand in his presence and take in his essential goodness. He could have held a *darshan*, the event where a holy person simply sits and acolytes come to sit near him, mutually, wordlessly, and partake of his goodness.

I saw Manoj Sir observe a poorly trained staff member hit a child on his back with a stick. He jumped up and immediately stood between the child and the offending staff member: "NEVER hit on the back. There isn't enough fat there and you will cause pain. We must never cause the children pain. Now put that stick away."

Manoj, age 56, has no illusions that he will save many of these children, "his children." He knows every child who has been through his program for the past twenty years. If he hears they have not shown up for school, he goes to their homes and takes them to school. He maneuvers scholarships for the motivated brighter students so that they can attend college, which is the equivalent of the American junior and senior years of high school. He lets nothing stand in the way of helping his children make progress and accepts with equanimity that most of them will not. He is realistic but unbowed.

Manoj comes from the street. As an adolescent and young man he was forced to live there. He knows what being a street person is. Now he is well educated and lives with his wife and beloved daughter, Priya. He extends himself fully for the sake of the children, even checking demolition sites and negotiating for materials to improve the shabby quarters of Friends of the Footpath. "His children" deserve his efforts. He even managed to equip a small playground with donated materials. I am sure he was instrumental in The Times of India providing food. Manoj Sir understands that if Friends of the Footpath can provide a solid meal, then there is a greater chance that a child's family will let her go to school instead of being sent to work at age ten. He knows that if he cultivates the education of the brightest of the Muslim youngsters, they are less likely "to be married off at eighteen instead of using their God-given brains." He has, on occasion, taken some of these children into his home for private tutoring if they are children of promise. He does all of this on the most meager pay.

Sir delights in his children's progress, takes personal pride in their growth, and mourns without despair the losses of children: children who move away, who leave school, who die.

<hr/>

Sanjay is a success story. I met him at Friends of the Footpath when he was twelve. He is now a handsome, vibrant, endearing, loquacious, curly-black-haired twenty-one year old. I saw him there recently, in 2013. He remembered me and came over, most animated.

"Do you remember me? Let me tell you something. I owe everything I am to Sir. He kept me going to school when I wanted to stop. He got me into college when we had no money.

"When I graduated I started working for a seller of fish to restaurants. Then I realized I could do this by myself. You have to really think, how much fish is coming in and how much fish will restaurants need? What day is it? Is it a weekend when people go to restaurants? You have to be smart and set your price so people will buy but you make money too. I'm good at it. I learned how to think that way in college.

"I make enough money that I pay for my younger sister to go to a private school and not the bad Municipal slum school I did. I have enough left to give my mother. But I have to be home every-day by five because my grandmother is waiting for me. It takes an hour and a half to get home. She says she won't eat unless I am home and she can see I am all right. We eat together. Then I go back out if I want to.

"Before I go home so my grandmother can see me and she will eat, I sometimes come here to Friends of the Footpath and do the art lessons when the art teacher can't come. She calls and asks me to help. Then I get to see Sir and help children like he does. Someday I want to do what he does, take care of poor children so they can make something of themselves."

⇒⋅⇐

Sir is one of the two authentically great people I have had the honor of knowing in India, perhaps anywhere in my life. Manoj would be deeply embarrassed were he to read this.

A DAY AT "FRIENDS OF THE FOOTPATH"

It is ten a.m. Children are milling around outside the closed building. They are both very young children who have come to have a safe, supervised place to play and a meal and older children with afternoon rather than morning classes who have come for a safe place to study or talk and to have a morning meal. They are waiting for Sir to arrive.

Manoj Sir drives up on his fifteen-year-old motor scooter wearing his signature white helmet. He opens the former church. The children run in. The little ones take down the small tables and stools and set up a carom board. The older ones turn on the fans and open the large dark wooden windows that have shielded the former nave for the evening.

Mornings are quiet at Friends of the Footpath. Children are safe.

It is in the afternoon that the place buzzes and hums and quivers with activity and energy. Sixty children, sometimes more, arrive from school, representing all grade levels (Standards). Six to sixteen year olds are bustling around, settling in with their age-mates to receive help with their homework. They are noisy until Manoj lets out his characteristic "*Eh!!*" with a deep resonant bellow.

There usually are volunteer tutors for the children, working with them in groups on their assignments. Tutors come from Canada, England, and Australia, rarely from America. They usually have no training and do the best they can. These tutors stifle their frustration and try hard, sitting on small stools at small tables in the large and dark former nave.

The children don't understand their lessons. The tutors come with Canadian, English, or Australian notions of what children these ages should easily know. The foreign volunteer tutors earnestly try to help. They may often be shocked at the poor foundations of the children's learning.

The children's world, however, is the Mumbai footpath and the immediacy of need. They have no place to study except Friends of the Footpath. They may try to read by streetlights or a single light bulb under a tarpaulin, but they must more importantly be aware of who is walking by the footpath space that is their home. Is it safe? Is there enough food? Is there enough clean water? Is mummy crying a lot today because there isn't enough money? These street children don't have the luxury of time to study the geography of Ghana or the conjugation of the English verb "to be," or to learn the modal auxiliary as a figure of speech. The insistence on including such things as the modal auxiliary in the curriculum for children learning English as a third language, living in communities where they never hear English, is symbolic of the Mumbai school system's backward-thinking, apparently uncon-cerned, colonial, unrealistic nature. There is no taking account of the children's context.

In school, the street children are often treated with condescen-sion. It is the rare and wonderful teacher who takes the trouble to notice a youngster's difficulty in math and try to help her. Why help a human piece of nothing, condemned to live a discarded life due to economics and politics? Her only use will be as cheap, poorly educated labor, perhaps the wife of an alcoholic who strug-gles to protect her children? No wonder this child's learning is fragile. There is nothing fragile about her capacity for resilience, however.

There are other tutors, however, local to Bombay. They are the Upper Standard students of several of the quite posh schools who receive community service credits by "helping out" at Friends of the Footpath. These students, with some exceptions, most often stand around together talking to each other, with looks of dis-taste and condescension at what and whom they see around them. Their drivers will pick them up in the family car soon, please let it be soon. They arrive late, look at their watches, and leave early. Manoj Sir has quite a lot to say about this and sometimes he will say it to them. This shapes up their attendance but does not penetrate the class hierarchy attitudes.

A few years ago, Sir hired an assistant. Veena is dedicated to Manoj and to the children. She is factotum, tutor, teacher, re-source, bookkeeper, and the strong female presence that, along with Manoj, helps create just a small sense of family within the confines of the former church that welcomes these children sev-eral hours every school day.

Friends of the Footpath is alive with the sounds of children talking, tutors trying to teach, Sir and Veena keeping things in order. Every time I enter that idiosyncratic make-do space, I am moved by how the children's eyes shine and their white teeth sparkle and curve into a smile, and their bodies move with grace and unbroken energy, despite the way they are treated out in their world and despite the fact that they are quite aware of how they are treated. They remain open when you would expect them to be closed, funny and impish when they should be bowed down with the weight of their lives, eager when they should be sullen. They are the unmined gold of their country.

Four o'clock: time for dinner. The food has been delivered. The children stack the stools on the low tables and clear the once-nave into an open area. They take turns sweeping the floor. They stand in two lines, boys on the left and girls on the right, ready to recite the Lord's Prayer. There may be a few Christian children, but most are Hindu and Muslim. Sir and Veena are devout Christians. The prayer is experienced as words pertaining to Something Greater. Its words serve to separate all the activity that came before, with getting ready to take a meal. It is a prayer of gratitude and the children in fact are grateful. In their moment-by-moment lives I am not sure that they are aware of their gratitude. But it is there. They are in a place, for these few hours, every school day, where they are safe, where they are cared for, where Manoj and Veena love them, and where they can eat.

After the Lord's Prayer, the children sit cross-legged on the floor and pass tin plates to each other. They are served, and take turns serving each other, a nutritious meal of rice, dal, and another vegetable. If it is the time of the Muslim eid of the goat sacrifice, those non-vegetarians may have the luxury of donated goat meat. They talk and gossip and eat, rinse their tin plates, sweep the floor again, close the windows, and head onto the footpath towards their rolled-up bedding, seeking the postcard of Lakshmi in the tree, and wait for their parents to return for the evening.

Manoj Sir and Veena stay to do paperwork; they are responsible to the civic organization that is funding Friends of the Footpath. They lock the building. Then Veena walks to Churchgate Station to take the train and Sir gets on his motor scooter and heads home to his wife and daughter, about whose education he feels so strongly.

OUR WORK AT "FRIENDS OF THE FOOTPATH," 2005

Asha and I began working therapeutically at Friends of the Footpath during our first year of collaboration. We decided to see selected children in small groups of six to eight. As at the Institution for the Aged Blind, these groups quickly became fluid. The six familiar faces of Tuesday might be four of the same and six different faces on Wednesday. One youngster may have asked her friends to join. Another may have had to study for an exam. Another might join a different group. This destroyed the Western group psychotherapy idea about continuity of attendance, but within the Indian street children's come-and-go context it made perfect sense to them and I believe something therapeutic occurred each session. As Asha was unfazed by all the shuffling of people, I knew that it was my responsibility to shift my thinking about groups. At Friends of the Footpath, with street children who live in the Ever-Now along the footpaths of Bombay where four or five million of its eighteen million people are children on the street, amidst the working chaos of this miraculous city that threatens to fall apart but never does, the comings and goings of group members were simply part of the way things were. I could either accept and learn to work within this framework, or judgmentally decide that the therapeutic situation was unworkable, pack up my marbles, and go home.

Although at first disconcerted, something I no longer am, gradually I even came to enjoy this "who the hell knows what will happen next" atmosphere. It kept me on a constant alert; it loosened my Western rigidity; and I started to learn three critical things that I have brought back with me to my work at home.

1. Always account for the context.
2. There are things that do not require interpretation.
3. Children, some of these children, have greater dignity and knowing than many adults.

The children wanted to discuss, actually I think they wanted to teach me, the foreigner, about what it was like to live the way they did. They were devoid of self-pity. They described their homes. The children in hutments had some pride in the relative permanence of their homes compared to the children who lived directly on the footpath. Nevertheless, they assumed an outside threat from the authorities to that permanence. They lived in a state of permanent impermanence. One of their great pleasures was Bollywood music and dancing. The Bombay-based Hindi film industry, Bollywood, markets yet-to-be-released films by placing the music and videos on the radio, in stores and on TV prior to release of the film. These are not teasers but rather the whole song or video. Going to the opening night of a new Bollywood film is a great occasion and an expensive one. Some of the children made extra money by being the street scalpers for overpriced first night tickets. The youngsters learned the latest dance moves.

The young and mid-adolescents in our groups did not have a sense of future. It was a meaningless tense. They lived in the moment; they learned in the moment; they acted in the moment. Grasping the idea that going to school could lead somewhere was difficult. We spent much time talking about what they might want to do, in just a few more years, once they had finished their nominally mandatory schooling. In other words, we wanted to convey that it was possible to have a future, to work toward a future, a goal. Most of the youngsters finally landed on such occupations as teacher, doctor, and, vaguely, engineer. They had some nebulous notion that you had to work, somehow, to accomplish these goals, but nothing more. Nevertheless, we tried, intrepidly but feebly I suspect, to instill the beginning of the idea of a future.

Both the boys and the girls felt strongly about teaching us about their lives. They described their homes in detail. They did not stress how crowded their living conditions were. They focused on permanence or impermanence. They spoke a great deal about their families, about their worrying mothers and frustrated fathers. Discipline was generally a cuffing, not a beating. We were told about how hard mummy and daddy worked, how they worried about paying off the police so they could stay in their footpath or hutment homes, how they never knew if there would be only rice or both rice and lentils (source of protein) when they got home, how daddy would hit them harder if he didn't have enough money for lentils. One boy liked to play the radio loudly. If his father came home upset, he knew that if he didn't lower the radio he would get hit. He did not lower the radio. He said he saw it as his right. He also, I think, wanted to provoke his father. It is my impression that he was helping his father save face about not being able to provide for his family by giving his father some specific defiant behavior to hit him for.

Here is Rosie, who wanted me to be sure to "tell everyone in America" her story. (She checked the following year to be sure that I did tell as many people as I could about her. I had.) "I worry about my mummy. She cries a lot. She has always cried. I was still in her stomach when she saw my father get knifed on the footpath where he had his shoeshine box. He wouldn't pay those men any more just for being allowed to shine shoes on the street there. That was his spot and the street was free and he wasn't going to pay those people because they didn't own the street. After he took the knife out, he went home. He was all bleeding. Then the men came and shot him dead and my mother saw it. She has been crying since then. She has been crying since before I was born. We don't have the same place to go back to sleep every night and now my mother cries because she worries everyday will I find where we will be sleeping tonight. What I wish for more than anything in the world is a place where we know we can sleep because maybe that will help mummy stop crying."

When Asha and I asked her how she felt telling her story, she said: "It lightens my heart to let you know my story."

They also told us about their cricket games played in empty lots, football (soccer) stars, and their pride in India as a prize-winning cricket country. In fact, cricket is now played more widely in India than any other country. We realized that they didn't have a sense of what India actually was, geographically. They were aware of the neighborhood they lived in, when they lived in it. They knew their city was Bombay ("Bombay" and "Mumbai" being used interchangeably, as I am doing as I write). They did not know that

Mumbai was part of the state of Maharashtra or that India had almost 30 states.

We found a map of India on the wall and taught them a song to perform on Friday night, a big night at Friends of the Footpath. It was a variation on Woody Guthrie's "This Land is Your Land," with Indian locations replacing redwood forests and Gulf Stream waters.

"This land is your land,
This land is my land,
From Maharashtra *(western state)*
To Tamil Nadu. *(Eastern state)*
From the Himalayas, (Him-AHL-ye, *farthest north*)
To Kanniyakumari *(southernmost point)*
This land was made
For you and me."

We were readying for the Friday night performance.

A SLEEPING BOY: BROOKLYN, APRIL 1947

*I*n the apartment, in my room, where the crib is placed near the middle of room, it is time for my afternoon nap. I am six months old. My mother has put me in the crib and put a blanket over me. Her eyes look at me and yet don't look at me.

What do I see? Something has happened to her eyes. I also see the edge of her mouth curl. I have learned to know what my mother feels by watching her closely.

My mother, at first simply unsmiling, has become someone dangerous to me. I know it; I just know it. I am not safe. There is no one to take care of me.

We are alone in the apartment. I know that, too. My mother's eyebrows narrow. Her lip curls. The look in her eyes is dangerous and mean. She turns away from me and comes back quickly. She holds one of the blue *pillows from the day bed. She holds the pillow right over me. The pillow comes down, not quickly, onto my face. I try to cry out.*

(My breath)	**uh' uh' uh' uh' uh' uh' uh' uh'**
(My heart)	tun *tun* tun *tun* tun *tun* tun *tun* tun *tun* tun
	tun tun

My mother holds the pillow even tighter against my face. I can't hear my own cry anymore.

Uhhhhhhhhhhhhhhhhhhhhhhhhhhhhhhhhhhhhhhhh
hhhhhh
tun *tun* tun *tun* tun *tun* tun *tun* tun *tun* tun *tun*

The blue disappears. There is only black. And silence. I feel pressure in my upper arms, pushing against the pillow.

Now I can see a little blue again;

huh huh huh huh   huh   huh   huh
tun *tun* tun *tun* tun *tun* tun *tun* tun *tun* tun *tun*

the black quickly returns.

Uhhhhhhhhh ahhhhhhhhh uhhhhh aaaahhhhhhhhh
aaaaaaaaaaa
tun *tun* tun *tun* tun *tun* tun *tun* tun *tun* tun *tun* tun *tun* tun
tun

My legs still kick, but my body and my throat are getting tired.

Uh uh   uhhh uhhhhh
tun *tun* tun *tun* tun *tun* tun *tun*   tun *tun*   tun *tun*

I stop screaming. I stop pushing. My legs are slowing down; they are al-most still.

Quickly I see the blue of the pillow again.

<u>Huh huh huh **huh huh huh huh**</u>
tun *tun* tun *tun* tun *tun* tun *tun* tun *tun*

The pillow is now gone. I can see the ceiling of my room and then I see my mother's face. Her curled lip has become even scarier. It almost looks like she is going to laugh. She waits. I breathe.

<u>Huhuhuhuhuhuuuuhuuuuuuhuuuuuuuuuu</u>
tun *tun*   tun *tun*   tun *tun*   tun *tun*   tun *tun*   tun *tun*

I flap my arms because they hurt. My tired legs hold still. She is done. It is over. This time.

FRIDAY NIGHT AT "FRIENDS OF THE FOOTPATH"

The doors are open every Friday night at Friends of the Footpath, when it becomes a neighborhood haven. This is the time for unschooled children and sometimes their mothers to come for a meal. Homeless youngsters without access to water have the opportunity for a weekly bucket bath. Children in rags receive clothing that has been donated. The "regulars" at Friends of the Footpath provide entertainment and, above all, these shelterless, hair-matted, sometimes disfigured, always hungry children receive a nutritious meal. They may be as young as three or as old as eighteen. My wife has joined Asha and me for this evening's activities.

The former church fills up with two hundred often-rowdy children. The fluorescent lights keep the once-nave dimly lit. A television plays for a while, a fleeting diversion from desperation. For many of these children, Friday night at Friends of the Footpath stands as their only reliable stability. These are the children seen begging, with no known place to sleep. These are the children who own only the clothes that are on their thin bodies. These are the children who cannot go to school because they must do some kind of menial work, as do their parents, to bring in even a dime's worth of rupees a day. Some have no parents. All are hungry.

And yet the mood in the once-nave of Friends of the Footpath does not reflect the desperation of the children and some of their parents. The place buzzes with activity and noise. The children play ball, dance, swing each other around. Once I was sitting on a table watching this scene when the four-year-old guardian of his one-year-old brother thrust the baby in my arms for caretaking while he ran off to play, relieved at least for a while of his duties. He returned ten minutes later to reclaim his charge. I felt like a benign baggage-check man. The children pull me up to swing them around or to try to teach me (impossible task) Bollywood dance moves. A seven-year-old Footpath regular surreptitiously slips a drawing into my hand and runs away. He knows this is our last day and although he doesn't know where America is, he knows I will be in an airplane for a very long time. His picture is of a plane flying over the former church of Friends of the Footpath, with a clear cross on the church. He is wishing me a safe journey. Clearly, the dim fluorescents don't matter; the children provide the voltage in the room.

Time for entertainment. The Footpath regulars have prepared a new dance, as they do every week. Everyone sits down in rows, boys on the left, girls on the right. The difference between sitting down and settling down is corrected by Sir's sonorous "**Eh**?!!!!!!" The fact that the commanding voice issues from Manoj's equally commanding physical presence helps maintain relative order.

The entertainers are in their saris and ready. The CD player starts to boom and the girls start to move. Their graceful arm movements contrast with their sharp-angled gyrations. The boys, with unbuttoned shirts, raised collars, low-cut slacks, start to join them. Their acrobatics are impressive and the audience lets out whoops when the dancing becomes both more physically daring and more suggestive.

After the dancing, the children anxiously ready themselves to sing the Indianized version of "This Land is Your Land." Twenty of them, with Asha and me with them holding timid hands, step up to the microphone and deliver the song. Shyness disappears after one line, and the children sing out full-throatedly to much applause, despite the fact that most of the audience doesn't understand the English they are singing or the geography they are singing about. The language difference does not diminish the pleasure.

As mealtime approaches, the children become more serious. I physically sense the need and the hunger, the respite from the desperation of tomorrow, contained by the formerly hallowed, now neglected space. I am awed by what is happening. The regulars and some of the adults pass out the tin plates to two hundred hungry children. Then the rice, the lentils, vegetables, and Maharashtrian square soft bread for sopping up the sauce. The children all sit cross-legged. Some eat very fast, as if their stomachs were internalized monsters that would eat them from the inside out if they were not fed. Others eat slowly, seemingly savoring each individual grain of rice and trying to retain the oral experience of food in their mouths for as long as possible.

This much hunger should not be allowed to exist. But it does and it is here. All one can do is to try to take the edge off it the best one can. What else is there?

When the children are finished, they get up, dip their now empty tin plates into a bucket of water and put them on the stack to be washed by the adults and some of the Footpath regulars. Then the children are given one small banana and a chocolate bar, a little something for tomorrow.

It is fully dark out. The children are leaving, some of the adolescents hanging around outside, prolonging their proximity to this safe place, and, I think, their closeness to Sir. The former church is empty. The lights are being shut. The space has, for this Friday evening, been re-sanctified by the children.

As Asha, my wife, and I leave and walk into the churchyard, several teenage boys come out of the dark and stand in front of us, looking. We wait. They offer us their bananas and chocolate, all they have for tomorrow, as gifts. We accept them and the boys leave. We continue walking and, sure that we cannot be seen, find three children to give our gifts to. Hungry children are easy to find.

PACKING AND DEPARTURE
OR
"ARE WE GOING TO GET THERE ALIVE?"

The next day is free for packing, generally putting things in order, dinner at Asha and Gopal's, and the trip to the airport at midnight for the two-thirty a.m. flight from Bombay to London, a flight clearly scheduled by a sadist at British Airways.

After breakfast at the guest house, during which much of the staff says goodbye warmly, we go to our room and take out our suitcases. Putting my things inside is arduous. Everything is heavier than it was when I packed this suitcase over three weeks ago in suburban Washington, DC. All my clothing is freighted with my sadness that we have to leave. The work for this year is done. Asha and I have seen how clear it is that we can, and should, work together. My wife has taken pleasure in supporting me and in finding her own way to be in the city.

I don't want to go home. I want to go home. I don't want to go home. I don't want to leave the blind men, nor the staff, at the Institution for the Blind Elderly. I don't want to leave Asha and Gopal and all the people we have met, so many of their friends and relatives. I don't want to leave Manoj or Friends of the Footpath. More than anything, I don't want to leave the children. No, more than anything I don't want to leave India. I have had the same feeling on previous visits when touring, but this is different. It is not the India of romance and spirituality and architectural and artistic splendor that I don't want to leave. It is the India of the streets, the homes that die by daylight and are reborn at night and the people who live in them. I know some of them now. I don't want to leave the murmuring heart of Mumbai that lives beneath its streets.

The suitcase, just one for three weeks, is now packed, most of the clothes much the worse for wear. The carryon, full of our regular prescription medications, a pharmacy of mostly unused "what-ifs" for infections, gastrointestinal explosions that never happened, bandages, and other possibilities, is reassembled. The books I didn't have time to read are back in their place along with the journal I didn't get to keep.

We go to Asha and Gopal's airy flat for dinner for the last time. We've spent much time together: dinners out, dinner parties at their home with so many of their cosmopolitan friends, English-speaking experimental theatre on which we walked out, dance concerts, and Gopal and Asha's beloved movies where we got simultaneous live translation while watching a film primarily in Hindi. I thought we would be bothering people, especially when the man behind us tapped me on the shoulder. But he said to

Gopal in American English, "Thank you so much for translating; it was a big help."

I will not miss the eunuch who works the street corner near the Colaba guesthouse, intimidating passersby into parting with Rs. 500 for the pleasure of his dancing on the street. I will not miss the beggars. I will not miss bathing out of a bucket despite my pride in learning how to get fully clean from half a bucket of tepid water. I will not miss the relentless hawkers on Colaba Causeway or walking down to the Taj Mahal Palace Hotel near the Gateway to India.

And yet at the same time I will. They are part of the enormous mosaic that is India. This place has a completeness that fills me to bursting and that I have not found and cannot find anywhere else. India's contradictions make for her completeness.

We are driven to the airport, a one-hour drive under the best of circumstances, two hours under usual circumstances, longer depending on the mood of the traffic. British Air says they want us there four hours in advance. We are compliant for the first and last time. Asha refers to our driver as "The Flying Sikh," and indeed fly is what he tries to do. He races for the airport, although we have left with time to spare. Honk. Rush...SLAM ON BRAKES. Breathe. Honk. Rush (somehow in traffic backed up for miles)... SLAM ON BRAKES. Honk. Jump the curb. Honk. Drive on the footpath since no one is walking on it. Oops; here comes someone. Honk. Slide back into traffic. Motorcyclist going too slow. Brush him aside and send him flying. Honk later. Rush...SLAM ON BRAKES. Honk. Scrape another car to create another lane. Much cursing but KEEP MOVING. And honk.

Arriving at the airport, I realize that I have examined my life three times in the course of the ride there, entered an altered state, and gotten a stomach so knotted that I can barely stand up. The Flying Sikh is very helpful in getting a cart and keeping the vulture-like aggressive red caps away from us so we can get into the airport. I give him a large tip for getting us there alive and off he goes, with a honk and a wave.

PART TWO

RETURN – 2006

My wife and I learned the year before that nineteen hours of flying, including a multi-hour layover and 1:00 a.m. arrival, is not the most sensible way to reach Bombay. We began overnighting in London and taking a red-eye from Heathrow, arriving in the early afternoon.

The pungency of the Mumbai air greeted us along with Asha as we emerged into the bright light. Asha, in her determined way, broke through the line to hug us hello, itself a breach of Indian protocol: a woman hugging a man hello in public. She capped it with a *Namaste*. The air smells of tar, car fumes, trees, and sweat, and somehow creates a heady, not at all unpleasant, dense aroma.

People are standing three or more deep, some with signs, some yelling names, some watchfully waiting for their returning family. The amount of luggage is staggering. When I see it carried on someone's head I wonder how he is managing not to stagger. The chaos is not really chaos, like so much else. It is carefully calibrated and leavened with the Indian penchant for unexpected kindness. If we had troubles with our month's worth of bags, a stranger would come along and carry it to our car. The same thing happens on the baggage carousels. People are standing five deep, fighting for space, shoving people out of their way. But if anyone notices that you've spotted your luggage, he will himself push people out of the way to retrieve it for you, unasked, and hand it to you with a flash of white teeth and the dazzle of the whites of brown eyes.

Asha met Lin and me at the airport. "Go to the white covered section, stand in the middle, and freeze. I will collect you."

How to get large luggage into the small cab? One look and it is clear that there are more bags than there is car. Asha advised calmly, "Don't worry. It will work." It worked. My original thought had been that the only way to accommodate the luggage would be to remove the engine and push the cab like a shopping cart to the Colaba Family Association Guest House.

Once in the taxi with the driver, the question is: will the one hour trip take forty-five speeding minutes or two and a half sluggish hours? The new driver was not the Flying Sikh and so, having maimed no one with the cab, we arrive one hour later. Not bad. A fleet of four houseboys are waiting, smiling, remembering us from last year. They spirit the bags into our room. Asha says goodbye and mentions I will see her the next day in order to firm up our plans.

"You have same room this year, sir," said with a big smile by the roomboys prying our luggage out of the taxi. After completing the handwritten paperwork in multiple oversized ledgers that look like Uriah Heep could have kept them, and paying in advance for our stay, we head to our room. It has been freshly painted and so the flakes coming off the walls are new and have this year's dust on them. Lin and I head out to the covered market we discovered last year and buy what the room is lacking: a bathmat so we don't fall on wet slippery tile, an extra trash can, crackers so we can make it to the 7:30 dinner time which itself is early by Indian standards, a case of bottled water, tissues, and toilet paper, about which the cleaning staff are oddly stingy. We unpack our clothes, offer a blessing over the dozen extra hangers I threw into my suitcase at the last minute, sit still for a moment, and head out to lunch.

Unlike Chinese food, which is much less palatable in China than in America, there is no culinary gap in India. The way to find a good Indian restaurant is simply to walk in to one. Many Hindus are vegetarian and all menus are laid out with "Veg" and "Non-Veg" sections. Selecting what to eat is simple. Close your eyes and point. Whatever it is, it will be delicious, albeit spicy. Sometimes I am puzzled why Indian food is so damned good. It favors oiliness, heavy spice, and extreme sweetness. This should not work for an American palate. However, it is irresistible. Even for breakfast. I am most surprised by the unlikely but delectable uniqueness of Indian Chinese food, a blend of Chinese ingredients and Indian spices that fuse into something extraordinary. It is almost as if the food delights in surprising you with its succulence.

We return to our room and rest. I review the plans that Asha and I have put together for this year's visit: a return to the Institution for the Aged Blind, to include training for university students and faculty on group therapy with special needs populations, a visit to Pune to a well-regarded orphanage and adoption agency where I will do training on play therapy and other topics for two days, and a return to Friends of the Footpath to do focused group therapy with the older children. I look carefully at the schedule and our meticulously worked-out plans that will undoubtedly go awry.

Now, one year later, is also the time for Asha and me to look back and try to understand just exactly what we did last year. With hindsight, what in fact are we up to? How can we structure our thinking about our joint undertaking? Last year we came to know each other, take the measure of how we work together, and in different settings. We developed more than a working relationship. Asha and Gopal and Lin and I are now friends. Asha and I discovered how seamlessly and respectfully we work together. Can we find an overarching meaning to what we are engaged in? After much talking—Asha and I are very good at much talking—it becomes apparent that we are developing without having realized it, a Global Mental Health Model. We are involving ourselves in the public service, social justice side of globalization. We are experimenting with how, or whether, a Westerner in the mental health field, can enter a uniquely rich Asian culture in such a way as to be helpful. Are we looking for a hybrid approach? It turns out that the answer is "not really."

The primary issue clarifies itself. Can a Western psychologist put aside his Americanness, but not his knowledge, enough to be able to enter an entirely foreign culture and work within its beliefs, customs, assumptions, and truths in ways that are helpful. Can he *submit* to the host culture, learn how to comfortably be *"the Other,"* so that he can have Indian lenses in his spectacles as much as possible, learn from the home context, cherish being the one who is not-at-home, and adapt his skills? Is this what it takes for a meaningful global mental health-based interaction to occur? This conceptualization defines the substance of the rest of my journey.

COMING HOME...TO
THE BLIND

As we approached the building, we had a brief but pleasant surprise. The Administrator of the Institution for the Blind Elderly, out of kindness, believed that she had arranged with a nearby wealthy out-of-town neighbor for us to inhabit his large cottage for the duration of our stay. We moved in with our week's worth of luggage and met the staff, including the man who would sleep on the floor outside our bedroom all night in case we should want anything. A vast improvement on the mold and mildew of last year's on-campus cottage.

Unfortunately, the Administrator's idea of the owner's generosity was not the same as the owner's. He believed that he had given us permission to use his place for one night, not seven. An industrial vice-president, he was coming up to the area for a week and had heard that there were strangers in his summer home. He gave orders that we were to be "out of there in one hour before I arrive or I will call the police." Lacking the skills of fast flight, we gathered our things as quickly as possible and, with much embarrassment and disarray, vacated the lovely premises. Another new experience: Lin and I had never been thrown out of someone's house before. Our first eviction.

We made our way by foot back to the Institution's campus, silently carrying our things and a bit confused about what had just happened. We were approaching three of the residents, all fully blind, who were coming in our direction out for their daily walk. They had been told that we were returning "sometime soon," but that was several weeks before. As we approached them, still silently holding on to our belongings, the three residents came up to us, stood at an appropriate personal distance, and told us they were glad we were back. They sensed our presence and certainly heard our feet on the gravel. We could not be identified by our voices as we weren't speaking. And yet these men knew we were back. Taking my hand in theirs, although I don't know how they figured out who was who, two of them said "Dr. Marc, welcome back. We have been waiting for you" in Hindi. Asha translated. The experience led me to wonder, how do we come to know something? And how do we know that we know? The three blind men were absolutely clear whom they had chanced upon.

We moved back into the cottage we used at the Institution the year before. It had been closed up since we had last been there. The linen was still on the bed; the towels hadn't been changed; the mattress hadn't been turned and neither had the bugs inside it although most likely they had multiplied. Asha and Lin took over with the only available equipment, hand brooms and rags, bending over to sweep the year's worth of dust off the floor, strip the beds, wash the dishes, and obtain help from staff to get the mattress into the sun for as much airing out as possible. The mildew and mold however had clearly if not visibly claimed the property as their own. And so we spent the week in a place to which we were allergic. However, the Administrator lost little time in coming up with clean towels and linens and assigning a staff house servant. The house servant was proprietary, yet also fond of us. Thus, when she gave us a Marathi tongue-lashing for washing our own dishes or making our own bed, she smiled and laughed. She did, however, make her point.

Our house servant took us under her diminutive wings; she could not have been five feet tall. She checked at various times throughout the day to be sure we had water. She had the knack of making particularly good Indian coffee: Nescafe, milk, and a great deal of sugar, and she knew how much we liked it. During our long workdays, this tiny eminence emerged seemingly from the air with cups of her coffee for us.

"THERE'S A PICTURE I WANT TO SHOW YOU"

B rooklyn, 1951. *It is quiet in the apartment. The sun is starting to go down. I like this time of day because when I look down six stories to the backyards of all the real houses, the forsythia is even more yellow than it was before. I am four-and-a-half and playing by myself in the room I share with my sleeping one-and-a-half year old brother. Playing quietly is always a risk as my mother often comes in then. But being noisy will always bring her in. Quiet is at least sometimes safer.*

I am confused because I'm not in her way or making anything "difficult" for her. She enters my room, and says in a sweet voice that I used to think was somehow oily: "Marc, come over here, I want to show you a picture." It is a small black-and-white photo of her in a two-piece bathing suit, sitting in the sun. Her feet are on a raft, her knees are pointed up, and her arms are behind her propping her up.

"I'm eight months pregnant in this picture. That means you've been in my tummy for eight months. You're almost ready to be born. That means

you're almost ready to come out of me. But you see how it doesn't look like it? You can't even tell you're there. I never wanted it to look like you were in there." Her voice is calm but I sense the coming harshness in her throat on the words "come out of me."

She gets a little louder. "I never wanted you in me. You had no right being in my body." She is starting to lose control. I recognize the signs. I am confused and don't really understand what she means "no right being in my body." It sounds like I went somewhere I had been told not to go, but I don't remember that. I don't understand what I was doing in her tummy in the beginning.

"WHY WERE YOU BORN? WHY DIDN'T YOU JUST DIE INSIDE ME? OR NEVER BE THERE AT ALL? YOU DON'T DESERVE TO BE HERE."

*I am frightened and start to walk away. My mother pulls my arm and keeps me close to her, pushing the photo in my face. **"LOOK AT ME. IT'S AS IF YOU'RE NOT EVEN IN THERE. I WISH YOU WEREN'T THERE. I WISH YOU WEREN'T HERE NOW. YOU'RE DISGUSTING."** She leaves the room with a dramatic whoosh of her skirt and all the air is moving around.*

Then it is quiet again. I am too confused to cry, but I do know that I am scared. What did I do wrong? Why was she so upset? But she is quiet now. If this is like other times she has yelled at me, she will be calmer when she calls us in for dinner. I know to watch my brother and make sure he doesn't cry and upset her.

A few days later, I hear my mother yelling at my father. She is saying things that don't make sense to me. I can't tell if she is saying bad things about me, or bad things about my father. She does that when she is upset.

My father comes into my room. My brother Ron is playing. I don't remember what he played because he was only one-and-a-half and what he played wasn't very interesting to a big boy who is more than four years old. My father quietly asks me to come over. Daddy only yells when he is mad at mommy. He is not mad now but he is very serious.

"Marc, I'm going to give you a big job. Keeping mommy calm is going to be your job. She listens to you." I was confused because she doesn't listen to me. She just gets calmer after yelling at me. "Mommy is upset now and I have to go to work. You talk to her and she'll feel better. I'll come home when I'm done with work."

It was a Friday night and I knew he never worked on Friday nights. He left the apartment. I know he came back because he was there the next morning. I was scared and I was alone. I think I was angry with Ron because he wasn't old enough to help me.

AT THE INSTITUTION: A GOOD WOMAN

Who can find a virtuous woman? For her price
is far above rubies.
The heart of her *community* doth safely trust,
so that *they* shall have no need of spoil.
She will do *them* good and not evil all the days of her life.
...
Strength and honour are her clothing; and she
shall rejoice in time to come.
She openeth her mouth with wisdom; and in her
tongue is the law of kindness.
...
Give her of the fruit of her hands; and let her
own works praise her in the gates.

Proverbs 31, Verses 10-12, 25-26, and 31.
King James Version

(Slightly adapted by the author, *in italics*, to suit the occasion)

Meenakshi, an old seventy, surveyed her flat before locking up to leave for the Institution for the Blind Elderly, where she was one of the Trustees. Widowed, she lived alone in a good neighborhood with numerous trees on her block in her city, a three-hour train ride to the Institution. She looked at the small spare bedroom and all was in order. Her living/dining room, with its bare white walls, sofa and two chairs, suited her high standards of cleanliness. The small white kitchen was tidied up. Meenakshi had nothing extraneous. Her needs were simple. One small statue of a Hindu goddess gave evidence of her faith. Her flat's sparseness conveyed her dignity, self-effacement, modesty, and pride in her duty to keep a nice home.

Locking the flat, she bent over on the landing and rubbed her knees, the source of much pain. She also suffered from vertigo but only let it interrupt her twice-weekly visits to the home if it was severe. She straightened up, still a bit stooped, and adjusted her modest sari. Holding on to the metal railing, Meenakshi slowly moved her aching knees down the three flights, one slow step at a time. She had allowed time to get to the railway station at her aging pace. As the train arrived, she raised one aching knee and, placing her foot firmly on the train's step, pulled herself up. Luckily she was able to find a seat.

Meenakshi is one of the very few of the Institution for the Blind Elderly's Trustees to come to visit and actually meet with the residents. She comes out of concern for them and for the overworked staff. She personifies respect for others and elicits the same from almost anyone with whom she has contact. She dislikes conflict but will stand up for the needs of the residents and will do what she can to empathize with an Institution staff stretched too thin.

Meenakshi's university training is in an area unrelated to institutions, psychology, or people with special needs. Yet she ceaselessly tries to understand the requirements of the residents. She feels, and perhaps shares, their loneliness and isolation and she makes the distinction between providing for their physical well-being and their emotional well-being. She perceives the psychological deficit in the Institution's approach to them. She has been a gracious bulwark in protecting the work that Asha and I, and later Shakti, were doing with the residents over the indifference of the other Trustees.

The residents trust her and come to her for help. Hers is the voice in the wilderness, speaking up for the residents and bringing their needs to the attention of the Administrator. Ironically, her caring stance sometimes prevents the residents from learning to speak up for themselves and not always turn their grievances over to someone else to solve.

Meenakshi's manner is quiet and reticent. Although I would never take her for a firebrand, I could see blue-fired rage in her brown eyes when she observes cruelty or injustice done to the residents. She speaks and carries herself with true humility and sees the residents with abiding respect. She does not perceive elderly abandoned blind people. She sees human beings with pain and potential. She is intuitively aware that the residents' difficult behaviors, squabbles, fights, and recalcitrance derive from decades of helplessness and resentment. Although untrained in the perils and needs of those who are in an institution for years—dehumanization and passivity—she observes it.

During our time at the home, Meenakshi took it as her duty to find additional care for the residents, thus her support of Asha and me. She generated ideas of ways we might be helpful.

WHAT DO WE DO FOR A SECOND ACT?

Asha and I planned two activities for our second year at the Institution. We would conduct groups as before, building on what we had learned both about the residents and about what techniques worked better than others. In addition, I would lead a daylong training for students from two nearby schools concerning group dynamics in a special needs population. The students' professors would also participate in the training.

There were two notable changes from last year. Residents sat together more often and talked to each other. They bound themselves less in the black loneliness. They also walked in twos and threes, more than before. The very large meeting hall just inside the front door had undergone substantial refreshing. It was less cluttered; windows were no longer blocked by tall furniture, and the whole thing had been painted a cheery yellow. The cows seemed to like the yellow as they came inside more often.

The residents, now including a handful of women, were happier to be with us than to settle into the mixture of psychological pain and pleasure of being with each other. Nevertheless, it didn't take a long time to help them talk. I don't know if Asha and I had honed our skills, or whether the wandering cows, wild pig and its five canine pursuers had some kind of magic, but the groups worked.

Several residents had died. One's family came to the cremation. Only other residents and staff of the Institution attended the other cremations. Their relatives had been notified. No one responded. We attended the service prior to cremation of one resident I recognized from the year before. The residents paid their respects but routinely were going through this ritual of death yet again, perhaps thinking of themselves and their next lives, perhaps lost in the "onlyness," perhaps wondering if any family would show them honor with their own presence at their cremation. Who would step into the river and cast their ashes into its flow?

During the groups, one man always sat next to me. He spoke of his discomfort at the Institution and of his loneliness. Between groups, he took me up to his dormitory space, offered me his bed to sit on, and gave me a box of crackers that he had purchased with part of the twenty-five rupees a week (50 cents American) he earned through his skilled labor in the Institution's knitting section.

At the last group, he again sat next to me. He took my hand in his and repeatedly took his index finger and placed it strongly into my palm, next taking his other index finger and placing it on the back of my hand. Eventually he removed it. He continued this motion saying, in English, "I can't do this anymore I used to do this I can't do it anymore this is what I used to do." Eventually I thought

I understood. I said, "This (his finger) is a rivet. You used to be a riveter. You were a skilled worker." He looked at me as if he could see me, took his hand, touched my heart and said, "I like you."

Anis, educated in Muslim schools, also spoke English. He had become blind at his work. He yearned to become proficient in computer use despite his blindness, and then to work on a public nutrition newsletter. His technological skills outdated, he needed to take courses to become current. He spoke at length and repetitively about this aspiration, enough so that I didn't know if his wishes were just bursting for an audience or if he was obsessively stuck in a fantasied rut.

To my surprise, three months later I received an e-mail from him. He had been saving his money as he earned it and was taking information technology courses. He had begun research into nutritional issues relevant to his context. I had another e-mail from him several months after that. His depression sounded much improved. Two months later I received a letter from the staff of the home. Anis, age 48, had died suddenly of a heart attack. Only residents attended his funeral.

Arvind, a wealthy industrialist, had developed a serious progressive eye disease, although he never told us its name. He did not want to be a burden to his family and so, despite the protests of his wife and children, he institutionalized himself. His family did come to visit him regularly. After a while, after months of weekly visits begging him to come home, he, with constant tears brimming at the edge of his eyes, insisted that he would not return and be a burden; that being a burden was shameful and so he would stay here until he died. Family visits became less frequent, his once proud appearance began to deteriorate and his immaculate turban become dusty and full of flies.

Peter, the English first name denoting a Christian, was perhaps fifty. He had a round sweet face, a good nature, and a beatific smile. He was Hindi-speaking. Asha was, as always, the translator of Hindi. For Marathi we again needed to bring in a third person. Peter and I sat across the circle from each other. He had something on his mind that he hadn't asked for several days. At last: "Do you have any American currency on you?" Aware that his curiosity was human, not monetary, that he was looking for a way to learn about this foreigner, Asha asked him: "Why do you want to talk about currency when you have a real American right here?" I asked if he would like me to sit next to him. He smiled and I moved over. Peter asked, "Can I touch you?" I said "yes," and he touched my feet, a sign of respect. A partially sighted resident moved Peter's hands from my feet to my knees so he could have a sense of a real person next to him. I asked, "Do you want to touch my face?" Peter replied, "You have to touch my face too. Then we will begin to know each other." He moved his hands to my chin and slowly began examining my face, as if examining a clay bust, trying to get a sense of what it looked like when unable actually to see it. I put my hands on his cheeks as he continued to seek me out. When he felt my glasses, his eyes brimmed over. I told him "Yes, I have eye problems too. I have glaucoma and I need glasses." He smiled and each eye dropped a tear. Then he abruptly turned and brought out a large Braille Christian Bible that he had next to him. He shuffled through the pages a bit to find what he wanted. He clearly knew the Bible well because he found the section he wanted quickly: Matthew 5, 3-4, from The Sermon on the Mount. He touched my arm then held the book in one hand and moved his fingers over the raised letters, speaking aloud.

Blessed are the poor in spirit: for theirs is the kingdom of heaven.
Blessed are they that mourn: for they shall be comforted.
(King James Version)

He put the Bible away, smiled, touched my arm again and then gently my cheek. In the three subsequent, brief visits to the home, whenever I first saw this man after my arrival I went over to him quietly, said nothing but put my hands on his cheeks. He knew this was my greeting, laughed out loud, showed his lovely smile, and placed his hands on my face. Only then did words enter our greeting, when he said "*Namaste*," and I placed my hands, in the Namaste gesture, inside his.

TO PLEASE THE DONOR

One day, a major donor to the Institution was visiting and observing, primarily observing me. He stood at the back of the room, his seventy-five year old eyes cruising up and down my body. I made mental note of this—how could I not?—and was relieved when he left the room.

The Institution's Administrator later mentioned to me that the Donor would be most happy should I join him for dinner. She asked me please to accept the invitation on behalf of the Institution because his contributions were substantial. I had not anticipated this as part of the definition of volunteer work.

To myself: "Oh shit, do I really have to go through with this?

The office staff called me to the phone a few hours later. The Donor indeed invited me to dinner at his home and mentioned that his wife would be away. I told him that my wife—long silence from his end—and I would be glad to join him for dinner.

Asha and the Administrator dropped us off at 7:30 and Asha, knowing his reputation, entered with us. She told him in her best proprietary mode that he must return us to the compound no later than 10:30 p.m. as we had much work to do early in the morning. His face became pinched and he reddened in anger, his cheeks looking like meat cooked rare. The donor then invited my wife and me into his bedroom, equipped with sofas and chairs, for a drink. I accepted, joining our host, a double Scotch. This was my limit and I made that clear. He looked at me with a "we'll see" expression. He then offered a second double Scotch. I took the drink, put it on the coffee table and left it there. He made it clear that he was disappointed and waiting for me to drink more. "I never start dinner until I've had four double Scotches. I do wish you would do me the honor of joining me." As his guest, I held the glass to my lips so they touched the liquid and put the glass down. The Donor shrugged and said, "We have time." Throughout, he ignored Lin other than peremptorily offering her a drink that she declined. He couldn't remember her single-syllable name.

The Donor asked why I bothered to become a psychologist when it took so much work and did so little good, especially since there were other things I could be doing that would be more interesting. I smiled and didn't respond. He gestured to his large bed and mentioned again that his wife was out of town. (Small wonder.) The Donor then recited a lengthy disquisition on the meaning of life and how little "common morals mattered."

He seemed to be talking to himself and as he walked around the room and had his back to us, Lin whispered to me, half-smiling: "I wonder if these drinks are drugged or if we're going to get out of here alive." In his circumambulations around his bedroom, the donor periodically looked me up and down, as he had done

earlier in the day at the Institution. He behaved as if my wife were
not present and certainly were irrelevant.

After an hour-and-a-half in his bedroom and the insistent im-
movability of that still-full glass of my second double Scotch, the
Donor invited us into the living room/dining room. Before leaving the bedroom, Lin asked for the restroom. This rather roomy
house had its single bathroom in the bedroom. As she got up, she
gave me a look of apology.

The Donor and I were alone. He had landed in a club chair
across from me after his discourse and slowly looked me up and
down again with his eyes. I stared at the increasingly interesting
coffee table.

When he heard my wife emerging from the restroom, he began speaking of his childhood farther south and the grand seven-
gated Hindu temple where he had gone as a boy, as if this had
been the ongoing conversation throughout her absence.

The Donor was clearly frustrated. My wife was present, which
was not his plan. I was not drunk. I showed no interest in his looking me over. I was rather proper and polite, spoke when asked a
question and initiated no conversation.

We walked into the living room/dining room, much more comfortable than the bedroom for entertaining, and air-conditioned,
which the bedroom was not. The lights were low and the Donor
dismissed the house servant. He invited us to the table, covered
with meat dishes.

My wife and I are pescetarians, which the Donor knew. As
his guests, and aware of the importance of his money to the

Institution, we placed some of each of the types of food on our plates and picked at it, complimenting the Donor. He proudly said that he did all his own cooking. I made note that it was 10:00 p.m., a reminder of when we needed to be back at the Institution and a way of implying "get me out of here" that the Donor—no fool—noticed.

The Donor showed us the way to the living room section of the area, with double sofas and club chairs, and offered us dessert, a pudding that could be taken with or without liquor. We declined the liquor. I mentioned that it was 10:20 p.m. He made a derogatory comment about "that bitch who is so controlling of your time." I quietly and politely told him that we really did need to get back and thanked him for the evening. He shot me an angry look that I pretended not to notice.

We got into his car, he insisting that I sit in front next to him, Lin in the back seat. He prepared himself some *paan*, a mildly narcotic paste made from betel nuts, ate it as he drove us, full of eight Scotches, liquor with dessert, and now *paan*, back to the Institution speeding over back lanes. The Institution's orange and white gate was locked.

The Donor said "Oh well, we can go back to my place." I commented that I was sure we could get someone's attention, which we did. The Donor dropped us off at our attached cottage and drove away. Lin and I were delighted to return to our mildewed, moldy accommodations.

IF YOU HAVEN'T WALKED IN MY SHOES, CAN YOU REALLY KNOW ME?

Students of psychology from two universities made the three-hour railway trip to the Institution for a day of training that I was to conduct on ways to work with special needs populations. Their professors were to join them.

I experienced the strength of the teacher-student (guru-shishya) relationship. Hierarchy drives Indian education at all levels, Asha taught me. Subsequent reading I've done, and personal experience within the Indian public school (American middle and high school levels) and university settings, has underlined this reliance and insistence on hierarchy. The few studies I've seen view this as one of the major problems with Indian education at all levels and at all strata. Students are taught their teachers' opinions that they are to feed back to the teacher without critique and thus receive their passing grades. I still cringe at this, even as in recent years we have been working within the educational system, and feel strongly that something must be done about the power of the hierarchy. Fortunately I arrived at this through extensive discussions with Asha and with one insightful educator. But this is a story for later. Now, back to the Institution and the waiting university students.

The students were traveling on their own time and money and arrived on time. The professors, also members of one of India's Humanist Societies, were late. I learned from later experience that they were supposed to arrive late, as their students should be waiting for them out of respect. However, these students also had trains to catch home, long rides, and a deadline for leaving the training that was scheduled for the requested six hours. When told that the professors would arrive at some unknown time and then have something to eat while the students waited, I unilaterally decided, more irreverently than not, to respect the students' schedule and to begin the training. I spoke in English to mostly good English speakers and those who spoke Marathi had a translator. The professors arrived one-and-a-half hours later. They took seats and observed, one of them commenting that she didn't know what this training was about, despite my having been asked to teach on this particular subject. I understood this as a matter of tit-for-tat and a protest at the lack of respect I had shown the professors by respecting the students' schedule.

I reviewed, with Marathi translation, how groups work and some of the techniques of group psychotherapy. I stressed the importance of recognizing the residents' context:

- The physical surroundings of the common areas
- The placement of tables, chairs and rugs throughout the Institution

- Dormitory living: all that was privately yours was a bed and a dresser
- Lack of privacy
- The shifting winds of the moods of the staff, Administrator, and fellow residents
- The walls and railings to cling to, heading to workplaces, dormitories, dining hall
- A ringing phone that was never for you
- Cows and dogs underfoot within the building
- Enforced heterosexual celibacy
- Lack of freedom of movement
- Repetitive work and empty days off
- Endless days without visitors
- A strict hierarchical environment: Administrator over staff over residents
- Imposition of taking the passive role within the home

We set up the role-play. This would take one-and-a-half hours from beginning to end, including setup. Both students and their professors would be thoroughly blindfolded after we moved them away from the meeting place where the training was occurring. Thus we began with dislocation. Each participant was given a piece of paper with a back-story of who they were. How old? Male or female? How did they come to be placed in the Institution? What did they do before they became blind? How did they feel about what had happened to them, being placed in an institution and rejected by their families?

We blindfolded one group of fourteen while another group of fourteen would first observe and then have their turn. Asha and I would be the therapists at a first meeting of these new residents of the home. While the observers stayed put under the tree outside, with the wild pig on his various forays being chased by his hounds (it was always hard to tell who had the power in that animal game), we shuffled the fully blindfolded participants. We made sure that they could not see at all, with the exception of one or two who had been left, in their stories, partially sighted. No one knew whom he or she was standing next to.

They formed a line, put one hand on the shoulder of the person in front of them, and were led by the partially sighted members to the meeting place. We helped each person find a place in a small circle, sitting cross-legged under the tree in the dappled sunlight they did not know was there. The observers made a larger outer circle and observed without comment. Asha and I sat in the center of the circle and led a "session" for newcomers to the home that was to last at least half an hour.

A half hour is a very long time. The group awkwardly began, really not sure about what to do. This awkwardness proved to be the more superficial manifestation of profound discomfort in experiencing the context of a blind person. The visual map is gone. One major faculty in perceiving and making sense of the world had been taken away. The hesitation and difficulty in getting started with the group session was really, then, fear. I believe that anyone in this circumstance would be frightened. However, I suspect that the utter destruction of the prevailing hierarchy added to the level of discomfort. No one even knew who was sitting next to whom.

Not to be cruel, we reminded everyone that they had been given a back-story, a specific role to play if they chose to, for beginning the session. The group settled down and became able to begin. Some participants could more comfortably enter into this process. Others could not; they could not overcome the terror of experiencing immediate blindness. Immediate blindness is what some of the residents had endured. Most of the back-stories were in fact the details of the residents, with ages and genders altered.

The most important concept I wanted these eager students to take away from the day was the concept that "the context is the teacher." If you don't understand another person's world, if you cannot comprehend his context, how presumptuous it is to try to be helpful. Therefore Asha and I had intentionally devised an extended role-play for both students and their professors in which the embedded teacher/student hierarchy disappeared.

The minutes passed. Slowly. The pain of the experience passed. Slowly. Then one courageous participant, in fact a professor, dramatically fell apart at the experience of being abandoned by her family. She keened and swayed. "Why is my family throwing me out? I've always done my part. I can't help what happened to me. I've taken care of everyone else. Why can't they take care of me? Isn't that fair? Isn't that what a family should do? Will they ever see me again? Will I ever see them again? Will I be alone on holy days and holidays? Will I die here alone? How many years will I be here? What will happen to me? Why did they do this to me?"

Still sitting, she threw herself into the lap of the person next to her, who patted her head and moved his head toward her helplessly, unseeing. It was time to stop and give the other group a turn, although it seemed clear that they weren't sure they wanted one. However, if the helper cannot even tolerate a brief enactment of the difficulty of his client, on what basis can she be helpful? How can she learn to hear, really hear, the pain and understand its impact?

We asked everyone to take the blindfolds off. They hurriedly untied the knots and fell into an impressive sense of release. The courageous role-player was in fact one of the professors, and the person she had thrown herself on was one of her male students.

This caused some brief embarrassment; India is a society in which traditionally males and females should not touch in public.

Some people broke out in tears: tears of pain, of release, and, most importantly, of empathy. We reviewed the experience. We discussed what the observers saw and felt. We examined what the participants found helpful, and not so helpful, from the role-playing therapists. And we did it again, observers and participants changing roles. Rather than being repetitious, the second run of the role-play enriched the discussion. I think this is because another hierarchy had been dismantled. Now everyone present had had the prolonged experience of being unsighted. A half hour is a very long time. Most interestingly, once everyone had had their turn, the group became more animated, especially the students. They were unafraid to explore what had just happened and how to apply it.

Shakti was the compelling, convincing, and quite gifted professor who was able to give full-throated expression to the pain she was experiencing in the role-play. When the training day was over, I was chatting with her and she said to me knowingly, "One of these days you are going to supervise me."

The next morning, Asha, Lin, and I moved on to our next stop, an orphanage and adoption agency.

A GRANDFATHER'S DEATH

*B*rooklyn, 1952. *I am a little over six years old. My brother is just three. It is almost winter. My Poppa Harry, my father's father, went into the hospital so the doctors could fix what was wrong with his stomach. I wasn't allowed to visit him but the day we took him to the hospital, I waved at him from the street and he waved at me from his window. There were still a few yellow leaves on the trees. I wondered why they hadn't turned brown and fallen yet.*

Poppa Harry was very proud of me, just because I was me. He made sure to see me every weekend and if I was sick during the week, he would take the subway during his lunch hour and have my mother take my temperature so he could see for himself if I was getting any better. Then he turned around and got back on the subway and went to work.

I used to go for walks with Poppa Harry. Just the two of us. My brother was too little. He told me stories of when he was a boy in Russia. He also told me about something he called "injustice." He taught me that word. He told me about rich men who didn't pay their workers enough money. The rich men lived in big houses and the men who worked for them didn't have enough money for food. He asked if I thought that made sense. When I said "no," he would always ask me to tell him why. "Remember, it's very important to be able to say why you believe something."

As we walked to the candy store, he told me about a man called Joseph McCarthy who he said was a very bad man. Joseph McCarthy was making people tattle on their friends and calling them names and not letting them work just because they tried to help poor people earn more money. Poppa Harry said that making people tattle and not letting people work were terrible things. He said there was a man helping Joseph McCarthy who was called Richard Nixon. When we walked and passed a place full of dead people, Poppa Harry would always say: "You see dat zemetery? Itz not so crowded dey couldn't make room for Richard Nixon."

Poppa Harry and I always stopped at the candy store. He would buy me something even though I heard my mother tell him not to. He told me to "eat it fast before we get home." I remember Poppa Harry and Grandma Reva and how much I loved them. He looked at me just as if everything about me was perfect. He looked proud but I never thought that I had done anything special.

When the grownups would talk, there were three languages. It took me awhile to figure out why sometimes the grownups spoke in each one. Grandma Reva and Poppa Harry talked in Russian when they didn't want anyone else to understand. They and my parents spoke in Yiddish when only grownups should understand. And they all spoke in English if it was all right for Ron and me to understand. My Grandma Reva, who liked to break rules, sometimes took me aside and taught me how to curse a little in Russian and Yiddish.

When they came to visit, I would sit in Poppa Harry's lap for a while and then I would play, always sitting very close to his feet on the floor. I *would go over and sit in Grandma Reva's lap that had lots of room for me. She also taught me a word. We had a picture of poor people picking cotton. A man was carrying a great big basket and was kneeling on the ground so he could hold that basket. A lady was picking cotton and filling the basket. They didn't look sad but they did look very poor. My Grandma Reva told me to look at the man's arms and how straight they were. She said that the man and the lady were doing their work the best they could even though they were very poor and weren't being paid a lot of money but it was their job so they would do it right. Grandma Reva said that the man and the lady had "dignity." That's when you do something well because it's your job even if it's not fair. She held me close and always smiled when she looked at me. She had grey eyes that seemed to smile too. Just because she loved me.*

When Poppa Harry got sick and went into the hospital, he was supposed to have an operation and then leave the hospital after a bunch of days, maybe a whole week. He didn't look sick when he went in. He just said his stomach hurt. Grandma Reva didn't seem too worried, just some. But the doctors made a mistake and Poppa Harry got something called an infection and the medicines didn't help and he died a few days after the operation.

I know that nobody expected this because I came home from school a few days after Poppa Harry's operation and I heard my father crying. I didn't know why but I started to feel sad too. Then I saw Grandma Reva stretched out on the couch and she was crying even more and she was making terrible long low noises. I began to cry too even though I didn't know what was wrong. But I knew that what was wrong was very very wrong.

My mother took me aside and into the bathroom, "where it's private," she said. I was wearing green corduroy pants and a red sweater. She stood me up on the seat of the toilet and told me "Poppa Harry died."

I asked if I would ever see him again and she said "No."

Then she seemed to think of something and said "but he'll be able to see you from the sky."

"I'm never ever going to see him again?"

"No."

"But I didn't even say goodbye."

I started to cry more. I didn't see that look come into my mother's eye. I wasn't looking out for it. **SMACK!** She slapped my face hard. "You're out of control. Stop it." She was yelling. I was surprised and didn't understand that I had done something wrong. **SMACK!** She hit my face again. I tried really hard to stop crying. That must have been what I was doing that was bad. **SMACK! SMACK!** It was hard to stop crying but I did. I didn't want to be hurt anymore.

Later, I sneaked into the rooms of the apartment that had pictures of Poppa Harry and turned them over so no one could see him.

ORPHANS AND ADOPTIONS

We moved from the unwanted elderly to the unwanted young. Several hours by train from Bombay stood a highly respected orphanage and adoption agency farther south along India's west coast on the Arabian Sea. We spent time there during two consecutive years.

The agency's blocky building stands three stories high in a fenced yard with an outside play area. It is clean inside, if not particularly bright. Children are brought here up to age seven: toddlers running hungry and naked in the streets; days old abandoned infants; five year olds who look like they are three due to malnutrition. Some were not abandoned but removed from their homes because of the level of abuse they endured, some too traumatized to speak for months.

However, a number of the children showed signs of being good candidates for adoption: taken in very early and thus better nurtured, better able to relate, and not as damaged by neglect or abuse.

Others had been too harmed to make an adoption a likely success. They would live at this orphanage until age seven and then be moved to another which worked with older children and so it would go until they were sixteen or eighteen, hopefully done with schooling and somehow able to cobble together a life on their own.

The clinical director, Meher, wanted to institute a modest treatment unit and asked if Asha and I would come down and teach. Asha turned most of this task over to me. The staff, many well trained and carrying Masters degrees in child development, sought to learn about play therapy and assess if they could do it. My task was to work with the staff, Asha always available for when I would get derailed from the Indian context. She also provided counterpoint observations.

The agency was the first in which the focus of our work was the staff rather than those who suffered. We were one step removed. I was delivering over two separate visits twenty-four hours of lecture and interactive workshop activities to trained staff (but not trained in what I was there to talk about).

The first year we stayed at a country club, courtesy of gracious Parsee friends of Asha and Gopal's, that was once a British army site for post-hospitalization recovery. Guests instead of ill and wounded soldiers had used these rooms. Our room was sparse and a bit dark despite having a window. It looked out on a sunless wall. The hard mattresses felt like they were stuffed with hay, not surprisingly, as the grounds had become a trotting area for local horse breeders. Long corridors, as in a hospital, whitewashed walls, potted plants, and a jungle of rattan chairs and tables. Obsequious waiters brought English-style breakfasts of eggs, tea, and toast with marmalade. We were in a different world than the one containing naked, abandoned, starving young children and babies.

I spoke about the principles of play therapy, stressing how young children use the way they play as their language. If you want to know what a child is feeling, understand his play. If you want to know what a child is thinking, ask him. Emotional problems are more naturally expressed in play. The staff was deeply attentive and their questions showed much caring for the children in their charge. Role-plays of difficult young children interacting with a play therapist (me) using toys, served as approximations of what staff would find happening in a playroom.

One young woman decided to take the role of the child she worried about the most, a four year old found wandering in the street, malnourished, naked, matted hair, dirty and covered with bruises. Mute. Six months later, now well nourished, physically sound, in a caring environment nothing like a warehouse, she still had not spoken. She grunted and willfully insisted on getting her way.

I arrayed the toys I'd been told she liked on the floor and added a few more potentially aggressive items as well: trucks, blocks. We played out a thirty-minute session with the role-played "child" approaching me and moving back, looking me over directly and walking around me, pushing me, trying to hit me. "Are you worried I will hurt you?" She picked up a block and threw it at me looking very angry. "You're hurting me first. Is that to stop me from doing something bad to you?" Clearly this role-play had taken on an immediacy such that everyone, including the staff member proxy, and I, had gotten caught up in this scenario. "I don't hurt children. I don't even touch them on the arm unless they want me to."

She circled around me, one finger placed in the center of my head. I didn't look at her as I didn't want to disturb her approach. She walked around me three times and then I looked in her eyes.

She withdrew, grunted, and took up a block to throw at me. Still silent, I simply watched. Would the wounded child emerge or would the tormented silent animal retreat? She retreated but fortunately didn't shy a block at me. She curled up, ever vigilant.

I stayed perfectly still and painfully slowly moved my head so that she was prepared for me to try to look in her eyes. Our eyes met. She angrily rolled a truck at me. I think she intended it to symbolically push me away. I decided to purposely misinterpret what she had done and take it as an invitation to play. As I rolled the truck back to her she was surprised. I was bypassing her anger; she hadn't expected this and I had done it from the distance she had dictated. I hadn't moved my body since we first sat down. She looked puzzled, picked up the truck, examined it, grunted again and made a motion to throw it at me. And then she stopped, examined at the truck, and rolled it back to me looking sullen.

I smiled and took the truck, waited a bit, and then rolled it to her. She looked me in the eye and sent it back to me, turning away. Since she now had her back to me, I took this to mean that she had had enough. (She actually had done a lot.) But I wanted to see if she could muster a bit more courage and come a little closer to play. I turned away from her, matching her stance on the floor, and started to play with the toys I knew she liked. Throughout all of this I alternated between not speaking—mute meets mute—and speaking simply and clearly as if I were playing alone with the toys. She became curious. She watched more closely. I shifted myself just enough that it because harder for her to see what I was doing. She didn't move for several minutes. She was still watching. I kept playing.

Slowly, she inched closer to see what I was doing. I kept talking to myself about what I was doing with the toys as if nothing had happened. She approached further until she was next to me, watching. She grabbed one toy out of my hand and started playing. I said nothing as I felt that drawing attention to her after she had worked so hard to override her vulnerability would push her away. She continued to play, silently but next to me, careful not to touch me, and watching to be sure I wasn't going to touch (i.e., hurt) her. But she stayed.

At that moment, I ended the "session." Everyone in the room started to laugh, including the "child" and me It was as if we, all twenty-five of us, had been in the midst of something real and had been holding our collective breath to see what would happen next. We had lost track that this had all been role-played. I considered what happened as a testimony to the empathy of the staff and the potential for people to undertake play therapy if regular supervision could be obtained from a qualified professional.

The following year, Lin and I stayed in a guest room in the adoption agency itself. An Indian breakfast was brought to us from the kitchen. The agency had built a playroom with a one-way observation mirror and a careful selection of toys, doing what could be done on a budget.

Staff had just begun to see some of the more troubled youngsters under the supervision of a local child psychologist well versed in play-diagnosis and play therapy. Our task this time was twofold: to deliver a workshop on mother-child attachment and to observe the supervising psychologist through the one-way mirror as she worked with a young child. I was to narrate to staff what she was doing and why, as well as point out aspects of child development noticeable from this child's behavior.

Another cultural knot was made. All the research I had seen on mother-child attachment and what facilitates healthy bonding had been done in the West. Its findings included the "fact" that eye contact was a critical element in attachment. As a mother looked in her child's eyes it caused the child to look in her eyes and this visual dance continued, enhancing brain development in such a way that it kept encouraging this visual connection. When I presented this, the staff angrily confronted me. "Indians do not look in each others' eyes for long; it's considered an intrusion." "Are you saying that all Indian mothers can't bond with their children because they do not keep gazing in their eyes?" "Are you saying something is wrong with us?"

I have since heard that this is not universally true across the subcontinent. Nevertheless, it most decidedly was true in this part of India. I quick-stepped and explained that of course this was not a criticism of Indian mothers. The research had been done in the West where eye contact patterns are different. We do look people in the eye for long periods of time. Clearly it did not mean criticism of Indians. I was sure, despite not having seen research, that the mother-child attachment bond was achieved through different, culturally normal ways in India. The result would be the same. The mother and child would do a dance of connection, be it visual or verbal or through touch that would facilitate secure bonding.

I am grateful for the anger sent my way during this presentation. It pointed out to me in the most immediate way that Western research findings and standards are imposed on cultures that do things differently. I apologized to the audience.

We all had lunch together and the opportunity to chat informally, stop being the presenter and become the guest, did much to lessen the tension. After all, what was sustaining this much-concentrated interaction and learning was mutual enjoyment of each other. The staff, all women, told me about their own children and wanted to know about mine. As we finished eating, I had to review my notes, and make corrections, so that I could continue to discuss the topic.

The following morning I spoke again on the principles of play therapy, going into more detail than the year before. We then observed their supervisor in action. She deftly worked with a timid three year old and skillfully brought her out of her shell so that we could witness some play. She also had the youngster do a few drawings. We gathered closely around the one-way mirror and I narrated as things were happened. We watched the interplay of therapist and patient, the progression of the child's expression of her feelings, the evolution of her thinking, as well as watching which of her behaviors were age-appropriate and which were not, and why.

After a debriefing with the supervisor, we all sat on the floor in a circle and I talked for a couple of hours on the interpretation of the drawings, being exceptionally careful to elicit comments about what certain objects generally meant in this part of India. I was not going to repeat a Western interpretation slapped onto another culture where it does not belong. This experience has sensitized me to how easy it is for Americans to apply, inappropriately, our own standards, expectations, and meanings to cultures where they simply do not apply. America is not "the standard" by which everything else is to be understood and measured.

It was time to leave to catch the train to Mumbai but staff wanted me to stay and talk about how to work with prospective adoptive parents. I could only manage to give a half-hour before rushing for the train.

My visits to this orphanage/adoption agency were in the second and third years of my work in India. I had no contact since then until the eighth year, when I received an e-mail from Meher. The play therapy unit was continuing to function and was doing well enough for the agency to offer treatment to neighborhood children who needed help. Proof yet again that relationships in India, once begun, do not end.

QUIET SPACE

*B*rooklyn, 1953. *I am seven years old. My mother is in the house but she is quiet. My brother is interested in his toy trucks and cowboys. It seems safe now and so I take out my latest book from the library. I should know not to trust the quiet and I do know not to trust the quiet but I try it out anyway. I am so tired of being On Guard all the time.*

In the room Ron and I share, there is one corner that the sun likes. It is in the corner farthest from the door, between two windows and right next to the steam radiator. In winters, this is my warm place. I take out my library book and smell the pages and the binding. I love the smell of paper. I open the book to where my bookmark is and start to read, glancing at the door to be sure that my mother is still quiet and not in the room. I don't want it to happen again. Not so soon after yesterday; that was the last time.

It seems safe and I begin to read, facing the windows so the sun can fall on the book's words and the words can become even more beautiful. I have wondered how lines and curves and dots become words and then mean something. I can't figure out how it works but I know that once I start reading the lines and curves and dots become people and places and action and feelings. It is better than magic. I read my book and the cowboy's horse is chased by nearby wolves. One time in another book the big red dog saved his owner from a lot of danger. I have forgotten everything else including where I am. It is like I have fallen into the lines and curves and dots that became words and then people and animals and action and feelings. Then I see the book become darker. The sun isn't touching it anymore.

I turn around and there she is. My mother. Again. She has waited until it was quiet in our room and sneaked in. She walks very softly, maybe because she is so short and small. She has the twisted smile and look in her eyes. She doesn't want me to be calm. She wants to ruin it. First she leans over me and stares. Her eyes look cold, like they were molded of clay ice. Then she squats next to me and I shiver because I know what she will do next.

She puts her face almost touching mine and she starts to yell. I know what she will say because it only changes a little each time she does it, but it scares me and she looks scared, too. Scared and mean at the same time. "I HATE YOU. WHY ARE YOU READING? WHY AREN'T YOU DOING SOMETHING ELSE? WHY DON'T YOU GO OUTSIDE AND GET OUT OF HERE. THIS ROOM WOULD BE NICER IF YOU WERE DEAD. MAYBE YOU WON'T GET DINNER TONIGHT. YOU'LL JUST HAVE TO WAIT AND SEE, WON'T YOU? I'M LEAVING THIS ROOM. YOU'RE DISGUSTING."

She kicks me in the leg. Sometimes she punches me in the arm or slaps me on the face. Then she leaves. I used to be confused when she said these things because I never could find out what I did wrong. Usually when she says I might not get dinner she still puts food out for me. Sometimes she doesn't talk to me for three days. Not at all. It's scary too, but I also like it because she leaves me alone. I put my book away because I don't want her to take it away and I want to remember the horse and the cowboy and not just the lines and curves and dots. Sometimes I hide my books. But first I take one last smell of the pages. Books help me feel calm, especially when I think of my mother, the angry hurricane in the kitchen. I wonder if she is also very scared about something.

BACK IN BOMBAY—FOOTPATH VISITS

W e returned to Mumbai, several hours on a slow-moving train. India has the most extensive rail system in the world, designed by the British, but the trains themselves move slowly, chugging at a leisurely place. We were riding First Class A/C, out of Asha's deference to the Westerners' reliance on air conditioning. Food sellers quietly make their way up and down the aisles. The tomato soup, of course spicy as we are in South India, is delicious, although to see it ladled out of a large tin into a paper cup deceives me into distrusting its savor. Most of the passengers read the newspapers, Asha and Lin their books and I, prone to motion sickness, people-watch. The teal vinyl seats have some slashes in them here and there; the luggage racks seem to sag due to their narrowness; the lighting is dim. There are two restrooms in each car, Western-style to the right, Eastern (squat) style to the left. The toilets open on to the tracks. When using a train toilet, it is the tracks that appear to move. I watch my aim most carefully as the margin of error is small. Trains often run on time. This one did and we arrived in Bombay with our small suitcases and headed straight to the Colaba Family Association Guest House. The desk clerk welcomed us back from our several days away, told us we had no messages, and handed me the key. As ever, our belongings were in our room where we had left them, the room had been cleaned in our absence and the daily papers had been saved from the days that we had been gone.

The next morning I walked the almost-mile to Gopal's and Asha's place. Asha and I planned for our working days at Friends of the Footpath. We would again work in a short-term group therapy framework, and I had selected another song. I had been asked to "bring us another song when you come back next year." After a couple of hours of processing our stay at the Institution for the Blind Elderly and at the adoption agency/orphanage, we spent the morning walking the footpath.

Many of the street vendors live in the distant suburbs and take the train in to central Bombay early every morning, unpacking their wares on the edge of the footpath perhaps an inch from the street. They reappear each morning on the main thoroughfares, rarely on the side streets. Their wives also wake up early, get the children to school, and prepare their husbands' lunches. By 10:30 a.m., they get on the Bombay Commuter Railway with their food-stuffed tier of tiffins, stacked tins that they hope to get to their husbands within one-and-a-half or two hours. The street vendors keep the same spot and look out for each other's goods if someone needs to take a break to find a pubic toilet. Otherwise, they are on their haunches all day until it is time to fold up for the night. For a fee, they can leave a table against a wall so it doesn't have to commute too.

The food stalls start to come alive closer to lunchtime. I regret the well-advised warning to travelers not to eat the street food. The smells of fried dough, sambhar, stir-fried vegetables, grilled meat, intensely savory sauces, hot mustard seed, lemon and ginger are intoxicating. Being in the dense crowd of customers yelling their orders, talking and eating, is itself intoxicating.

But we have to move on.

We are going to visit a children's shelter at Mumbai's Central Terminus Station.

THE RAILWAY "SAINT"

The Chatrapati Shivaji Terminus (CST), formerly known as Victoria Terminus and still referred to as "VT", gives a glimpse into the Indian love affair with the acronym. It is the central railway station in Bombay. It is a magnificent heap of Victorian architectural detail thrown together to make a train station large enough to fill a city block and accommodate between one and two million passengers daily. Its model is St. Pancras station in London.

VT contains pale brick, dark brick, archways without function, inadequate and illogically placed Arrival and Departure Boards, too few ticket stations, the garish flashing lights of what in America would look like carnival fortune-teller booths, fishmongers on the way to deliver the thrashing goods they balance so well on their heads, shoeshine boys lining the platforms—two rupees for a shoeshine, about a nickel—and people rushing to jump on trains that are standing still awaiting departure. This is choreographed railway bedlam on a schedule. And yet it works as long as you account for the fact that the trains run on Indian time.

This particular visit to VT was not to take a train, not the Bombay Commuter Railway nor the Intra-City Trains. Our goal was to find the shelter for railway children hidden away somewhere on the indoor outskirts of this vast complex of architecture, machines, and unending reserves of humanity.

We passed the Commuter Railway platforms and continued beyond the Intra-City train platforms. We moved beyond the crowds until we reached an inside-the-precincts but outside-the-common-boundary area within this enormous, barely comprehensible, people-filled complex. In a dusty, uncovered area next to the border fence, was a corrugated and windowless tin hut. The outside temperature was ninety degrees Fahrenheit. The heat inside the corrugated and windowless tin hut was incalculable. In a ten-by-ten foot space filled with meager pallets, twenty boys sleep, bathe, and grab a quick breakfast before being sent off, so they wouldn't be picked up by the railway officials as vagrants. The boys arrived daily, in substantial numbers, from their various villages, the early teenage bearers of the financial hopes of their families. They came to the big city to make money, somehow, and send most of it back to their families in the villages.

There was nowhere for these children to go, nowhere to find a job in a city of eighteen million people, perhaps half of whom live on the street. There is a distinction between a street child and a homeless child. A street child usually lives under a blue, sometimes dark green, tarpaulin that is supported by two outer bamboo poles and leans against a public wall in the back. The street child lives there with at least one and often both parents, each of whom works at least one job unless the father is an alcoholic. Then the mother carries the burden. Although these makeshift homes have to be dismantled in the morning, they are reassembled in the same place each night unless there is threat of "demolition" by the police who are looking for a payoff for "demolition prevention." As fragile as this existence is, street children often know that their "home" will be in the same place and that their family will be there. There is a modicum, albeit the barest one possible, of stability.

A homeless child has no such place. He has no special place on the footpath that is his. He has no parents. He has no benign adult on the streets to be concerned for his welfare, or care whether he is alive from day to day. These children will try to find whatever kind of work they can but then must to figure out where to keep whatever money they might possibly make. They are bait for disease, rats, thieves, kidnappers for the child sex trade, and beggar masters. The railway station is filled with rats and bandicoots. Sometimes the railway children are so hungry that they jump down off the platform between oncoming trains looking for castoff food, the rats their companions. Not infrequently, passing trains kill them.

And here is the corrugated tin and windowless shelter for the railway children, housing twenty children with no room for more. Asha and I arrive to meet the one paid staff and one volunteer who look after these castaways who are somehow their families' best hopes. We chatted with the two adults as the boys got themselves out of the hut, took quick baths and ate whatever the shelter could provide. We watched as these guardians maintained discipline with sternness but not harshness.

The volunteer was the more talkative. He had those beautiful Indian brown eyes that looked strong and yet seemed chronically near tears. He spoke eloquently of his concern for these railway children: what in the world would happen to them once Bombay swallowed them? He wished that their parents understood that the future was not to be found in a city with millions of people living on the street, more than half of them children. However abundant Indian kindness might be, and it is considerable, there are just too many children being disgorged into the city.

The volunteer became quiet, looked sad and yet seemed determined. He came to the shelter every day after working a late night shift and before going home to his own family. He received no money. Observing his overwhelming empathy for these children and the pain it was causing him, I asked him how he kept doing what he was doing. What kept him going? He silently looked at his colleague, then at Asha and me, and thumped his chest twice. His friend told us that he couldn't speak just then but he wanted us to know that he had two hearts: one for himself and one for the children and that was what kept him going. A saint in the squalor.

FOOTPATH HOME VISITS

Asha and I spent a morning paying visits to the Friends of the Footpath children in their homes, and visiting other street dwellers of an older generation. Protocol dictates that visitors stand at the curb and wait to be invited "in." We particularly wanted to visit a family originally from Tamil Nadu in southeast India. Three generations had lived on this piece of footpath for several decades. They saved a little bit every day so that when it was bribe time they had enough money to give the police and "demolition" crews their quarterly bribes. Two middle-aged sisters remained, their children having moved elsewhere nearer their jobs. Their home was the ever-present back wall, a blue tarp supported by four poles, and additional pieces of plastic that enclosed it on three sides. They kept their home up all day, no dismantling every morning.

The two sisters appeared to be in their forties. Several decades before, their grandfather had moved his family to Bombay hoping for greater prosperity. He raised his family on this same spot on the footpath and his granddaughters were proud of the continuity. Their home was spacious and well furnished by street standards. They possessed a large white wooden dresser, a bed, a washstand with blue and white pitcher, and one dark green trunk. A large photograph of their grandfather hung over the dresser, surrounded daily by fresh saffron and rust-colored marigold garlands. Both sisters worked and clearly had learned how to manage their small wages to provide stability and the small comforts that mattered. They took particular pride in honoring their grandfather with fresh garlands for his portrait.

The sisters invited Asha and me in, after we had stood on the curb—their doorway—and offered the bed to sit on. This is considered an honor to a guest. They offered us water and Asha made our excuses. The sisters' home, a neighborhood landmark, spoke of stability in the face of chronic and inevitable instability. The sisters told their family story, demonstrated their pride through their erect carriage, and we had a fifteen-minute conversation. We then said our goodbyes and whenever I walked by their home, I was greeted by one of them. They arranged their work so that someone was always home, protecting their beloved simple property. These sisters were the picture of pride and propriety.

One year, their space was empty. The bribe price had increased and what had once been an impossible-yet-true home had become partial rubble. I do not know where they went. Rather than referring to destruction, municipal "demolition" means making someplace unlivable. A home partially turned to rubble for lack of a couple of hundred rupees.

Two of the children from Friends of the Footpath took us with them to show us their homes, but more importantly to meet whichever parent might be available. Radina lived inside an actual building, with brick walls and four-sided rooms made of weak plaster. The family, six people, had two rooms. To assure the ability to stay there, they rented out one of the two rooms to another family, four people. Ten people in two rooms but the walls were solid and they had a real roof and a door to shut at night for safety.

Radina was proud of where she lived. It abutted a small hutment wedged between two four-story brick and concrete buildings. I have always found this particular hutment especially moving. In this small space no more than thirty feet wide and one hundred twenty feet deep, visible from Asha and Gopal's flat, more-or-less stands almost a mini-city, easily overlooked from the footpaths on either side. It teems with people pushed into crooked corrugated tin lean-tos with laundry drying on top, tarpaulins of blue plastic or scraps of tablecloths, and the inevitable bamboo poles, an incongruous cyber café, mothers babies rats, bread being kneaded on the concrete, smoking ovens, women washing their children, adults washing themselves, torn clothes still being worn, the competing sounds of Bollywood music from too-loud radios, children from infancy to late adolescence, adults staggering with drink, children playing while always at risk of abduction for the sex trade, adults fighting with knives, parents and children doing chores, and the impression of irrepressible full-spectrum vibrancy. Whenever I am visiting Asha and Gopal, I stare out their windows and watch this defiant demonstration of life that insists on being lived fully. Sureka lives in this hutment and plays with Radina every day after they help each other with their homework, if they can find a peaceful place and time after their chores are done. Their school treats them as if they were useless, unworthy, and barely human, but their life and vitality could power a city if they were properly educated and channeled.

"IF I HAD A HAMMER"

As we entered Friends of the Footpath, Asha and I were greeted by a large number of children who remembered us from the year before. "Last year you came on January 7th but this year you are here on January 8th." "How long are you staying this year? Until January 28th like last year?" "Are we going to learn a song in English?" "Are we going to talk together so we feel less tension?"

We blended the focused group therapeutic aspect of our activities with learning a song. The children, so self-conscious of the poverty of their English, took pleasure and pride last year in singing an English language song, even if they didn't fully understand every word. This year I had brought the lyrics for "If I Had A Hammer" and shortened them.

> If I had a hammer
> I'd hammer in the morning
> I'd hammer in the evening
> All over this land.

I'd hammer out danger
I'd hammer out a warning
I'd hammer out love between my brothers and my sisters
All over this land.

If I had a bell
I'd ring it in the morning
I'd ring it in the evening
All over this land.
I'd ring out danger
I'd ring out a warning
I'd ring out love between my brothers and my sisters
All over this land...

Well I've got a hammer
And I've got a bell
And I've got a song to sing
All over this land.
It's the hammer of justice
It's the bell of freedom
It's the song about love between my brothers and my sisters
All over this land.

I like its message, simplicity of language, rhythm, and melody. It is made up of one-and two-syllable words. It is also a song that I knew Manoj would like. We expanded the use of the song this year and talked about what it might mean. Social justice is not something street children know, and yet they understand *in*justice intuitively and on an appropriate ethical level. They understood, I hope, the basic core message of this song. They certainly loved the melody and the repetition and lit up when Manoj and his assistant, with guitar, came in to join them, harmonizing.

The children, ages eleven through sixteen, insisted on beginning each session learning the song, so that they could perform it on a Friday night in front of the children from the neighborhood who would be present for their baths, collecting donated clothing, having a meal, and receiving their banana and chocolate bar for the next day.

After song practice, the therapeutic work of the groups began. Again, Asha and I saw several groups sequentially and daily, keeping the numbers low to allow sufficient time for each child to speak and for there to be reasonable discussion of whatever issues arose.

One little girl, too young for a group, came in and asked to speak to Asha or me. She spoke enough English and so I left and talked with her. In the conversation that follows, I have smoothed her English somewhat so that our conversation makes ready sense. She told me "I want less tension in my heart." I asked what was the matter. She said that she had looked out of her tarp and bamboo house and saw a man walking across the street. Two men came up behind him "and they put a knife in his back and he made a noise like 'uuuuugh' and then he fell down and his back was all red. Was that blood? And then the men who did it ran away and he just stayed there until the police took him away. I scared to go outside now."

I told her that sounded very scary. She asked if I could "make it better." "Do you mean make sure everyone is safe?" "Yes." "No, I can't make it better. I wish I could." "But you would try if you could? The police don't try." "You want to feel safe to go out." "Yes and my mummy taught me how to see if bad people are near me and come home if I think so." "Your mummy is right. She's teaching you the right thing." "Will I not feel scared again?" "I think you'll start to feel that you can go out and play again." She gave me a hug and said "My heart feels better."

Rosie, the girl whose pregnant mother watched her husband being knifed and shot for refusing to pay extortion money to keep his shoeshine spot on the footpath; Rosie, the girl whose only wish was to have the same place to go back to each night; Rosie, who only wanted to be sure where to find her waiting mother each night, ran up to me smiling. "Did you tell people in America my story like you promised?" "Yes I did, I told a lot of people." "How many?" "Hundreds." Plaintively: "Did they like me?"

"I DON'T WANT TO MAKE THE WORLD A WORSE PLACE"

I returned to the group. These boys, eleven to fourteen, Muslim and Hindu, sat on stools around a large art table in their school uniforms stained from use and from a recent half-hour on the enclosed and safe but dusty play area outside the former church. They initiated a conversation about morality. "I don't want to make the world a worse place. There is already too much bad."

Asha and I asked him to explain. "I can make more money if I don't go to school and start to do things for the bad people and then my family will have enough to eat. But what they want me to do isn't good. They want me to take money from people selling on the street like they owe the money just for shining shoes or selling small bags there. They don't owe money but the bad people take their money and hurt them if they don't pay. My mummy and daddy work so hard so we all have enough *dal*. If I follow what the bad people want me to do then mummy and daddy won't be so sad. What should I do?"

All the boys took this seriously. "Could you get a small job that wasn't bad and give the money to your mummy and daddy?"

"I tried bringing *chai*" (tea with milk and spices) "to people but I didn't make much money. It didn't really help."

"What else could you do? Or maybe you should work for the bad men and take the money from the street *wallahs* (sellers).

The agonized youngster continued. "I feel like there are two angels, one sitting on each shoulder and they are whispering to me. One tells me to do the bad things and the other says I shouldn't." He became tearful and agitated: "The world has so many bad people. I don't want to make the world worse. I don't want to become one of the bad people but I want mummy and daddy to stop feeling sad and worrying about the food for us. I don't want to be a bad person. I don't. I don't."

The group ended in the silence of this boy's realistic and common dilemma. The other boys touched his hand or forearm as they left the room. I expected his anguished face to stay locked in its expression as he sat still and alone. His face brightened, however, and settled into its usual expression blending thought and play. He got up, walked over to us and offered a heartfelt "thank you," despite the lack of resolution. I envied his resilience and capacity for gratitude and marveled at how sad it is that all these children have learned of necessity to be aware of the evils in this world.

For the Friday evening open house, again close to two hundred street children received their meals and watched entertainment given by the Friends of the Footpath children, i.e., the children who go to school. As we left to go back to our guesthouse, one of the children ran out to the curb to say goodbye and show off his banana and chocolate for the next day. He was standing in front of a parked and gleaming, high-end Audi.

Is there something in India's ancient air that informs each evening's soft breeze and somehow teaches equanimity to her children?

PART THREE

THE INSTITUTION FOR THE BLIND ELDERLY: WE ALL TRIED SO HARD

Over time, Asha and I discussed asking Shakti to join us in what we believed had the potential to become a model for mental health intervention in the age of globalization. We struggled together to uncover the human, rather than the economic, side of collaboration in a shrinking world. We also saw that the residents of the Institution needed far more than an annual visit from Asha and me. The ongoing personally deadening effects of institutionalization did not limit themselves to the time that Asha and I visited. We needed a collaborator to provide year-round psychological attention to the residents.

We wondered about Shakti, whose mother had been partially blind, and who had some personal investment in the treatment of the residents. She was a qualified psychologist who already visited the Institution sporadically. We asked if she would like to join this project, take over the clinical work with my provision of ongoing supervision. We three would use Skype™, struggling through our cross-culturally shared technological ineptitude to experiment with this global model. Asha and I hoped to begin to build a network, beginning with the addition of one. We stressed that this was a collaborative effort among equals, and not, for example, part of the entrenched Indian hierarchy of supervisor and student.

In between my visits to India, we talked with Shakti about this: e-mail for me; phone for Asha. Shakti eagerly agreed. Although we fairly quickly ended up running into culturally based difficulties, Shakti stayed always intent on learning, on expanding her skills. She knowingly exclaimed: "You see, you *will* be my supervisor!"

I added, in order to stress the proposed collaborative nature of this relationship: "And you will be my teacher." She lived the Indian context; I was the visitor. She dismissed this with a cursory "yes-yes-yes," her problematic, albeit charming, way of ignoring input from another person. I'm not sure Asha and I expressed ourselves clearly enough. We aimed to build up a trial protocol for working cross-culturally, a model that would be collaborative and outside the typical Indian reliance on hierarchy. In retrospect, I understand that Shakti conceptualized a much more traditionally Indian model.

Shakti would provide bi-weekly sessions with the residents. Asha, Shakti, and I would then have a Skype™ conversation after each session, debriefing and thinking together about what had happened, different directions in which to head in the future, if any, and specific ways to get there.

There were no cultural differences in our shared difficulties mismanaging the technological problems. We floundered in cyberspace with utter equality. If only we had all been seven years old, we would have managed the technology without difficulty. However, we stumbled together, touching the wrong keys, restarting conversations, and dropping each other mid-sentence. Eventually, we entered a serious technological Indian-American pact: once we got the three-way Skype™ conversation started, we would all keep our hands off our keyboards until sign-off time. Frustrating, but very funny. Three people, two in cities in India and one in America, were equally taking turns pressing wrong keys: International technological cluelessness. Asha spoke from her private home office space. I was on the computer in my clinical office. Shakti was at her kitchen table with her family bustling around her and tuned in to the conversation. Her pride in being "supervised" by an idealized American was evident in her tone. I culturally misunderstood what she sought from me, and I experienced myself in an Indian minefield that took me some time to understand.

WHAT I THOUGHT I KNEW
WAS NOT WHAT I KNEW

Shakti is a more traditional Indian than Asha, with less exposure to the West and the peculiarities of our thinking. Shakti, Asha, and I are all approximately the same age. Shakti is always meticulously dressed, traditionally, often in turquoise or burgundy and saffron, looking stately although diminutive, and composed, even when sitting on the grass holding a resident's hand. When we visited her at her university, she exhibited a touch of hospitable *hauteur.* Her hair dark, her smile seemingly open, I often wondered what was unstated. Earnest at times, charming when she wanted to be, Shakti's dedication to her work shone. Still, I thought I saw a steely quality.

The problem arose with the question, "how does one learn?" By being told what to do? By internalizing the "received wisdom" of the supervisor? By being mentored? By entering into serious discussions with colleagues about different ways of thinking about and approaching a problem or differences in philosophy of treatment?

Professionally, Asha based her method of learning in respectful and informed conversation and even confrontation with knowledgeable people. She and I spent much time "ironing things out" and airing different viewpoints until we arrived within a shared, jointly achieved space. She was aware of the distinction between striving for a quick fix and letting matters take their time.

Shakti based her model of learning on the reception of received wisdom from teachers. She had learned a series of techniques and stressed action in her clinical work, often disappointed if treatment lasted more than four or five sessions. On the other hand, she also based her work on the lovely Indian belief that immediate and unfettered genuine empathy will cause healing by itself. And sometimes it did. She was trained in a series of techniques aimed at quick alleviation of suffering rather than exploration of it. I would consider this as primarily palliative. She would see it as true healing. She would sit closely, deeply empathically, take an Institution resident's hand in hers. After sitting quietly for a minute, silently sharing sadness and grief, she told the patient about how much he had to be grateful for. She was in Indian fashion trying to join the good to the bad, not letting the good get lost.

I found this moving but incomplete, bringing brief relief, at best, from my Western psychoanalytic perspective. My understanding was that the residents had the same experience. Shakti moved quickly from a resident's suffering to his strengths. In America, I believe we make the opposite error. We risk minimizing a patient's strengths and overstress what is wrong, what needs "fixing." Thus, Shakti and I each had something to learn from each other.

I experienced Shakti's approach refreshing at first. It offered a useful contrast to the American overemphasis on suffering and angst. I marveled that the shift away from overstressing pain was generated from a country with so many people who hurt so badly. Nevertheless, I still believed the residents experienced an emotional abandonment when Shakti darted so quickly from their grief and pain to a position of "everything is going to be all right," especially with people for whom everything was not going to be all right, was never going to be all right. My impression was that Shakti was uncomfortable sitting with a resident's pain for as long as needed, neither wallowing in it nor brushing it away, but letting it take its time.

After explaining this, Shakti surprisingly and enthusiastically agreed with me. I was taken aback at the speed with which she accepted my suggestion, as it ran counter to her years of training and her background. We also had no discussion during which we might have come up with an intriguing integration of viewpoints, despite my inviting this kind of conversation. I wondered if my English, although otherwise seemingly fine, lacked clarity. Asha translated into Hindi. Shakti speaks fairly good English, good Hindi, which is her second language, and her native tongue, Marathi. Occasionally, Asha's translating me into Hindi helped communication.

Shakti's too-ready agreement with me was a warning signal of a serious cultural difference of expectations. It was no one's fault, but I didn't pick it up. I didn't even realize yet to take a "wait and see" attitude for the next collaborative session, to observe if this were to become a pattern or just a single instance.

Since Shakti was trained and accustomed to working with activities and techniques, I began by making suggestions regarding how to help the residents tolerate putting words to a wider range of feelings: good and bad, happy and sad, pride and regret, appreciation and resentment, while Shakti could continue with the type of activity that she was trained for.

Shakti, thoughtful and creative, decided to have the residents, illiterate for the most part, "write" a poem together as a group. They decided its theme and Shakti elicited their thoughts. They reminisced about growing up but mostly talked, understandably, about growing old. She was their amanuensis, and they spoke with simplicity, humility and wisdom, expressing their Indian philosophy of life: We go through the stages of life, and as we age our tasks shift until the time arrives to leave our soul's current receptacle, our current body, and move on. The last stage of this life is withdrawal and readying oneself for the next life.

These abandoned, generally elderly residents, most of whom could neither read nor write, managed with Shakti's loving guidance to produce this poem:

"What is Life?"
(Informally translated from the Marathi by Shakti.
The author used Shakti's translation and smoothened it.)

What is life?
Life is uncertain.
Just like a bubble.
For a moment it is there
and then it disappears.

To be displeased with friends at one moment
But again live with the bond of friendship
These days of youth when we used to dream,

> Date, have friendships, chat.
> But nothing happened.
>
> Now only old age.
> And we have become helpless.
> Blindness is with us like a shadow.
> Now we are here only for blessing others,
> Because now we are walking on the path of spirituality.

Touched by the poem and the lovely work Shakti had done, a project she also felt justly proud of, I was taken aback when asked: "Tell me what to do next." Shakti asked this question seeking guidance when I saw no guidance being needed. It was the beginning of her asking me to perform hierarchical supervisory duties with a hint that I was coming up short of her expectations by withholding my "received wisdom" from her.

Instead of answering Shakti's question, I attempted to start a conversation as colleagues, about how she had arrived at her idea of the poem, and how in the world she had evoked such lyricism from unschooled people, most of whom would not recognize an alphabet, any alphabet. She adamantly stuck to her position: "Tell me what to do next," seeking guru guidance. A collegial discussion clearly was off-cue. Shakti strictly sought more concrete direction, or "wisdom" from me. The reluctant guru was failing the aspiring disciple.

As it became clearer that the residents were more capable people than assumed by others, I started paying attention in the attempted collaborative sessions to how often Shakti would listen to the men's and women's grievances about the institution and take them herself to the Administration. I suggested that she help the residents to understand that they were not helpless, to convert their passivity into actively taking responsibility for themselves. Yes, the Institution staff cared for them and thus they were in a subordinate position. They had nowhere else to go, and no one who wanted them. But that did not necessarily mean that they had to accept daily frustrations such as not being served meat. This was a religious issue. Some people ate vegetarian; others wanted meat. Why always go in the vegetarian direction, they wanted to know. If meat were occasionally served, those who were vegetarian could choose not to eat it. The residents needed to learn that they could speak up for themselves.

Shakti and Asha and I worked on teaching the residents how to speak up for themselves on matters such as this. Shakti would teach them whom to speak to, what kind of language to use, and how to develop a rejoinder to the knee jerk "No" that they would receive from staff out of habit, on any issue. Since Shakti very much has a mind of her own, irrespective of the heavy burden of academic hierarchy she had accepted, she did a superb job of empowerment. As an Indian, she easily identified the contextual factors and figured out how to address them.

INTERMISSION—A PLAY
PERFORMED BY THE
RESIDENTS

O nce, one of the residents came up to Asha, Shakti and me to announce that it was time for us to watch the play that they had prepared in Asha's and my honor, with Shakti's help. The play was another of Shakti's well-calibrated techniques to help the residents: they felt engaged in a project that took them out of their institutional sameness. They had created an occasion and an activity, one that required memorization, improvisation, rehearsal, and pleasurable anticipation. I mentioned this to Shakti as we walked in to the main building that had been set up for performing and viewing, but her only response was an irritated "yes-yes-yes."

The play worked with the theme of substance abuse and demonstrated multiple scenarios in which alcoholism, in particular, occurred. It was performed entirely in Marathi, of which I knew one word. A young man, played by an old resident, took up with unsavory people who introduced him to drinking. Another man abused his aunt, with whom he lived, and persisted in using drugs despite her unheeded threats to evict him. A married couple argued so much that the husband took solace in nightly drinking to blind drunkenness with his buddies. The wife and the aunt independently called the police, who arrived and took the offenders to court where they were remanded to rehabilitation centers. After an indicated passage of time, the men were discharged, repentant and wiser.

Granted, a bit of a fairy tale. More accurately, an important tale told with awareness and relish by simple people. Alcohol use was indeed a problem at the Institution, as it is in Indian society, a problem that is in fact, along with drug use, growing among the young. The Institution's staff shared much concern about residents' drinking.

The residents' performances showed that they cared how good a job they did. They had thoroughly rehearsed and they had left themselves leeway for improvisation that was quite funny—laugh out loud funny. Residents I had never seen smile were laughing; usually disengaged people were completely involved. This small event was, for participants, staff, and blind audience members, a triumph of humanity over institutionalization. Shakti was responsible for facilitating it.

I was shown by one of the fully blind women residents where to sit, as she took me by the hand negotiating her way around the uncharacteristically arranged large entry room with a still willowy grace. This was the first time I had seen her smile. When the play, which lasted twenty minutes, was over and bows were taken, this same woman came over to me and said: "You are one of us. I know because I listened to you and you knew what was funny and when to laugh and you knew what was serious when we were showing problems. Thank you for enjoying us."

THE FAILED GURU AND THE AGGRIEVED SHISHYE

Now I clearly saw the extent of the difficulties in collaborating that Shakti and I had. I more acutely felt the tension between us, as well as her growing frustration.

Asha, I believe, was stuck in the middle, fully understanding how contextually bound Shakti was, while yet working to appreciate my perspective. I don't think she saw, until I pointed it out and a light bulb went on, that Shakti wanted access to me and that Asha was "the other woman" standing in the way.

Shakti's, Asha's and my differences in styles, expectations, and assumptions were increasingly clear. Addressing our fraying differences bluntly was futile. The Indian art of indirect communication, noting true meaning by tone, timing, gracious wording symbolizing the opposite, or omission of response, is so different from American directness, at times brusqueness, at times perceived as impolite, rude, arrogant, or bullying.

I saw, through foreigner's eyes, different ways that Shakti and Asha related to their Indianness and how I related differently to each of them. Shakti inhabited her Indianness without reflecting on it. She did not articulate it, although she wore it beautifully and proudly. She is highly traditional, impeccable in style and always traditionally dressed. Shakti epitomized the strong Indian woman while living within an academic environment of extreme hierarchy, usually highly dominated by men whose approval she sought. She functioned impeccably within this context. She would expect her "supervisor" to be her guru (teacher) and her to be his Shishye (disciple or acolyte). The guru is the conduit for the transmission of specific techniques and wisdom. The Shishye is the recipient who will receive self-realization through the guru's knowledge. Shakti had not been exposed extensively to non-Indian ways despite visiting America to stay with relatives. When in America, she stayed within an Indian orbit. The American context, as near as I can tell, did not factor in her daily life there. Her only comment to me about it was that it was difficult to do without the house servants so readily available in India.

Asha, an exceptionally proud Indian, is insistently self-reflective. She has a good deal of experience of the non-Indian world. Asha also has specific exposure to the West, which does not make her any less selectively critical, and yet she discerns the point of view of the non-Indian. Asha is fully saturated with her Indianness, but she articulates it, or at least she articulates it to me. She readily voices the reasons for her joy in being Indian, as well as her grievances about her country's failings, cultural and political. Asha's traditional but relaxed Indian blouse is worn over jeans. She always wears a traditional *dupatta* (scarf around the neck and over the shoulders), but casually. Asha despises hierarchies while Shakti assumes them and generally relishes them. Asha is irreverent and iconoclastic at times. She learns by discussing, particularly by friendly disagreements and we have had many. She has a

Vedanta guru, thus showing comfort with hierarchy in the spiritual/philosophical, not the professional, realm. Professionally, she is outspoken and forthright, brilliantly observant. As a psychologist, she does not seek a guru. I doubt she would countenance one.

I was the foreigner. As an American supervisor, I brought my own style. I offered ideas, attempted to open new windows, and certainly didn't dictate or pass on "personally received wisdom." I like and expect to be questioned by my students. I don't know if I'm wiser than my students. I know I've been around longer and have more experience and training. I am decidedly no guru professionally. I find the idea inherently repellent and presumptuous. I don't want disciples. I think the idea of cultivating followers in my field is destructive and bears resemblance to a cult. It doesn't help new therapists to use themselves more knowledgeably and with more self-awareness in the service of helping patients heal. The concept of acolyte is repugnant to me in my own culture, not only in my field. It implies that my supervisees give up their selfhood as healers, instead of refining who they are to be better healers. In supervision, loosening the student-teacher hierarchy does not imply less respect for the teacher, it implies a collaborative atmosphere for learning.

I am intensely uncomfortable with the status of guru, and once threatened to discontinue supervising an intern because he refused to challenge me: "How do you expect to learn if you are just going to accept everything I say? What if you have a better idea? What if I am wrong? How will we know if we are understanding each other?"

Shakti and I found ourselves, therefore, in a cauldron of disappointment, discomfort, and disillusionment, with Asha as witness, occasional nurse, and often caught in the role of the Other

Woman. This played itself out over two more years of supervision and brief visits to the Institution. We all respected each other, and this kept the swirling undercurrents contained. Eventually, however, they simply had to overflow the river's banks.

Shakti finally angrily demanded: "Why are you not helping me? I am doing all the work myself. When you visit you watch me but we do not do anything together with the residents. You need to show me techniques." I understood the angry dissatisfaction as translating into: "You are not performing with me as you should!"

I tried to explain my approach yet again. My psychotherapeutic philosophy does not lend itself to "technique" other than letting the patient take the lead and talk about whatever he wants to talk about. No imposed activities, no poetry, no roleplays, all of which lent themselves to the Institution's context far more suitably than an American psychoanalytic approach. "But you must teach me what you know and we should do it with the residents together." I took this as a statement of disappointment in our failed collaboration and Shakti's anger at my withholding myself.

Shakti felt used. I understood this and described again how we were not using a typical supervisory approach, nor an Indian hierarchical one, but that we three were trying to engage in a collaboration, one that would use approaches that would best help the residents at the Institution for the Blind Elderly. She and I understood different psychological ways of working with people and thinking about people. I was supposed to share my thoughts about her sessions and the residents and she was to join in a conversation about what she thought. "I know I know I know, but you're not working with me and showing me anything."

My approaches to people and to work in other Indian contexts were all yielding rich results and warm relationships. With Shakti there was tension and disappointment. I don't know if she understood the respect I had for her work despite differences of contextual opinion.

Our collaboration ended...not of our own doing, however. The Administrator of the Institution for the Blind Elderly decided unilaterally that Shakti's ongoing mental health services would no longer be needed. I was relieved that our apparently unbridgeable conflict would end, and yet I was also sad and saw this termination as an insult to Shakti's devotion to the residents and dismissive of her hard work.

Meenakshi and Shakti are longstanding and very close friends. Shakti checks in on Meenakshi at home, to be sure she is all right. They often lunch together. Until Shakti was told to stop coming to the Institution, she and Meenakshi traveled the three train hours together whenever possible. When our work came to its end, Meenakshi was most troubled, upset by the severed collaborative relationship (although we stay in touch by phone and e-mail), but I think what most troubled Meenakshi was the loss of much needed psychological intervention for the Institution's residents. She remains ever their quiet but implacable advocate.

My thanks to Rajiv Malhotra and his book, *Being Different: An Indian Challenge to Western Universalism*_(Harper Collins India), 2011, for his discussion of the Guru-Shishye relationship.

PART FOUR

OUR BOMBAY NEIGHBORHOOD: COLABA CAUSEWAY TO THE GATEWAY OF INDIA

Mumbai is a peninsula reaching into the Arabian Sea on both sides. Colaba is its southernmost section, bordered on its north by the area known as "Fort," where Asha and Gopal live. Colaba's main commercial street is Colaba Causeway, running more or less parallel to the sea, which is hidden by too many buildings. This is where we stay for a month each year.

Colaba is filled with tourists from the city's most prestigious hotel, The Taj Mahal Palace down by the water. First time visitors stand in dazed bewilderment from the heat, the hawkers who do not hesitate to work the streets and grab someone by the arm to drag him into one of the uncountable shops, and the sellers of oversized speckled balloons as long as a man is tall. Pickpockets work this area and families come out for a visit to the Gateway of India, built to receive the King of England early in the last century. Genuine religiously dressed men (*sadhus*), in orange garb and barefoot, seek alms. False religiously dressed men are on the lookout for an easy mark. The Bombay sunlight shines down intensely. The street noise is insistent but not deafening, and the constant movement of cars, taxis, motorcycles, buses and pedestrians mingles with the smells of food, gasoline, engine oil, and the accumulated fragrance of too many people for the space to hold them. It is not an unpleasant smell. It is merely densely human.

Voices other than hawkers add to the intoxication or repulsion, depending on how one takes to this. It is impossible to speak softly while walking on the footpath or in the street. Once inside a store or a cybercafé, it is quiet and people speak in a conversational tone of voice. Not so in the restaurants teeming with people waiting for their orders and waiters rushing around trying to serve. Busy restaurants are a microcosm of the street action with the addition of good food, until the end of the meal when the pace slows and rejuvenation begins.

Human traffic is often forced into the street, dodging all manner of vehicles, because the footpath is full of parked motorbikes and yesterdays garbage piled high waiting for today's pickup, racks of t-shirts, slacks, dresses, street combers more properly understood as customer-catchers walking the streets and starting up conversations with people who represent "possibilities."

I now enjoy this cavalcade. At first, I was overwhelmed by the colors, human proximity, restaurant aromas, smells of the sea, people, animals, and oil, the barking of the hawkers, the balloons, Western spiritual seekers in Indian dress, sharp daylight, honking cabs, the incessant undercurrent of buzzing but indistinct conversation, random arguments, lineups of restaurants on every street, sightseers and sharpsters at the Gateway. The initially overwhelming too-muchness now invigorates me although I remain cautious. Bombay is not a place where I ever let down my guard unless I am in someone's home. Bombay is India on amphetamines.

The area is filled with pickpockets, some quite respectably dressed. One deft slice of a back trousers' pocket with a razor blade and a wallet falls out of its own accord. The victim doesn't even feel that it is missing until he reaches for it. Some pickpockets keep the razor blade lodged between upper and lower teeth. One highly practiced move from mouth to hand to back pocket, and back into mouth. Evidence hidden. Other pickpockets work in pairs, one the distraction and the other the snatcher.

A profusion of beggars uses Colaba as their daylight working turf. Women with infants who are often rented for their compelling effect on the passerby, four year old urchins in rags alone on street corners, lame or maimed ten or eleven year olds, young men and women, old women and men, some grey with dirt and others clean, many in clothing worn so thin that one more dunk in the river and smack on the rocks would destroy it, adolescents in groups wearing the latest in jeans and t-shirt fashion, all share the footpaths and the streets of Colaba.

There are different begging styles. Very young children simply stand with an outstretched unwashed palm. "Mothers" with often-rented infants in arm ask for food, but when my wife gave one woman some actual food she sneered and threw it on the street. The eleven year olds have so much vibrancy and urgency that is hard to resist, but handing over a small bill or a coin invites a flash mob of youngsters. People often must take refuge in the nearest store, becoming the captive of an eager salesperson. Some beggars follow people for several blocks, repeating their plea over and over while pecking at their arms with one hand. It is a firm but not strong touch. The only way I have found to stop it is with a very terse and loud "*Nae.*" Then they will walk away.

I have wondered about the lame beggars of all ages. They seem fewer in Mumbai than in Delhi, but nevertheless have a clear street presence. Are they lame from birth due to home or street deliveries without medical help? Did they not receive physicians' care at the public hospitals in time to treat the damage? Were they maimed intentionally so they would enhance their beggar-worth on the street? Who would have maimed them? There is independent begging, and begging with the oversight of a beggar master, a phenomenon described in Rohinton Mistry's novel "A Fine Balance." This system reminds me of Dickens' Fagin, the pedophile master of a passel of pickpocket boys all well trained and forced to account for their daily gains.

I don't like the beggars but that is presumptuous of me. They form part of the fabric of street life in their own country where seeking alms is an ages-old activity. I have wondered at times whether children of the slums are part of the begging scene. I will learn shortly the error of my assumptions.

And so the street life of Bombay throbs. It caresses, assaults, invites, and repels in the midst of its crowds' smells, vitality, venality, goodness, generosity, and evil. All are people trying to live another day. Life is lived so much in the street it seems there can be very few secrets. But that is my misperception.

It is early evening and the light over the sea and city is waning. Large money street deals are being made upstairs in Restaurant

Bloom on Colaba Causeway, in a back room. Elsewhere plans are in place to steal beautiful street children aged nine and ten so they can become human chattel in the sex trade. There is no shortage of stunning children, both boys and girls, and no end of repellent sexual predilections of predatory adults. The law of supply and demand easily maintains its balance. Assignations between Western businessmen and young boys are being made with sex dealers. The pick-up of a child for sexual acts occurs at night, just two blocks behind five-star hotels on an attractive tree-lined street. The adult sex traffic and the nightclubs where business gets done are readying for the evening.

And fathers are heading to their footpath or slum homes perhaps in silent, unstated despair because they cannot provide enough food for their children. Each family waits for its man: Is he safe? Is he drunk? Did he get stabbed or arrested for not offering a bribe to an official? Was he knifed for being unwilling to pay extortion money? Will mother need to go looking for him at the local hospitals? Was he robbed on the way home? Or did he shine enough shoes or sell enough cement or bring in enough customers to his boss's shop so that there will be lentils and perhaps vegetables with tonight's rice?

A BIRTHDAY PRESENT

*B*rooklyn, 1953. *I am going to turn seven in three days. I don't know if my parents will be giving me a present or not. My mother speaks to the neighbors as if she were proud of her seven-year-old son. In the apartment, when no one else is around, she tells me in a singsong voice "you have a birthday coming." She is not playing with that voice. I know that she is thinking something mean.*

There is a model of a tiger's head that I want. You put it together and then you paint it to make it look like you trapped a real Bengal tiger and you hang his head on your wall like you are an explorer. It cost five dollars.

"Can I have a present this year?"

My mother says in that singsong voice that I know means trouble: "We'll see. How much to do you want it?"

We are alone in the apartment. Except for my three-year-old brother and he is napping. No one else can see us. "Do you want a present very very badly?"

162

"Yes."

"What do you want and how much does it cost?"

I tell her and I somehow realize that I should try not to show her how much I want it. If she figures that out she will be meaner.

"If you want that tiger so badly you'll have to beg for it."

"Please, mommy, can I have that present?" She tells me that I must not want it that much because I don't sound like it. "You're not begging enough."

"Please PLEASE can I have a birthday present?"

"No," she says. "Not until you beg harder. I want you to get on your knees and fold your hands and look up at me like you love me and almost cry because you want that tiger so much."

I don't like this. When I am older, I will learn that what I feel is "humiliated." I just understand that she has gone too far in being cruel. But I know her and I know that if I don't do what she says she will start to get upset and then she will scream in my face and kick me and punch me and so, hating myself, I decide to do what she has asked.

I am beginning to understand that when she gets this way, which is a lot, it is because she is worried or scared and that even sometimes I think it has nothing to do with me except I am there and we are alone. I don't know why she picks me. She doesn't do this to Ron unless she does do it and I'm not there. And sometimes I think she just hates me, really me. Then I want to get away from her and get safe.

That is what Gram is for. She is my father's mother. She loves me. Poppa Harry is dead. He was my father's father. He loved me but once you are dead you don't get to be alive anymore. My Aunt Isabelle loves me. She is my father's sister. Sometimes she even pretends that I am her own son. Aunt Miriam and Uncle Reuben love me. They are my mother's youngest brother and his wife. But I don't think my mother loves me even though once in a while she tells me she does. She even kisses me on the lips once in a while. When she's not looking I sneak into the bathroom and wash her kiss off my lips. I don't like when she does it. I feel dirty. Otherwise, the only time she touches me is to hit or kick me.

I get down on my knees. I hate it I hate it I hate her I hate this. I wonder, does she ever hate herself? I wish what was happening wasn't a secret.

I look up at my mother's face. She has that crooked smile. "Please, please, mommy, can I have that present? I'm going to be seven years old and I'd like a real present for my birthday. Can I please have it?"

Three days later I receive my present. My father gives it to me. I don't think he knows what happened, but I'm not sure. Sometimes I hear him in the bedroom with my mother and he cries. He says to her: "I don't know what to do to make you better."

I don't either.

MUMTAZ AND THE
FISHERMEN'S SLUM

Mumtaz Mahal, the best-loved second wife of the Emperor
Shah Jehan, died in childbirth in the year 1631 in northern India. Her husband spent the next twenty-two years building
perhaps the world's most beautiful building to serve as her mausoleum and his monument to her memory. Shah Jehan and his wife
were reunited in this building upon his death in 1666. They are
still there in peace, although not where the public can see them.

The Taj Mahal, this majestic resting place for two people, dom-
inates in its sheer scale a square of four buildings: a large, arched
entry, an important mosque, a building to match the mosque for
symmetry's sake but otherwise empty, and the monumental yet
perfectly scaled Taj itself. Made of translucent white marble and
covered with delicately inlaid semi-precious stones of blue, red,
and green forming floral designs and quotes from the Quran,
surrounded by formal Persian gardens with walkways of trees

and formal rectangles of emerald grass, the Taj is its own oxygen. There is no need to breathe on one's own. The Taj does it for you. All that is missing is perfume in the air.

The overwhelming spaciousness peacefully dazzles those who come to be overcome. Staring at it from any angle, its perfect symmetry produces a dance of straight lines and curves. Although the Taj itself is not the mosque on the site, its minarets are their own call to prayer, and its five domes are prayer itself. At sunset the white marble turns pink and gold. As the sky darkens further, the great white dome shimmers in the deep navy sky. At sunrise, the domes and minarets emerge from the grey mist, become pink, pale yellow, and then gold before the dazzling white of the marble emerges in its purity.

And all for two people in death only.

⇒—⇐

To the south, in Mumbai's Machimar slum, in the first decade of the 21st century, another Mumtaz lives. Husbandless yet not widowed, the matriarch of a three generation family of women, all of whom sleep in a single room that is eight feet long by five feet wide and not quite six feet high, she presides over the household. A small table pushed into a corner, holding a small television and stray papers, stands opposite a small flank of small shelves that hold all the family's goods. Folded clothing, shoes, schoolbooks, paper and plastic bags, nostrums keep close company. The family's Quran, bound in simulated leather, sits separately on one shelf. There is no other furniture. The family, as with all slum-dwelling families, sits, eats, entertains callers, argues, and hugs on thin-woven mats laid out on the floor. In the morning, they are rolled up and put away on the shelves.

This Mumtaz of the 21st century is in her fifties. She wears an old orange and white sari, covering her head with it when in the presence of strangers. She has two daughters who are in their thirties. One older son has been married for several years but has not brought his wife to live with Mumtaz. The younger daughter, recently married, moved to live in her husband's parents' home in keeping with Indian custom. Her mother-in-law, if she approves of her, will be her friend and principal companion. She will help raise the children and there will be amity. Her mother-in-law, if she disapproves of her, will be her taskmaster and abuser. She will take over the raising of the children and there will be discord. One hundred and fifty years ago she could have safely set her daughter-in-law on fire if she fully disliked her.

The other daughter, Jaya, left her husband and ran away from the regular beatings inflicted by her mother-in-law as her husband watched and vilified her. Humiliated, she brought her eleven-year-old daughter, Ghina, back home with her to Mumtaz. She had to leave her two older sons with her husband and her mother-in-law. She agonizes over them. They are fourteen and sixteen. She is ashamed and burdened by conflict for having so publicly broken the cultural norm. She also must contend with her mother's, Mumtaz's, anger, disappointment, and strongly voiced disapproval.

Mumtaz lives in the Machimar slum near the tip of southwest Bombay. By hutment standards, she is comfortable. In addition to the family's one-room home at the end of the lane, she has constructed a kitchen four feet by three feet. This kitchen has a great slum luxury: a small window. Kitchen access is accomplished by stepping across the three-foot square opening for the narrow, steep ladder that serves as the doorway to Mumtaz's living quarters from the dank lane below. The family's upstairs space is closed off at night by lowering a plank over the ladder. This serves as the door.

The odor of fish permeates Machimar. As the slum curves around, the backs of its structures form a dramatic cliff rising directly out of the Arabian Sea. From the front, Machimar slum is protected from the six-lane public street by a chain link fence that the residents nevertheless move as they need access to the street. The narrow concrete footpath forces people together.

Machimar houses several thousand people in a small, dense area. There is an optical illusion at work. Behind what looks like a straight line of two-story concrete rooms, each its own home, lies a shadowy maze of lanes, flanked on one side by the public toilets and showers and on the other by the drop-down to collect the fish. The smell of the fresh fish being gutted by women at one end and the stench of the ill-kept public toilets and showers at the other meet in the middle, along with the odd dead rat or bandicoot lying in its urine and shit. A bandicoot resembles a rat that has swallowed several other rats. Due to the fence, there is nowhere for the residents to move this offal and so they shovel it into piles which will eventually get collected on no predictable schedule. Machimar's residents live in a human warehouse.

Each dark lane may be two feet wide, an odiferous blend of fish, urine, soap, rat shit, and the soft smell of babies. Most of the one room windowless homes open onto these lanes (*guhlees*) as they wend their way back from the footpath to the drop-off to the sea. The ocean, often a symbol of dreams and wishes and freedom, in Machimar is just background. With "only" several thousand people, most everyone knows everyone else. Toddlers in the *guhlees* wander from home to home, Hindu or Muslim, makes no difference. Someone is looking out for them. They will be welcomed into any home they choose. One crawling Hindu child likes hanging out with Mumtaz, who beams when she sees him. There is no religious tension. The baby's mother simply requested Mumtaz to refrain from teaching her son to bow to Allah with each call to prayer from the local imam. Mumtaz is careful to comply.

I am lucky. Asha has done much advance work: appearing in Machimar and meeting people, asking the residents if it would be all right if a white American psychologist joined her in coming to talk with people. The residents know what a psychologist is. "Talking to a psychologist makes the tension in one's heart feel better." Asha has even gotten written police permission for me to visit Machimar. (In years to come, we don't bother with the police or with permission from authorities. We just go to various slum areas throughout Mumbai.) Machimar just happens to be only a ten-minute walk from the Colaba Family Association Guest House, so Asha and I begin here. The residents would like it if Asha and I visit for a week or more, as long as "the American is not someone who wants to tell me that Jesus is better than my religion." Asha assures them, with a knowing smile, that I am most decidedly not that kind of American. Reassured, several people ask for our help spontaneously. Mumtaz is one of them. She is expecting us.

Mumtaz waits for us in her room, along with returned daughter Jaya and granddaughter Ghina. She sits, half-filling the room by herself. She leans against the flaking turquoise wall in her full sari. One leg is bent and the other is held with the knee up and foot flat on the floor. Mumtaz has her elbow on her knee and cups her chin with her palm. Jaya dresses with even greater desperation in a grey, once white, sari with green, now black, paisley, the product of too many washings for one inexpensive piece of fabric. She looks resentfully and fearfully at her mother who is furious with her for breaking tradition and leaving her husband and two boys.

Ghina is wearing her tan and white school uniform. She attends a regular school despite the presence of a *madrasa* within the slum. (Mumtaz attends the *madrasa* to try to learn enough Arabic to be able to read the Quran herself.) Mumtaz and Jaya speak Hindi. Ghina speaks Hindi, good English, and is able to read the Quran's Arabic and translate it. Ghina has a soft round face with dimples and a ready smile. She has been taught hospitality and when we are all in the room, she takes out mats for us to sit on, cross-legged, and looks to her mother and grandmother to see if she should make tea. Although I cannot imagine how she could not take in the tension between her mother and grandmother, it is not discernible. That may be because underneath Mumtaz's severity and Jaya's distress, their caring for each other is subtly present. Warmth exists.

Mumtaz asks for our help. "We are not getting along. My daughter should go with her husband just like my other daughter did. I will share my home with her but I want her to choose to go back to her husband. It is shameful what she has done. We argue." Jaya tells us, "I couldn't be beaten and called those names anymore. My husband did nothing but laugh and yell at me "whore" and other terrible things. I was able to get Ghina out but I feel so bad that I left Rasheed (age 12) and Ahmed (age 17) there. I abandoned them. Should I go back there and be beaten so I can be with my sons? I am not bringing Ghina back there. What do I do?" Mumtaz's absent, unmentioned, living husband haunts the room and hovers above us all.

Asha and I meet with the family every day for over a week. Since we are treated as guests in accord with Indian hospitality, I don't know whether to call our time together "sessions." We may spend one hour, or sometimes two hours, deep in conversation. Either Mumtaz or Jaya will want to talk to us alone afterwards, perhaps fifteen minutes, perhaps an hour. The Hindu toddler downstairs makes his way up the steep stairway helped by a child in the *guhlees,* knowing that Mumtaz will watch him while his mother runs an errand. She rubs his back while speaking. A neighbor may stop in for a quarter of an hour, listen, and offer her opinion. The best I can do is consider this as "working openly."

Mumtaz offers us tea during the first two sessions. By the third visit she has baked a variety of cookies and places them in the middle of the room in which we all sit cross-legged. She mentions that the water has been fully boiled so the tea is safe for me to drink. On the fourth day my knee is damaged.

I had been mugged the evening before, walking home to my wife waiting for me in our guesthouse. A young man violently pushed me from behind and sent me sprawling into the street along with the traffic. I landed on my knee. Realizing what was happening, I grasped the small travel wallet in my front pocket, covering it with my hand, and clutched the book Asha and Gopal had just given me. The predator quickly frisked my pockets, couldn't feel my wallet, and ran away empty-handed. Thirty seconds had passed. When I got up, my slacks were intact but my leg was bleeding in several places and as I walked, my knee increasingly hurt. (It has since been diagnosed as a bone chip directly below the knee. I have made friends with it, and call it my Bombay Bone Chip.)

When visiting Mumtaz and Jaya and Ghina the next day, Mumtaz noticed how I moved my knee and was concerned. I told her the story. She arranged for me to sit against the wall and stretch my knee out during our session. My foot touched the opposite wall, hence my estimate of the room's width.

The session begins. We clarify the issues, and try to make sure that Mumtaz and Jaya understand why each one feels the way she does. There are no problems getting feelings aired. Actually, the conversation is much more direct than many Indian discussions, which tend to be oblique: the meaning is between the lines and in the silences; agreement may well imply disagreement. Not so much here.

Again Mumtaz's missing husband hovers above. Asha and I can discern Mumtaz's raw feeling beneath the surface that seems not quite connected to Jaya. Mumtaz and Jaya make it clear when our time is up, usually by starting to clear away the tea and biscuits or cookies they have supplied in the middle of the tiny room where the five of us huddle.

After several days, our presence in Machimar is well known. As we walk on the footpath to talk, as we do daily, with the gentle and ambitious young father who runs a public telephone service and sells cement on the side, a tall man who may or may not be clutching a knife approaches us menacingly. "What are you doing here? Why is a white man here? What are you planning to take from us?" He starts to hover over me and several men rush over and gently pull him back. "He is an American visiting us. He is a psychologist. He is taking nothing. He is giving to us. He is good." The man changes his minatory posture, harrumphs to save face, and then rather humbly apologizes to me, offering his hand.

A street discussion with all these men develops as they want to tell Asha and me what their lives are like, what they do for a living, how they are exploited by their landlords (they most decidedly are), how hard they work and how little they bring home for their families. The women cleaning fish look on, as do children in the street. Asha and I then get an escort to the end of the gate and people say they will see us the next day. One man tells us he wants to show us his home and the photograph of his dead child.

I am surprised how family therapy with Mumtaz, Jaya, and Ghina seems to be occurring amidst neighbors' visits, toddlers, beggars calling up the ladder for money, stray dogs and cats, sessions of indeterminate length, tea, cookies, sitting cross-legged on the floor and in a context where everyone knows what is happening with everyone else. I shouldn't be surprised by now.

We return the next day. Now we are greeted by many, but not all, people on the Machimar footpath. The women cleaning fish remain suspicious. We have trouble finding the right lane because the shard of mirror hanging by a string on the *guhlee* opening had broken. We figure it out eventually but our difficulty is noticed, for the following day a new shard of mirror is up and the woman who provided it comes out of her windowless home to show us that she has done this for us. She smiles simply and is pleased by our gratitude. This is warm Indian hospitality that permeates the culture and crosses social strata.

As a Western psychologist, I still don't know whether to call what we are doing "therapy" or not. It appears to have a therapeutic effect. The emotional tone in the home is lower. Voices have hints of kindness, although when Mumtaz becomes stern it still is most impressive. On this day, Mumtaz repeats, "If you have a husband you should be with him. Other circumstances don't matter." But today her sadness is low-lying fruit; it is more accessible. Something is going to happen. We wait. Ghina is at school; only adults are present.

"I will tell you my story but first you both must tell us a very sad story that happened to you." She is asking for reciprocity. She wants not to be the "subject" and seeks a human joining in sorrow. Mumtaz is asking for the gift of our own hurt. Asha tells her own story of sadness and regret and mists over. I tell the story of being beaten after my grandfather's death, with a few soft tears. (I recall being trained never to disclose anything about myself. But this is India and not America, and this is Mumtaz and her family, specific people with specific needs in this particular moment.)

Mumtaz is satisfied. No, she is not satisfied, because she hasn't been sitting in judgment. She is moved, and aware that she has been respected. With tears in her own eyes from our stories, she tells us hers. She was married. She still is married. Her husband deserted her for another woman, a blind woman, an implicitly unsavory woman, an unattractive woman. He no longer acknowledges Mumtaz when their paths cross. This is an internal humiliation made public in the all-knowing environment of a slum. Her tears in reaction to our stories haven't stopped when they are renewed with tears from her own stories. We all are experiencing the intermingling of human woe. I know this because when she finishes and dries her eyes (and we dry ours), she looks at Asha and me and says, ever so delicately, "Thank you. I am not ashamed."

As we leave for the day, a woman whose one-room home we pass daily stops us. She looks frantic and asks us to come in. Do we have time to talk with her? She is terrified because her husband did not come home last night and this has never happened before. They had moved to Bombay from a northern Rajasthani village a year before. He is a vendor near the central railway terminal, the CST. She doesn't know if he has been robbed, murdered, or run away, although that would not be like him. Nor does she know what to do. She has called the police, costing the equivalent of ten cents, a lot of money. The police were dismissive of her because of her uneducated village accent. She can't leave home because of their baby. It is cold at night and her husband has no jacket. She has asked friends to ask friends—the wonderful Indian social network at work—and still can find out nothing. She just wants to tell her story. After an hour and a half, she thanks us for listening and says she feels calmer. The next day she makes a point of finding us to tell us that he has been found. The police mistook him for someone else and had kept him overnight. They have let him go without expecting a bribe and he is now home. She thanks us again for listening to her. "I felt better just talking."

On the way to Mumtaz, we stop to talk with the man who runs the public telephone and sells cement. Perhaps thirty, he has a wife and two young children. Despite being a practicing Jain (a non-deistic ethical "religion" almost exclusive to India), he has a small shrine in his open area shop that includes Jain symbols, a card of Muslim quotations, the marigolds and candles needed for Hindu *puja* (daily service to a god), and a postcard of Jesus. He smiles: "I want to cover everybody." He asks me to help him to put up the flowers and other items to ward off the evil eye "for those people who believe in that," and we work together. He talks at some length about the need to get ahead so that he can be a good father and husband and give his wife a better place to live and his children a better neighborhood where perhaps the schools might be better. (I visited him over the next several years. He had since purchased a sari shop in a different part of town, and was preparing to move.)

As Asha and I finish talking with this charming, ambitious entrepreneur, several men walk up. One is heavily bandaged across his bare chest, the other two are his friends. He has just come from the public hospital. A homeless street sleeper, he had been mistaken by a group of Bombay gangster goons for someone else because he had the same first name. He had been punched, kicked, and sliced with a knife in the stomach. As he is telling his tale, a truck comes by to pick up an order of cement. Trucks are not allowed to stop on the street in front of Machimar. The religiously eclectic entrepreneur asks for some help moving cement bags onto the curb to make a driveway so the truck can drive up, and off the street, to the disappointment of the police who are deprived of a bribe. Everyone around helps, including the bandaged fellow until he is in too much pain. They load the truck; it drives away, the cement "driveway" removed, the fence replaced. We have to leave to meet Mumtaz, Jaya, and Ghina. Again, from the group of men: "Thank you."

During this meeting, Asha and I mention, delicately, that Mumtaz's feelings about her husband might be influencing how strongly she feels about Jaya returning to her husband. Jaya has a husband and she left him; Mumtaz had a husband and he left her. It is hard for her to tolerate the comparison. It is quiet as Mumtaz thinks and Jaya observes. Ghina wisely places herself outside the tight circle.

Six more people join us. Mumtaz's relatives from the south are in town and stop by to visit, bringing Jaya's newly married sister with them. They are Mumtaz's nephews' relatives and Mumtaz appropriately considers them her own. She invites them to join the conversation. We now have eleven people in the eight by five foot windowless room, all sitting on the floor, and all participating. This conversation proves very useful. Mumtaz hears varying views about Jaya's leaving her husband and sons from her own family and not just though Jaya's protests. Jaya's relief at being joined by others is palpable.

The next day is our last. We walk through the gate and are greeted with hearty hellos. The man who runs the public toilet asks if I want to use it as he has just cleaned it. The eclectic entrepreneur has finished his set-up for the morning and smiles: "You are too late. Come back next year? Visit?" and he offers me some of his water: "It's all right for you. It's bottled."

We meet with Mumtaz and Jaya alone. Ghina is getting ready for school and is still in the room. Jaya has decided to return to her husband's and mother-in-law's home to be near her sons and try to watch over them. Ghina will stay with her no-nonsense but loving grandmother. (Actually, Jaya has a plan that she is keeping secret.) Mumtaz and Jaya are deeply grateful. As is Ghina. With an open smile, she then looks most serious and takes down the family copy of the Quran and covers her head. "I will say 'thank you' by reading for you from the Quran." She devoutly speaks the holy Arabic words and when she is finished, looks up at us with a wide smile. We thank her for honoring us. Mumtaz and Jaya beam and we all say goodbye.

We visited the next year. Jaya had indeed returned to her husband. Her older son was now safe and out of that house: he was eighteen and working. She had, after several months, arranged for her younger son to transfer to a different school so that he would spend after-school hours with Mumtaz, minimizing his time at his home. In a few years, when he graduates school, Jaya plans to return home to Mumtaz and then look for her own place. Mumtaz has made peace with this. She has come to feel that it is all right if Jaya leaves her husband because of the abuse as long as she has taken care of her sons. The children will be safe and will have their mother. Mumtaz gained supportive distance from her own pain. She said to Jaya: "You don't want to end up with a husband like mine." We said our last goodbyes to Mumtaz and her family.

No one will build a glorious mausoleum to this 21st century Mumtaz in a fishing slum in Bombay. She is no Emperor's beloved wife. She is a wife but not beloved. But she is full of life and has learned from her suffering. As with all the slum dwellers, she does not bemoan her poverty. She knows, as does everyone there, and best articulated by the eclectic entrepreneur, that they were "One

Stars" and not "Five Stars" (using the hotel rating system). The entrepreneur says to me: "Yes, we are One Stars. And we do wish we had more and want more for our children. But that doesn't mean we are unhappy. There are Five Stars who have a lot more. Are all of them happy? It all depends on how you choose to look at how you live."

When I try to organize my thoughts about India, to think about what I have seen as a tourist and witnessed in close personal situations during my volunteer work, when I look at the whole picture in all its layered density, its colors, smells, movement, philosophy stated or unstated, it's sheer humanity, the Taj Mahal does not come readily to my mind. The people of the slums are foremost. Without sentimentality and with clear eyes, they have my deepest respect.

Not two people in a mausoleum, but thousands in small rooms permeated with the smell of fish.

Lonely Planet INDIA was a useful resource on the background of the Taj Mahal.

"THIS IS WHAT'S WRONG WITH YOU"

*B*rooklyn, 1956. *My mother is out for my blood. She has started stalking me around my room, fists flailing trying to find my face, legs looking for a good opportunity to kick me. I am ten years old now. I try not to listen to her words because I have heard them since I was three and four. They don't change. I move more quickly than my very quick mother and so I am a more difficult target. She gets increasingly frustrated because she cannot release her terrible internal tension by hitting or kicking me so easily. I have learned how to get myself out of the thin rope she has used to tie me to my closet doorknob. She tried, with my helpless father's assistance, to tie me to eye screws that she put in the wall over my bed so that I would be tied to the wall while lying down trying to go to sleep at night. I quickly learned how to get out of those ropes and put my hands back in when it was time to get up in the morning so she wouldn't know. Eventually she found out and gave up on tying me to the wall.*

She has started screaming new things and blending them with the old. **"I wish you had never been born. You are an evil monster."** *I have* *heard her say this in different ways for years now. I try to ignore her more but her words still hurt and I still haven't figured out how I am a monster. She adds something for the first time, or this is the first time I notice it as I've worked so hard to tune her screaming out.*

"IF YOU HAD BEEN BORN A GIRL EVERYTHING WOULD HAVE BEEN ALL RIGHT. BOYS ARE PART OF THE EVIL. IF YOU WERE A GIRL, I WOULD HAVE SOMEONE TO TALK TO. I WOULD HAVE CALLED YOU "MICHELLE" AND YOU WOULD HAVE TAKEN CARE OF ME. YOU WOULD HAVE LISTENED TO ME TALK. YOU WOULDN'T BE INTERESTED IN YOURSELF.

"YOU ARE SELFISH, INCONSIDERATE, AND DEMANDING. IF YOU WERE A GIRL YOU WOULDN'T BE. YOU WOULD KEEP ME COMPANY. *Instead you are a boy and a monster and you should never have been born.* IF YOU WERE MICHELLE I WOULD HAVE WANTED YOU. I WANT YOU TO GO AWAY. SOMEONE SHOULD TAKE YOU AWAY!"

Hearing this, I slow down as I still circle the room as if I were in a cage with a hungry tigress. This is a mistake. **SMACK**! *I am cracked on the side of my face once, twice. Then I get away. I've regained my speed. My mother makes her movement to kick me. I am angry and place myself in front of my bed with its metal bed stand. I purposely hesitate. She makes a quick move to kick me in the shin and I dart quickly away so her shin will hit the metal bedstead. She is furious. I feel hurt and angry but also vindicated. I also know I had better leave quickly now. I run for the apartment door as my mother tries to stop me. I get there first and run out. I don't remember if it was warm or cold out or whether I needed a coat or not. I just knew I was away. And although I felt angry and I felt good that my mother got hurt for trying to hurt me when she kicked me, I also felt sad.*

I stay away until dinner time. She is quieter then.

MUMBAI: THE WHITE "FIVE-STARS" LIKE BROWN BOYS

Bombay can boast a thriving child sex trade. Beautiful nine and ten year old children, mostly boys and mostly homeless, are kidnapped, stolen off the street. They become sexual chattel, often for Western businessmen staying in the Five Star hotels. The predatory businessmen pick them up at night several blocks behind the big hotels, in good neighborhoods, and are provided rooms to do with these boys whatever they wish. No one is watching. No one cares. This is reputedly primarily a gangster activity but I suspect independent operators as well. The children are kept and used until they are older adolescents and look more adult. Then, with no schooling behind them, they are let go, released into the hard streets of Bombay, uneducated, without marketable skills and with no place to sleep.

Asha and I worked in a Youth Shelter with several of these boys-now-grown-up, eighteen to twenty-two. They stayed there safely at night while they looked for unskilled labor work during the day. The Shelter consisted of two floors, one large room on each floor. Light linoleum tile, light walls, few windows, no furniture. Just a place to put a bedroll and a suitcase. A small kitchen allowed the young men to cook small meals or at least make tea. The Youth Shelter is intended for temporary use, a place to be safe overnight until someone finds work and a room to rent.

We enter the Shelter and two young men smile and welcome us in, inviting us up the stairs where the boy-men sleep. Each temporary resident has a shelf for his small suitcase and basic toiletries: razor, soap, toothbrush. Anil takes down his suitcase and one other and offers us seats. I tell him I will break it if I sit on it. He breezily says, "No you won't and I'll find another if you do. Sit, I'll bring tea. Sugar? Milk?"

He returns as a small group is forming to talk with Asha and me. I expect sullen, broken-looking, ill-kempt young men, their oppression made visible. Instead I find the effects of oppression in well-groomed people who can smile through pain: feeling lost, not knowing where to turn, having no plan or even the conception of how to formulate a plan. Most can read and write at the fourth grade level, the time in their schooling when they were kidnapped and forced into childhood whoredom. They tend to be rather dark-skinned: "The white Five Stars like dark boys."

Together over several meetings, we talk about what a plan is and how you make one. One fellow looks out the window at the sea and muses with a wistful humor, "I'm sure there's someplace where I'm good for something. I might even have a family." He is the only one who could think that far ahead. The others live in the moment. They have to. What kind of job could they get? How do you look for a job besides walking in shops and begging for one? Where will I find a meal for lunch?

Anil also lives in the moment, but with success. He has found a job delivering pizzas and has had that job for two weeks at that time. He is confident this will last as his employers like him, as do we. He conveys intrepid optimism, loves to talk, and is an appealing human being. During one of our visits he is particularly excited because he has advanced in his job and has been entrusted with a motorcycle and helmet, both dark blue. He jokes about how he makes his way through Bombay traffic (actually something worth boasting about) as he makes his deliveries. In fact, in the ensuing two weeks he spotted me walking on the streets in different parts of the city and flashily pulled over to stop and say hello.

Most of the boy-men believe their greatest hope lies in becoming cabbies. We talk about driver's licenses and how to get them. They recognize with some humor that they don't know their way around the city "but we learn, we get you where you going," they say earnestly, with bright eyes, and conviction. Despite how lost they are, these abused former sex bait are not without optimism. Somehow they are confident they will make it all work out.

To offer truth to the optimism, two young men from Karnataka, the next state south, came to the Shelter. They came to Mumbai for greater opportunity, as do so many millions. All they knew about Bombay was that they had a cousin who lived there and he had told them he would help them find jobs if they came. The Karnatakans only knew his name. They had no address. They thought he might be an auto-rickshaw driver. Bombay has eighteen million people spread out over an immense area. One can commute for two to three hours at a reasonable, perhaps wild, pace and still be within city limits. They had absolute confidence that they would find him.

It took the Karnatakans less than a day to find their uncle. They learned that auto-rickshaws are only allowed in the mid- and outer sections of the city and so they made their way there. They asked where the auto-rickshaws could usually be found. A helpful man on the street told them that they tended to be in two neighborhoods of the city. Heading toward the first section, they stopped in many shops and asked auto-rickshaw drivers if they knew the uncle. No luck and so they went to the other section where there is a concentration of auto-rickshaws. In thirty minutes they found their uncle and planned to move in with him in two days. These two smiling Karnatakans gave the residents of the Youth Shelter hope.

On the day they left the Youth Shelter for their uncle's place, they came looking for Asha and me at Mumtaz's home in order to say goodbye and to thank us for listening to them and for being interested in them.

FOR A FEW RUPEES MORE

A sha and I made our way to Friends of the Footpath for our annual period of work with the street children. We walked through the gate at the back, off the grey and reddish-pink brick footpath and onto light brown sandy earth on the side of the Friends' building. We passed street families, washing and cleaning up the evening's evidence of life. A pail of water here, freshly washed tattered clothing hanging there. The bedrolls were tucked away. A street cat sniffed around while a dog torpidly watched. Mid-February had marked the shift from winter (85 degrees) to summer (95 degrees or more). The monsoon had been almost six months ago and the dry dust of rainlessness sat lightly on everything. Nothing would glisten with the freshness of water until mid-June, when grey stone buildings would become pearly, footpaths develop a sheen, leaves turn an emerald green, and the wet bark of trees glisten in shades of brown like newly polished shoes.

As we entered the building Veena, looking severe, came up to us and whispered that eight-year-old Praveen had died the night before of meningitis. Would we talk with the children, who had been informed, about her death and their feelings?

Asha and I consulted with each other briefly ("briefly" is all we had) and decided to break the children into two groups by age: eight to twelve year olds, and thirteen to seventeen year olds. We started assembling the smaller children in a circle but all the youngsters, in their urgency, would have none of this. Within less than a minute we had a single group of fifty children surrounding us. The youngest were on small stools, a few of the older ones were on full-sized chairs, and the rest were standing. Asha and I sat on small stools as part of the circle so that all of the children could see at least one of our faces. The sun filtered into the building, highlighting the dark brown shutters and illuminating the dusty specks floating in the light. And so we sat, a circle of living children and two adults in the high-ceilinged room, dark but for the piercings of the sunlight, and discussed the death of an eight year old girl.

The children had all seen death before, in their makeshift homes, in street violence, in public hospital corridors where there is a space in the hallway for a patient's family to become welcome squatters during the illness of a relative. Nevertheless, an eight year old had died. Since death should come after many years, Praveen had not been allowed to live out her full life. A parent had to bury her child. The sequence of life had been cracked.

The children were most disturbed by this dis-order. They spoke of their sadness about Praveen. They reminisced. They would miss her. The children also understood, I believe, the closeness of the possibility of their own premature deaths because of Praveen's story. She had become ill on a Friday evening with a high fever. Her mother gave her home remedies to lower her temperature, unsuccessfully. She spent most of Saturday unsuccessfully trying to come up with enough rupees (American equivalent perhaps fif-ty cents for two people) for bus fare to the nearest public hospital. The best she could do was amass enough rupees to get them partly there. She picked Praveen up and put her on the bus, taking her as far as their rupees would allow. After disembarking she carried her feverish eight-year-old the rest of the way, alternately holding her in her arms and heaving her over her shoulder. Praveen died in the hospital early Sunday morning.

The children sat soberly. While death was not quite common, the comings and goings of people were. Some families lived in the same cobbled-together home for years. Others moved frequently. Praveen had moved. The children continued their day.

THE SOUTH INDIAN PSYCHOLOGICAL ASSOCIATION

O ne year, The South Indian Psychological Association held its annual convention during my regular time in India. Asha decided that we would attend, as the theme for the meeting was globalization. We had not registered for the meeting. Upon looking at the program Asha and I both noted the preponderance of presentations pertaining to the business of, rather than the human factors involved in, globalization.

We looked at each other. Asha had come armed: "I've brought my slide show of our work with the blind. We're going to get ourselves on the program and you're going to make a presentation. I'll run the photos and add to your comments."

"How are we going to do that? We have nothing written prepared. We're not registered. We wangled our way in. We're not listed in the program. There is nowhere in the program where we fit."

"Marc, *you* are going to make it happen. Everything in India happens through relationship. I've met the President of the South Indian Psychological Association. I'll introduce you and then I'll guide you in what to do next. We'll get ourselves on this afternoon's program. First she needs to know you." Although unsaid, Asha was implying that just a touch of obsequiousness on my part wouldn't hurt.

Asha introduced me, stressing my being an American. The President's eyes lit up. I showed the correct level of pleasure in being present and in making her acquaintance. Asha and I then sat down. A few moments later the day's proceedings began…with an announcement that an American psychologist was in attendance. Applause. Further announcement noted that the convention was now international.

By this time I was beet red and feeling panicked that perhaps I actually would end up speaking this afternoon. Paperless, scriptless, naked. I said to Asha "surely you must have, in your huge knock-off Gucci handbag, a sheet of paper, or anything on which I could write down three talking points?" I had learned this standard technique years ago for performing in the electronic media and in print interviews. Asha found an old envelope in her bottomless tan purse. I borrowed a pen from the person sitting next to me, who graciously added, "How nice to have you with us, Doctor." I wrote down my three talking points, folded the tattered envelope, and hoped I wouldn't have to use it.

Asha told me that I would be walking over to the President of the South Indian Psychological Association every fifteen minutes, saying something different each time. She would guide me in this process and I was not to worry. In fifteen minutes, Asha suggested that I get up and go over to the President and simply mention that, having heard one presentation, I was most happy to be able to attend the convention. It would be fine to make pleasantries but I was not to mention anything further professionally. I did this and the President thanked me most graciously. I think she understood completely what was going on and that, if I followed the unspoken Indian protocol, she would find a place in the schedule for Asha and me to present our work. I found this interesting in that we had not mentioned our work yet, nor our wish to present. Instead of playing an underhanded game, I was enacting proper protocol to get something accomplished. There were no fools here.

Fifteen minutes later, Asha told me to go up to the President and mention that Asha and I were doing some very interesting work with the elderly blind that was an example of globalized mental health. She advised me not to express any wish to make a presentation. I followed my marching orders, unsure whether I was receiving an *in vivo* lesson in Indian formalities that would serve me well, or becoming a trained dog. It subsequently became clear that Asha was giving me a useful lesson in how things work in India. Relationship trumps all.

In another fifteen minutes, I returned to the President, who by then was expecting me. I mentioned that if possible, I had material to share that would be relevant to globalization and psychology. As directed, I didn't press the point. The President told me "that is most interesting." I returned to my seat and Asha matter-of-factly said to me: "Two more visits to the President and we'll be on the program."

Another fifteen minutes passed: "When you go up to the President this time, mention that you'll only be here today. (Not true.) The most important papers are being presented today. You might now add that you would be very grateful if the President might possibly find a way to allow you to present your work to the audience today. Leave it at that."

I did so. The President nodded her head knowingly. Little else was said, except I noted to myself that each time I went to speak with her, the President smiled more broadly and became friendlier. She remained aware of her position and of my use of Indian propriety.

Fifteen minutes later, at 11:30 a.m., Asha gave me a look. "Just go up to her. Say nothing. She knows what you want, you have built a suitable relationship, and she will graciously accommodate you." I followed through, by now really enjoying this process. As I approached, the President nodded and told me that Asha and I had been put on the program for that afternoon at 1:30 pm. Two hours away. Would we please join her and other Association officers for lunch?

The afternoon programs began, more or less on time. At 1:50, Asha and I were the first presenters, my having been placed onstage at a panel dais. I walked over to the podium with my old envelope. Asha manned the power point and held a microphone. We presented the first material concerning the human side of globalization of the conference thus far. Our allotted fifteen minutes became forty by audience request. They kept applauding when I tried to end after fifteen minutes. I saw the President nod her permission to continue. By the time I returned to my seat in the auditorium, Asha showed me a handwritten invitation to tea with the President during that day's afternoon break. It was beautifully done in gold-colored ink on delicate rice paper. Everything in India works by relationship.

SAGAR'S BIRTHDAY PRESENT

Sagar was turning eleven. In his bedroll on the street, he had dreamed for years of riding on a train. He wanted to feel the rumbling throughout his body that his friends had told him about. He wanted to stand by the always open doors; the windows had bars, which wouldn't be as much fun. He could feel the rush of the air, he imagined, if he stood by the door. The train would move him faster than his only means of transportation, his feet. His family does not have enough money for both food and a train ride (perhaps eight cents in rupees).

Sagar's best friend had been saving for three months to take Sagar on a train ride for his eleventh birthday. He had just made it, the exact number of rupees for the two of them to ride one stop, get off, and walk home. After school on the big day, he said to Sagar, "I have a surprise for you; let's go this way instead of going to Friends of the Footpath yet." They walked to the nearest train station. Sagar beamed. He looked as vibrant as his green cap. He was a little confused about the ticket lines and which side of the platform to stand on to be sure to get a train going in the right direction. The two boys didn't want a long walk to their street homes.

The train arrived. Sagar felt a bit frightened by the people rushing off the train and the people pushing to get on the train simultaneously, but he and his friend made it on. He stood near the door. The train looked like what he imagined but never having been on a train, he didn't know what to do. He wanted to feel the air on his face and the windows had bars.

The train left the station and picked up speed. It went into a tunnel and Sagar couldn't see what was outside. No one had told him not to put his head out the door when in a tunnel where you can't see what might be there. Sagar held on to the door handle and leaned his head fully out the door.

The train passed a steel pillar in the tunnel. Sagar's face was ripped off. His neck split open and his head hung backwards. He fell, although the train was so crowded that he never reached the floor. He was already dead. Everyone around him supported his limp body and dangling head, their clothes dripping his fresh eleven-year-old blood. When the train stopped at the next station, passengers created a human wall, not permitting anyone to rush onto the train until they gently carried Sagar's body off and his friend joined him. Then they soberly got back on to continue their journey home from work. Everyday Indian kindness in adversity. The trained pulled out of the station. Horror had become part of a day.

Asha and I happened to be spending several days at Friends of the Footpath when Sagar took his birthday ride. Our job, once again, was to help the children understand the end of a friend, what had happened. They could talk about it if they wanted to, or simply sit with caring adults if that was what they needed. The violence of Sagar's death shocked the children. This was not something they had seen before. They were stunned and their words came slowly, but they did.

The children's primary worry was what would happen to Sagar's soul. He, like Praveen, hadn't had the opportunity to live out his life, hadn't had the time to accumulate in this life the balance of karma that would determine his next life. He had been cut off in more than one way. They did not make the connection between Sagar's and their own poverty and the horror of what happened on the train: had Sagar not been poor, he would have known how to ride a train. He would have done it many times. Trains are cheap in Mumbai.

But not cheap enough if you are Sagar.

DISOWNED

Silver Spring, Maryland. 1963. We moved to the suburbs of Washington DC a few years ago. Leaving Brooklyn behind, I felt newly alive. Being a teenager helped. I had lots of friends who mattered to me more than my family did. We all felt the same way. We were our Chosen Family; our "real" families had been imposed on us and we were stuck with them. Sometimes that was all right. Sometimes it wasn't. We were starting to drive, starting to hang out, starting to date, starting to do things on our own with or without our parents' knowledge.

My mother hated being moved from New York because she had left her family behind. She believed my father had persecuted her by taking her away. When she cried, I wasn't surprised that my brother, my father, and I weren't the family she cared about being with. She still yelled, or wept, and she was openly bitter more of the time, always blaming my father for what he had done to her.

I am sixteen now. I share a different bedroom with my brother. I don't understand why we keep living in two bedroom apartments when three bedroom apartments can't be that much more expensive. My father is a podiatrist. He makes a good living, better than in Brooklyn, but my mother insists that we can't afford three bedrooms and we certainly can't afford a house. I get a smaller allowance than my friends, but I make it last by walking when I can't drive the car, or having a friend pick me up. My friends are naturally generous. My mother is losing control of me.

When I go to the theatre, I often go alone because most of my friends aren't interested. I hope someday they will be. I can save a quarter each way if I walk the ten miles in each direction from our suburban apartment to the downtown Washington theatre and then home. I also just discovered ballet. I went alone because my friends thought it entirely too weird, something for girls only. I saw Suzanne Farrell dance. She and I are the same age. I never saw anyone look so beautiful when she moved.

Last Saturday night I went out with my friends. My mother didn't want me to go. She didn't like it that I had a lot of friends and that I didn't stay around our apartment. I also didn't invite friends over very much; I wanted to be at their houses. They had their own bedrooms and privacy. They had parents who seemed at ease.

The reason my mother didn't want me to go with my friends last weekend is we had "family coming in" for a visit. They were distant cousins I had never met and their children were all grown. But they were family and "family is always more important than friends." This was a mantra I had heard ever since I had become very social and a mantra that my parents did not follow. Ron and I had been left alone often for years. Back in Brooklyn, I was his babysitter when I was eleven. When the TV caught on fire I had to deal with it myself because our parents were out and hadn't told me where they were going or how to reach them. They were with friends. There were also a few Thanksgivings when my brother and I were sent to the movies in Brooklyn while my parents were at their friends' parties. Children not allowed.

I didn't want to miss being with my friends just to be with cousins I had never met and who didn't even have kids my age to hang out with. My mother yelled at me not to dare leave the house. She took the car keys and hid them. I called a friend who drove over and picked me up. She tried to block the door but I walked around her. I got home around midnight.

The next day my mother didn't talk to me. She no longer threatened me with no food, because she knew I could take care of myself in the kitchen. Her only weapons by then were scorn, scathing words, silence, and hatred. But that Sunday she didn't say anything. Nor on Monday.

Today is Tuesday and I've just come home from school. When I walk in my mother glares at me and is silent. Then she coldly says, "There's some mail for you; it's in your room." I hang up my coat, go into my room and find a letter from her to me, delivered by the U.S. Postal Service.

Dear Marc,

Your behavior last Saturday hurt me to the core. How can you consider your friends more important than your family? Do you think they would help you if you were in trouble the way your family would? Do you think they really care about you? How could you not be here to meet your cousins? You are abominable. You disgrace me. I regret that I have to sleep in the room next to where you are.

I never told you this before but I have wished for some time now, since we moved, that you would slit your throat. Then you couldn't talk. Your friends seem to enjoy what you have to say...oh I hear you on the phone! Don't think I'm not listening. And if your throat were slit, you couldn't talk and no one would be interested in you. You would be alone and I wouldn't care. After all, I'm only family.

I am writing to officially inform you that I disown you as my son. Expect nothing more from me. I will provide only food, clothing, and shelter for you. Otherwise, you are nothing to me and you never will be. You won't be in my will so don't expect anything even after I am dead. I don't consider you part of this family anymore.

Officially,
Rose Nemiroff

A CAKE FOR SIXTY CHILDREN

On a Friday evening, Sagar's mother comes to Friends of the Footpath. Asha and I are there with the children. It is his birthday and therefore the first anniversary of his death.

Friends of the Footpath throbs with energy on Fridays. It seems like a sturdy ship in the Bombay storm, safe enough that its passengers needn't huddle. Instead, they dance rather than do homework, sing rather than recite lessons, and as always, those white teeth and sparkling brown eyes of the children brighten the interior against the evening sky peeking in at the windows. The exuberant children are their own night lanterns.

Sagar's mother, whom everyone knows, has come this Friday to commemorate her lost son. She carries a slightly oily white bakery box and nothing else. She has on her best sari, an inexpensive expanse of elaborately folded fabric, fabric worn so thin that her dark skin shimmers through the once-bright green. There are remnants of gold-colored striping along the edges. Her hair is meticulously combed and parted in the middle, with the red dye on top of the part that signifies she is married. She is trying hard to smile, even when she fails and the tears gently shimmer on her cheeks. She has saved enough money to buy a birthday cake for Sagar to share with the children at Friends of the Footpath. Sagar was only one of her several children whom this place has succored.

The children say hello to her, briefly stopping their activities and then returning to them. She greets each one by name. Sagar loved this place. His mother wants to honor him by treating the children to a piece of cake. She opens the bakery box. The cake she has been able to afford is six inches round and topped with icing in Sagar's favorite bright green. Six inches round for sixty children.

The children stop playing. It is time for the special Friends of the Footpath Friday night dinner. Everyone stands at attention in rows. Boys on one side; girls on the other. Under Manoj Sir's direction—his affectionate bark—they recite their prayers before meals and sit on the floor that they have swept clean with short-handled brooms. Adults and volunteers serve the food and the bread. Sagar's mother helps.

While the children eat, Sagar's mother goes to a corner and meticulously cuts the diminutive cake into sixty small-diced pieces. She is proud of what she is doing for her son. I believe the children are moved. She is ready to offer each child a small piece, perhaps the size of a sugar cube. I wish every piece could have some frosting in Sagar's beloved green. Instead of beginning with the children, Sagar's mother comes over to offer Manoj, Asha, Lin (who has walked over and joined us) and me a piece of cake first. I stand, impossibly trying to figure out a quick way to count the pieces to be sure that I am not going to take something away from a child. I take the smallest piece I can see.

I experience an Indian conundrum: I do not want to dishonor Sagar's mother by taking too little of what she is offering—she is offering the best she has, this is heartfelt generosity—but I do not want to deprive a child of a sweet morsel.

After everyone has his piece of cake, Sagar's mother wishes us well, looks at the children, dries her eyes with a piece of her sari, and departs. The children begin to clean up their dishes from the floor and get out the hand brooms to sweep it once again. Soon Friends of the Footpath will be dark and will stay closed until Monday morning. It will be quiet. Someone will arrange for the dusty dog to be fed. The street families who live by the side of the building will erect their wobbly evening structures and gather inside them.

The windows are shuttered, the lights put out, the floor swept. The counter where the food is prepared is clean except for a neglected bit of green icing. By Monday morning it will be gone. Perhaps a mouse will have found it.

PART FIVE

A TUMOR IN BIHAR

Roopesh works in the Bihari fields, near Nepal but not in the mountains, driving his water buffalo to create furrows for the wheat or barley and hops that will be used to make beer. He wears one of his two pairs of clothes as he sweats for hours behind the type of plough that would have been used half a millennium ago. His tawny skin and black hair shimmer in the cruel and endless sunshine that will ease only when the annual rains come. He has walked miles from his village to the fields. He is twenty-six and has worked the fields for twelve years. He is illiterate but has the remarkable skill of being movingly articulate with few words.

Roopesh married Nabah four years ago. He was twenty-two and she twenty. Nabah walks five miles from her village everyday to split stones by the dirt road, to clear the stones so the road can be paved. She works with women from several other villages, all in their saris of brown, yellow, and blue beneath the dust that has obscured the colors. She splits the large rocks with a hammer, picks up the smaller hand-sized, stones, and carries them either in a basket on her head or in a wheelbarrow to the growing mountain of rocks a half-mile away. Then she walks back, picks up her hammer and continues. Nabah is also illiterate but, unlike her husband, she is shy. The relentless sun and sand have, over the four years since she married, left her village and went to work, added ten years to her appearance. Her oval face and high cheekbones remain beautiful.

Roopesh and Nabah had their first child a year after they married. Three-year-old Poorti is the center of their lives. After walking miles home to their village when the sun starts to go down, they eagerly take turns scooping her up. Poorti likes to climb up her daddy's legs and into his arms for her sweaty hug. She licks her father's arm and savor's his body's salt. She prefers her mummy to pick her up and kiss her with the residue of the day's dust on her lips. Roopesh's mother, with whom he and Nabah live, cares for Poorti during the day. Their village has perhaps thirty houses. Some are of brick, some of concrete. All are configured the same: one large room with a kitchen set back from the living-sleeping-eating area. Outside is the toilet: a deep round hole dug for squatting over. Water is piped into the village and there are two communal pumps in the center.

Roopesh and Nabah wash when they come home, releasing their bodies from the sweat and dust, and change into their other set of clothes that they will also wear tomorrow. They wash this day's clothes, slamming and rolling them on the rocks to help remove excess water, and hang them on a rope on the side of their house. Then they eat dinner. Roopesh, Nabah, Poorti, Roopesh's mother and father, his father's brother, his own brother. Nabah and Roopesh also have a new six-month old son. Nabah takes the baby with her to work, carrying him on her back in a sling while she works. Then she can breastfeed him. She regretfully looks forward to the time when he is weaned, when he can stay at home with her mother-in-law and sister. His life will be easier and less harsh. Her toil will weigh her down less. But she will miss him. She won't see his smile all day and she won't be able to offer him an ongoing narrative of what she is doing. His six-month old incomprehension of her words doesn't matter; she is talking to her son who is with her.

All eight people sleep on the floor of the single furnitureless room. Poorti and her brother are nestled between their parents most of the time. The door must be closed at night to keep out intruders human and animal. However, Roopesh and Nabah's village is safe because it is so remote. Their house has a window.

Poorti has seemed ill the last two weeks. Her parents have tried home remedies but she still cries when she tries to eat and says her tummy hurts. She says her tummy feels hard inside although no one can feel it from touching her stomach. The next week, Poorti goes to the nearest "OC," Outpatient Clinic. The doctor there says something seems very wrong. He recommends an x-ray and after looking at it thinks he sees something growing inside Poorti's stomach that shouldn't be there. He recommends that she be examined at the nearest hospital, requiring a bus ride for several hours and a fare. Roopesh and Nabah examine all the money they have saved. Whatever is left after regularly daily expenses, they and the rest of the working adults in the family put into a box kept hidden at home. Twenty-five dollars.

Nabah, Roopesh and Poorti take the bus to the hospital. The baby was left at home so they won't have to pay an extra fare. Roopesh's mother so wanted to come but she understands that the family can't risk paying more money. What if expensive treatment were needed? When they get to the hospital the person at the desk gives them papers to complete. They tell her they need help because they cannot read or write. Will she help them? Although a bit short at first, she softens when she actually looks up and sees their faces and worried brown eyes. Once the forms are completed they wait two hours for the doctor.

The doctor talks with both parents. He is unnecessarily surprised how articulate Nabah and Roopesh are, especially Roopesh. The doctor should know better than to confuse illiteracy with ignorance or intelligence or expressivity. He sees it every day. The doctor examines Poorti and explains that he is going to "run some tests." He kindly explains as basically as he can what he will be doing. Poorti is taken away from her parents who stare helplessly at each other. The doctor returns and tells them that they will have to come back in one week for the results. He tries to console them by saying that Poorti won't have to come back, just Nabah and Roopesh and so the trip will cost less.

They return to the hospital. There are no papers this time and so they do not feel embarrassed. The lady at the desk is the same one as before. This time she greets them with a sympathetic smile and tells them that she asked the doctor if he could see them as soon as possible because she knew how worried they would be.

The doctor comes into the waiting room, offers a *Namaste* in greeting, and asks Roopesh and Nabah to come back to his office, a Spartan room with basic metal furniture and white walls. The parents are confused because the doctor is smiling but his eyes look worried and sad. He speaks softly to them, touching Roopesh's arm but respecting Nabah's cultural privacy by not touching her. He says that he thinks Poorti has cancer. They don't know what cancer is although whenever they have heard the word before everyone has become somber. The doctor tries to explain that something called a tumor is growing inside Poorti and that is what is making her stomach hurt. He says that tumors, which are cancer, get bigger and then they spread and people become sicker and sicker and can die. Nabah quickly and forcefully drills her fingernails into Roopesh's arm.

The doctor tells these now comprehending parents that there is treatment. It involves using needles to put very serious medicine inside Poorti. It is medicine that itself will make her sick but then might…might…make her better because it will make the tumor shrink before it has a chance to spread. This is called "chemotherapy." He tells Nabah and Roopesh that Poorti's case is serious. They both look frightened. But then he tells them of a place, a hospital, for children like Poorti. "Parents bring their children there from all over the country. Parents are allowed to live in the hospital with their children while the children get their chemotherapy and they can help care for their children when they are sick from the chemotherapy. Sometimes the chemotherapy takes as long as a year but the parents can stay there." He waits. He senses the money worry; it is palpable. "And this special hospital is free for parents who don't have the money. You just have to prove that you don't have the money to pay for the treatment."

The doctor adds, still serious, "You do have to pay to get there. It is in Mumbai, all the way across the country, and the train ride is very long. They will talk to you and ask for papers to be sure that you really don't have enough money. Do you have relatives in Mumbai you can stay with? No? Then you might have to live on the street until the hospital tells you if they will let Poorti in and let you stay there. If they do let you stay, though, they will pay for everything you need and you will even have your own stove for cooking Bihari food. I recommend that you go there and I will write letters about Poorti and how much money you have. I understand about the money from the papers you had to complete the first time you came here. Why don't you talk with your family about this? They can't come. Only the two of you. Your baby will have to stay here. I'm sorry. The hospital in Mumbai is already crowded."

Nabah and Roopesh know what they must do. They discuss this with their family. They will have to leave the baby. Maybe somebody in the village who is still nursing can feed their baby for three more months. They will have to leave their jobs and the family will have less money. After two bus rides to see the doctor, the family's savings are $ 23.50. It costs much more than that to ride the train, third class, to Bombay. How can this be done and how does the family feel?

Nabah's mother-in-law walks over to her and kisses her forehead. "If this were my daughter, the way I feel that you are my daughter, I would do everything I could. We will help you." Roopesh's brother hugs him. "I will work a second job on my day off." Roopesh's father just touches his shoulder. Coming up with the train fare becomes a village project. People give what they can. They sell what they can. Roopesh's employer assures him he can have his job back when he returns. Nabah's employer is less forthcoming; he hedges, and so Nabah will go to Mumbai not knowing if she has a job to come back to. But what is her choice?

Poorti and her parents arrive in Bombay and present themselves at the Hospital of the Holy Virgin, a highly regarded center for pediatric oncology. The receptionist takes their paperwork and gives them more papers to fill out. Roopesh and Nabah explain that they can't read or write. The receptionist yells out, a bit harshly, "Nirmala, come here and help these people. More illiterates!" This is not as cruel as it sounds. The receptionist has simply seen this too many times. With the paperwork done, the receptionist asks, "Do you have someone to stay with while waiting for your eligibility interview?" She has to explain what "eligibility interview" means. "No? Then let me tell you the best places to stay on the street. I know you brought your blankets and clothing and cooking things with you. Guard everything, but if you go down to the area three blocks from here, that's where families waiting to get in stay. It's a little better there."

Nabah and Roopesh make their way, never having been in a city, let alone one with eighteen million people in it, with perhaps half of them living on the street. They have never used a footpath, crossed a street with traffic on it, or heard so much noise. They will live here for one week. Other people have to wait longer but the receptionist was moved by this couple and the area she sent them to was one where the hospital uses runners to find waiting families. That is, they will not have to receive a written notice they cannot read. This is invisible generosity.

They receive word that their turn for an eligibility interview will be this afternoon. They wash for the second time in the public showers and put on the cleanest of their clothing, the ones that carry their history of sweat and dust more lightly, and walk over to the Hospital of the Holy Virgin for their interview.

A severe young woman in western dress meets Nabah and Roopesh at the doorway of her office. Poorti is in the hall and comes in and out, checking on her parents. The young woman looks at them with disdain but not eye contact and asks them to sit down. She has their papers in her hand. They feel like numbers, not people. The eligibility worker asks them why she should believe what is in those papers. Nabah, surprisingly, is the one who speaks. "Because it is true."

The worker harshly adds: "Why should I believe you?"

Nabah responds with dignity. "I do not lie."

This determiner of eligibility for the cancer treatment of a three-year-old village girl curtly stands. "We are finished. Thank you for coming in. I will meet with The Team and let you know their decision. Both Roopesh and Nabah look puzzled. They ask what "The Team" means. The worker softens slightly—it is visible in the corner of one eye—and says, "I will send someone to let you know if we can accept you as soon as I can."

Two days later a runner finds the Bihari family on the street in the space they have staked out as their own. The police leave these people alone. The police refer to them as "Those who are waiting for the sake of their sick children." Roopesh, Nabah, and Poorti have been accepted into the Hospital of the Holy Virgin. They should come to the hospital with all their belongings before 5:00 p.m.

The people who work in the pediatric oncology program are kind. Once the family exits the elevator, another first, they are brought to the doorway of the large ward where they will be living. Roopesh thinks, "What am I going into? I know how much I have left behind. I won't see my son and my family for so long."

The director of the program invites them in with a smile. The atmosphere of judgment so noticeable in the eligibility department has disappeared. This is a place of acceptance. The director explains how the ward is laid out, where the family's curtained space will be: one single bed, a locking metal supply closet, and a chair. Mother, father and daughter will share this space. She shows them their kitchen burner and where Nabah can keep her pots and utensils safely.

The director reviews the rules of correct behavior, all of which are benign and easily understandable. For example, if you eat meat please make sure that your pots and utensils and dishes do not touch those of someone who is religiously vegetarian. She points her finger at the window so both mother and father can see that the major hospital with which the smaller Hospital of the Holy Virgin is affiliated, the place to go for medical emergencies at all times of day, is right across the street. "No bus fare." Then she walks them around the floor-sized ward.

There are impoverished families from all over India and dozens of languages being spoken. Hindi is the glue, in general, although there are some families who don't speak it. A handful of people can speak a little English. Many children, aged two to ten, are running around, bald from their treatment and wearing masks. Others rest or sleep, tired from their chemotherapy. One or two are throwing up. But the children have both parents with them with the exception of the few single mothers.

There are activity programs for the children, suited to their ages. The parents only receive a lecture that describes cancer and tumors at an appropriate level, but otherwise have much free time. Asha and I had been asked to spend a week working with large numbers of parents in therapeutically grounded groups.

⚔︎

We decided, with the director, to see the fathers and the mothers separately and then put them together at the very end. We felt that the mothers would not feel free to speak openly in front of their husbands and that the men would feel the need to be strong in front of their wives.

We met with the women in smaller groups of perhaps twelve, as we did with the men. The mothers turned out to become most expressive when working on an art project. We put plenty of small bottles of tempera paint in the middle of the circle on the floor and gave each mother a piece of paper and a brush. Dishes of water were scattered all over, as were active children—those healthy enough between treatments to be vigorous. The mothers concentrated on their paintings and took their time.

Each began, in random turn, to talk about her painting. As they spoke, they became increasingly emotionally expressive. Tears of worry, and fear, tears for the rest of their families so far away for so long, fell from the fresh colors of their paintings by way of the mothers' words. The critical moment came when Nabah held up her drawing that, from a distance, looked like a green collection of vines with colored blooms. It had a firm dark green border. Shy Nabah said with a slightly trembling voice, "This is Poorti's tumor. I painted it smaller than the doctors' pictures so it wouldn't grow anymore and the medicine would make it shrink. It is dark around the edges like a fence to keep it from growing."

Most of the women began talking simultaneously. "My son is getting better and the doctor's didn't think he would live." "My daughter is going to be well enough to go home next week!" "The doctors don't know if my son will live. I am so scared and I am scared it will make my husband crazy." Asha and I spent the last fifteen minutes talking about living with the unknowable, an issue every woman shared. When the session was over they hesitated to leave and stayed to chat for some time.

Next we met with the men, again in groups of twelve. At first I misread their facial expressions and assumed sullenness and resistance. This was not true. After introductions, I asked, "What was it like to come here?" The men said, "It is good in here." "People are kind." "They do not treat us like dirt, like those social workers about proving how poor we are. She made me feel like I was not a man." "She felt she was better than me and disrespected my wife and I could do nothing." "She humiliated me." Vehemence ruled.

I had a thought, turned to Asha and said, "Will you trust me with this? And if it's a bad idea, just stop it. I'll need translation." Asha nodded curiously and with a smile.

I got up from my place in the circle we all had formed cross-legged on the floor and put myself in the middle of the group. "Let's pretend that I am the person who did the evaluation on you and decided whether you were poor enough to come into this program. What would you like to say to me? Do you think I'm doing a bad job and should be removed?" I thought a saw a touch of near-fear on a few faces. "I'm not going to tell anyone outside our circle what anyone says in here. This is private."

Silence. The men did not know what to do. They had never been in the position of speaking up critically against authority. We waited in uncomfortable silence. We had heard these men around the ward. They were naturally loquacious. We were not in the kind of spiritual silence that Indians are so comfortable with. These fathers were uncomfortable with the uniqueness of this situation. More silence.

"How did you feel you were treated by those (eligibility) workers?" Silence, and then suppressed loquacity won out.

"How can you treat poor people that way? We used everything we had to get here and you acted like we were nothing."

"I am not dirt. I am poor but I am not dirt."

"How can you expect me to prove what I don't have? How can I show you nothing?"

"You should be kind. We all have sick children. We are living on the street far away from our villages and our families. We miss our other children and you act like a judge who doesn't care."

"Now that we are in the program, I can see how different you are. The people in the hospital treat us with kindness and respect. They like us even if we disagree with each other. They treat us like men. You act like I am nothing. I don't think you should have your job until you have a sick child."

Everyone looked stunned at what they had said. I stopped role-playing the Eligibility Inquisitor, and smiled. The emotional temperature in the room lowered, and a sense of reciprocity slowly filled the room. The endemic Indian penchant for useless burdensome hierarchies had been broken in the role-play and in reality.

⇌ ⇌

The following day, when we met with the men in their groups, they were more at ease and entering into conversations with both Asha and me as if we could understand all their various languages. Asha can speak English (her first language), Rajasthani, and Hindi. I can only speak English and know a few Hindi words. The fathers were speaking the languages of Orissa, Bihar, Rajasthan, Assam, Andra Pradesh, etc., with beautiful facial expressiveness assuming we naturally understood.

We formed our circle, my less nimble hips and knees sore by now but determined. The men did not like to talk about feelings and so we avoided it. Rather, they showed their feelings by the way they described events. We asked if they would be willing to put on a play ("role-play" is a nonsensical term) about being in the hospital. Everyone was smiling and willing. An English-speaking Bihari sitting next to me put his arm around my shoulder, smiled and said, "After yesterday, of course!"

Asha and I asked these dads to put on a play about what it is like to be in the hospital with their sick child. Silence; a thoughtful, understandably sober silence. We told them to take their time to think about what they wanted to show and how they wanted to show it. There was no rush. (We would do our two groups of fathers and two groups of mothers that day but we would not run by the clock. It would take whatever time it took. Somehow it all works out, something I feel about India in general.)

The men were busy talking in the back of the room, gesturing, posturing, and making private jokes about what they might do. They started by firing an eligibility worker for being disrespectful, and laughed.   And then they unfolded their drama with gusto and deep feeling. A group of fathers was helping one man bring his very young child to see the doctor for his first chemotherapy treatment. Roopesh was this child because he was the short and compactly built. As he was being carried to the doctor's table, he was frightened and crying. A quiet but gentle nurse helped them put the child on a treatment table while a gentle doctor stood by. The doctor said nothing and Roopesh screamed as he received an injection for a long time. The men, these rough rural illiterate men, held the baby down and stroked his free arm and hair trying to soothe him. The child cried. The men, looking so sad and helpless, nevertheless unceasingly tried to soothe him. The treatment was over and the men carried Roopesh away.

Asha and I thought this was the end until one of the men said, in English and Hindi, "Part Two." He explained that this was now the child's second treatment. The men again carried Roopesh in from behind the curtain they had created. Now they were miming explaining to the child what was about to happen. They physically enacted that he would be put on a table, that a nice nurse would be there and would smile. Then a man in a white coat who was a doctor and was a kind man was going to be there and was going to give the child an injection. They mimed what the syringe would look like and that it might take a long time. It would hurt a little, but it was a medicine that was going to make the bad thing that was growing inside him get smaller. He would probably feel tired when it was over.

The carriers reached the "treatment table" and put Roopesh down so tenderly that I suppressed a gasp. The nurse came in and smiled. The doctor entered and administered the chemotherapy as gently as possible. Again the fathers stroked this pretend child as if he were their own, talking to him throughout the "procedure." One then put his hand on Roopesh's belly and imitated a shrinking tumor. All the fathers stood around the treatment table and stood guard over the now-sleeping child. The English speaker then said "The End," but it took a few moments for the sense of timelessness to be broken.

The group was over. I have no idea how long it lasted. As the fathers filed out of the room, a group of them, including Roopesh, came over and bent down to touch my feet and offer a *Namaste* with their hands. I took their hands in mine and put them to my head. The English spokesman said to me in English and Hindi: "Thank you for giving us back our dignity." I replied, again with moist eyes, "You have always had your dignity."

Several of the men started to weep, smiled, and left the room. They waited for us to finish with the next group. They brought in some of their children for us to hold, and invited us down to the street market to help them and their children pick out that evening's vegetables for cooking upstairs on the ward.

In the taxi on the way home I was silent. Asha asked me if I was all right. I told her that to be given witness to such dignity, kindness, tenderness and generosity from people who materially had nothing, who were treated by society as if they weren't worth existing, was overwhelming. She said, "This is why I will never live anywhere but here."

A SHARED LOAF OF BREAD

The social workers in the pediatric oncology unit of the Hospital of the Holy Virgin, all women, are well trained and deeply caring. A few favor Western dress but most are in saris or *salwar kameez*. One tells me, "I dress traditionally because most of our families here are more comfortable when I do." All have caseloads of too many families and all work long hours to try to help their families. We are told they are so busy that they have never met as a group before. Each worker carries her own outsized burden of families' worry, sorrow, fear, hope, and anticipatory grief. Many of the children at Holy Virgin come with very poor prognoses. A good number do improve. Some do not. After working all day with "their" families in hospital, the social workers return home to their own families and their own, healthy, children.

After meeting with the director of the program, we add a day to our activities at the hospital to provide a "workshop" with the social workers. The topic is ostensibly Burn-Out Prevention, but as we begin to work it becomes clear to both of us that something different is needed. These are women to whom attention is due. They understand burnout. What ails them is the burdensome loneliness of the varieties of sadness they enter and endure daily. They know their families well. They understand what gives their families comfort, what hurts them, what their soft spots are and what makes them impatient and angry. They know all the children. They sit with mothers and fathers whose bald and masked two and three and seven and eight year olds are running around the ward if they are feeling well, or sleeping weak, or exhausted. While we are sitting in our circle on the floor, a bald four-year-old boy welcomes himself to my lap and nestles in for twenty minutes.

The social workers, some of them so dedicated that they are yet another variation of the saints I have found in India, need to share their experiences with each other. An experience, once told to an empathic person, becomes a lighter burden because more than one person holds the sadness or grief. Joy and hope become greater when it is no longer held only within one person. This group needs to talk, to tell their tales. And they need to come up with a "loneliness prevention" plan. They ask the program director to join the group. They have nothing to hide and she has earned their trust.

Initial stories are ones of hope and success: a seven-year-old boy whom everyone thought would die had in fact improved and discharge planning had begun. However, it doesn't take long for the toll of caring to show itself. The air in the room, already heavy with humidity, begins to weigh more. Time starts to slow. The women tell of their attachment to the children. Yes, they feel joy at the recoveries, but there are always the deteriorations. Often these are slow, and a social worker will sit with a mother and father for months watching the daily diminution of life until the last exhalation.

One woman tries not to weep as she listens to the others, but she can't help herself. We ask her if she would like to talk. She nods, as a tear drops onto her sari. She speaks of a three-year-old girl to whom she was particularly attached. She loved the girl. The parents were so grateful that they came to love this woman. She was a great comfort to them. Their daughter's prognosis was "guarded." She had been in hospital for months experiencing ups and downs in her treatment. She was particularly fond of a special type of bread. Whenever mother baked it, the girl would save a piece for her social worker.

Her birthday was coming and the social worker spent her Sunday at home making some of this bread as a present. She wrapped the bread carefully in tissue paper and giftwrapping that she had bought. She came to work on Monday carrying the gift and went looking for the family in their cubicle since she couldn't find them out and about the ward. She looked inside the white-draped space and saw father facing the metal storage cabinet with his face in his raised arm. She turned to the right and saw mother holding her dead three years old in her arms, crying. Quickly, she kneeled down next to mother and offered her condolences while she started quietly weeping herself. Mother saw the gift and knew: "Did you make bread for my daughter?" The social worker nodded. The mother said, "Let you and me and my husband share it while we still have our daughter here. They will take her away soon. She would have loved for us to eat it together."

The room is hushed. Most of the social workers, as well as the director, are in tears. There is a long silence and then slowly other, similar, stories emerge. These caring, skilled women are cohering into a group. The director notices it.

Asha and I, by now after years of working together finishing each other's sentences, comment. Asha begins: "Now that you are talking together".... I continue: "where do you think you can go from here?" Several people speak simultaneously. "We should do this more often." "We should do this regularly and have it in our diaries (schedule books) so we know it will happen." "I feel so much less alone." The director exercises her benign prerogative. "I think we should have a meeting monthly, let's say on the fourth Friday in the morning, and not let anything interrupt our schedule." And, as near as Asha and I know, this is what happened.

PART SIX

MUMBAI MORNING

7:00 a.m. The sugar cane juice machine has just started churning. Years of yellow paint coat the steel housing of the gears that grind the cane into juice. Newer machines are clean unpainted stainless steel. This is the first early morning noise, followed by the soft, almost weak meows of starving kittens that hold their own posts on the footpath waiting for fallen or discarded scraps of food. Footpath traffic is light and vehicular traffic, while much less than it will be an hour later, is nevertheless a clear presence. The traffic signals are officially ignorable at this hour and while the one-way street signs are generally obeyed, it is never surprising to find anything with wheels moving against traffic. Crossing any street at this hour is an exercise in 360-degree pedestrian turns to check for oncoming traffic.

The public buses are already full of people on their way to work and students on their way to their private schools. Every bus disgorges one- or two-dozen youngsters aged seven to seventeen in their pristine uniforms of green, or blue, or red, or beige/white/

red plaid. The uniforms are pressed and fresh. These children's schoolbooks are carried in smart satchels or modish backpacks. The youngsters are talkative, warming up to receive their teachers' admonishments and requests for quiet in the classroom.

From the gaps between buildings, where the hutments house hundreds of people, perhaps more, in makeshift houses shoved between the walls of two large brick permanent structures, come the other children. These are the children, as clean as their well-tended counterparts, whose uniforms are equally clean but stained. There isn't money to replace them. Their uniforms are from different schools unless they are "charity cases" at a posh school. Their uniforms are threadbare and patched and have strands of fabric hanging from them. The red ribbons holding the girls' braids have no sheen left to them. Their battered schoolbooks are in cheap canvas backpacks. These children, too, are chattering among each other as they emerge from their gap in the buildings. They don't ride buses because bus fare might pay for part of this evening's lentils. Their talkativeness is a warm-up for their teachers' often contemptuous warnings for quiet, offered with a sense of superiority and an "I'm doing you a favor by being your teacher" tone.

From an educational and social point of view, these children are the "Should-Be-Discards." However, they are no less bright than their upper-class counterparts. They have no less energy. What they have is a more fragile educational base. When they get home from school, there is no space for homework; there is no time for homework. There is time for getting water while the public tap is on, washing clothes if it is possible, helping with the cooking and cleaning. When not in school, a hutment child's world is in the moment. Thus hutment and street children cannot consolidate their learning. The educational system "confuses" this for stupidity and lack of motivation. But right now it is 7:00 a.m., and the children are smiling and chattering and walking to school separately, perhaps a few steps behind, their well-to-do counterparts.

The street sweepers are out, stooped using hand brooms; long-handled brooms have never taken hold here. Last night's trash is being removed even as this day's trash is already beginning to accumulate from the early morning pedestrians. Vendors set up their stands on the pavement: this morning's newspapers; current newsweeklies; ill-bound photocopied knockoffs of current books; shoeshine stands. The sunglasses and motorcycle helmets and glasses cases and t-shirts and shoes are starting to be put on footpath display. Some cabbies are waiting for fares while others are flying to their destinations because they already have a fare. People wrapped in blankets are still sleeping on the footpath, as yet oblivious to the waking city. Those from blue tarpaulin homes are coming out of the public bathing places with towels wrapped around their waists. The light is bright. Whenever I walk in Bombay in the early morning, which I love, I feel like some grand, awful, awesome, beautiful, evening-dangerous, morning-safe, Goddess Beast is rising.

"YOU SONOFABITCH"

*S*ilver Spring, Maryland. 2007. *It is Sunday, late in the morning.
Time for my regular visit to my mother in her retirement community where she is desperately trying to continue in Independent Living and
avoid "stepping down" to Assisted Living. She is living alone right now.*

*My father has had a major stroke and is in the nursing home on the
community grounds. He is in a semi-vegetative state, although when I see
him and ask him his wife's name he sometimes smiles and says "Rosie," as
he tries to reach out his hand. Otherwise he is unresponsive. I cannot tell
if he sleeps or is comatose. I do know that he is going to die there. I don't
know when and neither does anyone else. His physician and nurse practi-
tioner expected him to die months ago. He silently wastes away except for
the occasional "Rosie."*

*My mother prefers not to visit him, saying vehemently, "I don't want
to see him like that." Once in a while she slips and adds, "**I don't care if
visiting helps him or not.**" I know she knows she has slipped because she
quickly retracts her comment. As always, she refuses to acknowledge having*

said something hurtful that she has just said. She has done it since I was a child.

She knows that I am aware of how she feels, that I heard those words escape her mouth. She is angry with me; I know her secret. I've arranged for her home health aides to take her to visit my father. He lies in a bed only two buildings away. With her walker and their help, it is not difficult for her to go and see him. Almost every time an aide comes to bring her to my father she has an excuse. She has narrowed the frequency of her forays out of the apartment to see him to twice a month.

Today I tell her that we are going to visit dad. I've already seen him but I don't tell her. Instead, I tell her that I want to see him and she is going to come with me. "I am **not** going over there. Everyone is sick there. They will keep me there." I explain that nobody is going to keep her there because there is no reason to keep her there. "They are going to do it anyway." I assure her that I won't let anybody "keep" her there and that I will bring her back to her apartment. "I'm not going."

"Yes, you are. You're coming with me. Here's your jacket," and I hold it open for her so she can put it on easily. I try to be careful to keep my tone of voice even and calm. She complies and I set her walker up and help her align herself properly. Her assisted mobility is fairly good. I explain that we're going in my car to the building my father is in. She glares at me and stands defiantly immobile. "Mom, it won't work. You're coming," and I very gently and slowly pull her walker so she has no choice. She looks docile and then turns to me: "You sonofabitch." But she walks.

We arrive at my father's building and then at the entrance to his room. She won't move. Again I gently, slowly, pull her walker and she has no choice but to follow. I can see a member of the nursing staff in the hall, who has been watching, nod her head at me. Her tiny gesture of support helps *me feel less cruel, for I know my mother experiences me as mean or somehow vindictive for inflicting this visit on her.*

My mother stops halfway towards where my father lies. I take her walker away. She must now wait. She has no choice and I am close to getting her near to him. I bring a soft chair and help her sit down. Then I push her next to his bed. She says nothing but he senses something. His hand moves slightly. "Dad, I've brought Rosie to see you." ("Rosie" was his pet name for her when they were teenagers.) She is silent and immobile. His hand tries to move ever so slightly toward her. I think he knows where she is because I make sure that when I speak, it is from right next to her. She doesn't move. I take her hand and move it toward him. She pulls it back at first, and then sees my insistent look. Then she lets me put her hand on top of his. He smiles and I think mutters "Rosie." I tell her to let him know she is there, that she is holding his hand. She does. "Marc, I have nothing else to say. He can't hear and I'm leaving."

"No, you're not leaving. If you don't know what to say, that's o.k. Sing an old song to him, something from when you were both young together. He'll hear you." She softens and says, "Joe, I'm here," and then sings a verse of "A Bicycle Built for Two." Dad's eyes are still closed but he has smiled. I tell her that it's o.k. if she doesn't know what to say. She just needs to sit with him for a while. She does.

When it's clear that enough time has passed, that she truly can't tolerate any more and he is asleep, I tell her that we can go whenever she wants. "Now!" I move the chair back, help her stand, hold her jacket open for her again, and set up her walker. Since we are leaving, she moves on her own. Quite well. When we return to her apartment, we visit for a while and then I kiss her goodbye and tell her I'll see her the next time.

As I approach the door, I hear her hiss, "You goddam sonofabitch." My Sunday morning is over.

LET NO CHILD GO HUNGRY

Janya, now seventy-five, was eleven years old when India became independent in 1947. Her Hindu family lived in what had become, through Partition, West Pakistan. Sensing the coming carnage, as almost everyone did, her family picked up and moved across the Divide into the refugee camps of India. With nearly a dozen siblings, Janya was last on the list of daily priorities and spent much of the time in deep hunger. The memories of her sustained hunger still well up from within her. Her father said "No" to higher education for her. Her lost education, with which she has made peace, has created a quietly fiery determination to try to assure proper education for children of poverty who show promise and dedication. From these experiences, Janya resolved to dedicate her life's work to assuring that no child would go hungry and that children would have access to education. If she could, she would feed and provide special teachers for them all. As it is, her new organization must select those children most likely to succeed if given the opportunity.

After marrying and raising a still close-knit family, she decided to establish a private non-profit organization that would select promising children from the various slum areas of Bombay. Thus, Janya gave birth to her last child: *Learning and Eating Together* (LET). *Learning and Eating Together* identifies children of poverty who have academic promise and subsidizes their education in the local schools. It pays for uniforms and provides its own skilled teachers as an adjunct to the regular teachers. It also feeds the children a protein-rich lunch, so there is one less person for the parents to worry about feeding properly at home. *Learning and Eating Together* works with parents in the slum areas to encourage sending their children to school and has put special effort into getting girls educated. It also offers enrichment opportunities. Janya has made sure that *Learning and Eating Together* stretches each donated rupee as far as it can go.

Janya is charismatic. When she asks for donations, her inner radiance makes it impossible to deny her. Her intrepidity when it comes to "her" children, whom she truly claims, has brought *Learning and Eating Together* considerable credibility in Bombay. She manages to keep it endowed although salaries still are necessarily low. Until recently, Janya would visit each school regularly to observe the teachers at work and to learn who the children are. A few younger children are seen in their schools, but the bulk of *Learning and Eating Together*'s resources go toward the eleven to sixteen year olds, Sixth Standard through Tenth Standard. Then the students, better prepared than most, can apply, if their families can afford it, to go to College, equivalent to American eleventh and twelfth grades. University is the next step (equivalent to what we refer to as "college"). *Learning and Eating Together* has a record of greater success at helping children escape slum life than many other non-profits. This is in part the result of the staff's utter dedication to Janya, referred to by everyone as "Didi" (Auntie).

I believe Janya to be another of India's saints, one of those healing counterpoints to India's pain. While personally warm and at times earthy and impish in a lovely way, with a touch of residual elegance, she has always seemed to be made of the same stuff as Mother Teresa. Tears still come to her eyes when she speaks of the children. She is loving, clear-sighted, humorous, and big-hearted, and yet a gracious pit bull when it comes to providing the best program possible for children in impossible circumstances. She is an Indian Lady With the Lamp, looking for slum children of promise and offering them the light of escape.

Asha and I were affiliated jointly with *Learning and Eating Together* for three years. (For the ninth and last year of my annual work in India, I worked without Asha, who had pressing family matters that required her full attention.)

The day usually starts at Janya's flat. She makes sure that Asha and I have morning coffee and something to eat before we get started. We, accompanied by a staff member of *Learning and Eating Together*, make our way to one of the more than fifteen schools in Bombay and several in remote villages that Janya has brought into the fold of her care. We spend close to a week in each school, somehow squeezing three or four schools as well as teacher and staff training into the time of my visits. Work with *Learning and Eating Together* occupies much of the last four of my annual visits. We squeeze in any other activity later in the day. The children treat us as teachers, although our work is therapeutically grounded. Teaching and group therapy combine in a unique blend. We then visit the children's homes in their various slums/*bustees* and meet whichever parent might be home, usually the mother, and spend time walking the lanes of the slums and meeting other people. I am a benign curiosity because of the light color of my skin and because I am clearly there to meet people and not take pictures. I never carry a camera, as I don't want even the appearance of the "wealthy" Westerner come to take pictures and take pity on the poor. I am accepted fairly readily, I think because I am in the company of Indians, but once this is established I remain accepted when I wander my own way, perhaps to meet the man who runs the tea stall or the fellow who is ironing laundry.

Asha and I then invite all the parents to a meeting at the school and we have the children explain what they are learning. Sometimes these meetings exclude the children so their parents can voice their concerns in a group that evolves into something therapeutic.

GOING TO SCHOOL

Asha and I, accompanied by a *Learning and Eating Together* staff member, enter our first school. It stands, all four forbidding stories of it, across the street from a *bustee* and is surrounded by a footpath of solid and cracked concrete. Its central courtyard is graced with some of the few bits of greenery in the area: three trees that would make an excellent place for children to play. In some schools they do; in others, this space is eerily empty but surrounded by active children playing on the blank concrete.

We enter the dark halls and climb the equally dark and musty stairs to the fourth floor, making our way past peeling and flaking paint, cracked and exposed walls where the paint has given up trying to adhere, dusty handrails. We go down a hallway that remains dark despite the atrium configuration and the presence of those untouchable trees. I feel as if this school does not want air to enter it or sun to shine on it. The walls are a color that I think was once yellow, but now are greenish brown. Missing is the smell of cleaning fluid or floor disinfectant, those smells associated with normal upkeep of a public building. This building doesn't want the children anymore than society does.

After removing our shoes, we come in to the classroom, Standard (Grade) Nine, with uniformed children ages fourteen and fifteen. This classroom is assigned to *Learning and Eating Together* and is cleaner and brighter. We are introduced in Hindi and Marathi, the official language of the State of Maharashtra, of which Bombay is the capital, and then in English. The youngsters stand and speak as they have been trained to speak: "Good morning, Madame. Good morning, Sir." Once we say "good morning" in return, they sit cross-legged on floor mats at small, eight-inch high "desks" that are more like low stools. Asha and I introduce ourselves by first names only, and explain that we will be working with them, avoiding the word "teaching" so they do not confuse what we will do with a lesson that has homework and a grade associated with it. We will be together for four days and at the end of the week we will meet with their parents. *Learning and Eating Together* staff workers are already busy with them, encouraging them to attend.

The students have been trained to speak all together, to stand in lines, to recite by rote, and in some classrooms, to expect to be smacked or at least threatened with a ruler for misbehavior. The definition of misbehavior appears to me to be anything the teacher thinks might possibly lead to a disruption in the residual British definition of "order." To my Western eyes, this notion of misbehavior is soul killing and antithetical to originality, creativity, playfulness and simple but fleeting tension reduction through movement. It suggests that teachers are afraid of children since discipline can be maintained in other, benign ways and without weapons.

Learning and Eating Together has given us much latitude and has encouraged each teacher to stay and observe. To make the point that our work will be different, Asha and I ask the students to re-move all their desks to the hallway. We then ask them to reconfig-ure their sitting mats into a square for all of us to sit together on the floor. We join the students on the floor and (for this first year) explain that we are here to talk about school and to talk about *bustees* (slum neighborhoods). Children from backgrounds like these are often hesitant to talk about where they live and particularly reticent to discuss their families. Asha and I have kept the topic to *bustees* in general so that we do not intrude or end up embarrass-ing anyone.

To further decrease the Dickensian pedagogical hierarchy, I begin by telling the story of my grandmother being denied educa-tion in Russia, becoming a cleaning lady in America, and how she taught my father about the importance of education. He taught me the same, and now I am a doctor. I omit the distinction be-tween physician and psychologist as not important in this context; I clarify if asked "what kind of doctor?" The importance of educa-tion is the point of the story. So in my family we started with a cleaning lady, like many of the Bombay slum students' mothers, and now we have a doctor. The youngsters smile and spontane-ously applaud. I mention that my grandmother (i.e., a woman) is my hero. They nod their heads.

We try to help the children speak about their aspirations. These are sadly vague. "Education will help me progress," with no ability to define what progress would look like. They are stuck repeating the party line, saying things that sound good but have no foundation: I want to be a doctor, a teacher, an engineer, etc. They don't really know what people in these professions do, except for teachers who are within their experience. There is lifelessness in the room. Asha and I give each other a look and shift into a role-play. We set up groups of youngsters who will demonstrate what people in their aspired professions actually do. They work at this and are at a bit of a loss. Asha and I join their groups and mime what a doctor does, an engineer, etc. They brighten and create scenarios on their own, such as visiting a doctor's office. Add a nurse. Create an examining table (teacher's desk; teacher intrigued/appalled), a treatment room, a syringe, and a consultation room on the floor where the doctor gives a diagnosis and instructions. Now they are enjoying themselves and thinking about their future. Asha and I ask, "What do you need to know to be a doctor (teacher, engineer, etc.)?" Slowly, because they have never thought this through before, the kids come up with the appropriate background knowledge.

We are all having fun now. "Who should go to school?" I say, clearly playfully, "I think only boys should go to school. Only boys can be doctors or engineers." As a group, they all start arguing with me at once. I see the teacher getting ready with her ruler to restore order. I ask her to please let me handle discipline and that this is far from disorder. As the onslaught of objections to my comment about girls' education continues, I pretend that I can't hear. The kids get louder. They are having a wonderful time. Then we ask for quiet. The children settle immediately as the teacher's jaw drops.

"Do you think I really meant it?" "No," they respond. "OK, let's talk about why girls should have an education, too." An orderly yet heartfelt discussion of how girls have been treated in the past ensues. They are quite articulate.

"IF I RULED THE *BUSTEE*"

All of Janya's children live in *bustees*, slum neighborhoods. They are often ashamed to speak of them, just as they are hesitant to speak of their families. They are well aware of their poverty; most importantly they are aware that the world only wants them to grow up to be cheap labor like their parents. Society relies on them to continue to live in these circumstances uncomplainingly and to be grateful for an underpaying manual job that requires long hours. These children and their families are expendable. There are so many of them. If a laborer father dies in an industrial accident, in an industry that should be regulated, is possibly nominally regulated, but more likely is unregulated due to much money crossing many hands, that father is replaceable.

Labor fodder. The fate of the family is irrelevant. The poor are needed to maintain the workings of society, but they are needed poor. Poor is cheap. Lose one underpaid worker and there will always be another. This is the unstated social agenda. This is Janya's fight: escape through education and education is best achieved when children do not go hungry.

After further discussions with the children, many questions about who *is* this strange white man and what is he doing in their school, and a good deal of playfulness, we then tell the Ninth Standard that they will put on a play. A group of them are going to be the Bosses of the *Bustee*. Everyone else is going to be the people who live in the slum neighborhood. Hindi and English are both used. Asha translates a great deal. However, the students don't try to shy away from English during a role-play. They do their best.

"Now, who wants to be a boss?" This idea is both a bit thrilling but somehow a little awesome to the children. Therefore, it is the bolder children who volunteer. A few are girls. "Wait a minute, everybody. Can a *girl* be a boss of the *bustee?*" Much discussion, beginning quietly and becoming louder as I offer mock arguments why not. These youngsters had claimed the concept of girls' education as told to them. But Asha and I want them to internalize it, to articulate it as well as they can, as vehemently as possible, and so I take the role of devilish advocate against girls' rights. This approach also defuses some of the fear of even pretending to be a boss. The children's lives are not without fear.

"OK, bosses. You go into the hallway and decide proper rules to make your bustee a better place to live." Off they go and the buzz of their earnest and excited voices made its way down the hallway, bringing some life to the institutional deadness. "Now, people who live in the *bustee*, let's set up the room for a meeting about the new rules." They bring the teacher's desk to the center of the room and add four benches, which become something for the bosses to stand on so that they will be taller than everyone else, because they are bosses.

The bosses enter the room. "The rules are these. Each boss will give a new *bustee* law and say why it is a good idea. If the people living in the slum neighborhood like it, they will approve it as a Good Law. If they don't like it, if anyone doesn't like it, he will stand up and say "Objection" and give his reason why he thinks it's a bad law. Then everyone will discuss it with the bosses and we will see if a not-so-good law can be fixed and become a good law. After that, you will all vote: Good Law or Bad Law. If it good, it becomes law; if it is bad, it does not become a *bustee* rule and the boss doesn't win."

Boss Number One: "We will separate the wet trash from the dry trash. That will keep the rats away." The class discusses whether this is a good rule or a bad rule. They add something to it: the trash receptacles will be kept farther away from where people live, especially people with babies. The *bustee* residents take a vote. It passes. The children have made a rule that will improve their bustee.

Boss Number Two: "We will get a grocer who doesn't charge us too much." Merchants may often overcharge the poor because the parents can't read the signs with prices. They are dependent on what the seller tells them. "No objection, but I have something to say. How can we do this?" Asha and I interject: "See if you can all talk together to see if you can figure out how to do it." There is a great deal of discussion, a blend of helplessness and defiance.

"Sir and Madam, we have two solutions. One is that we can go shopping with our parents and read the signs for them. If the prices are too high, we will shop somewhere else. Another is we will not shop in a place with too-high prices. We will shop somewhere else. Then the stores will fight and the one with lower prices will win and stay here."

"Good Law?" "YES!"

Using this same format, the children bring up problems of public drunkenness, alcoholism in the home, harassment of women, entry of disruptive strangers into the *bustee* at night (one reason the doors must be locked at night in each stifling windowless home), and arguing and fighting.

We end our four-day visit at this school with excited, articulate, and empowered children all talking and moving around. To bring some order to the end, we ask them to sing the national anthem, as loudly as possible, for my benefit. An ear-splitting *"Jai Hind"* (the salute at the end of the national anthem: "Victory to India") rings through the halls. As we leave, many of the students accompany us down the dark staircase now made lighter by their presence, and hold our hands, making sure we find our way out.

We will meet with their parents tomorrow and then move on to the next of four schools this first year with *Learning and Eating Together*. Now we will walk until we pick up an auto-rickshaw, allowed in this part of Mumbai, and then walk until we are at Janya's place for lunch. It is important to her that we not go hungry after so many hours at the school, and she would like a de-briefing. She would also like a several hours long workshop for her teaching staff after we have visited all four schools. The food is endless and delicious. Her is cook very attentive and loves what he does. It is apparent that he has fallen under the spell of Janya's benevolence and dedication. She draws people to her with her mixture of charisma, savvy, grit, and determination, all gently wrapped in her humility. It is never of herself that she is thinking.

AWAY FROM THE FRAY BUT
STILL AT WORK

Asha and I now must de-brief ourselves and plan for a teacher's workshop. I have learned over the years. We always start with a clear, beautiful plan for our work. However, it is not what we will end up doing. It will be added to, deletions will be made, there will be new people to meet, invitations, cancellations, new tasks. So The Plan is an "At-Best, It-Might-Be" outline.

I walk over to Asha and Gopal's place. Their flat, on the top floor of an old, block-long office building, is a haven, the only non-business space in a commercial building. After ducking into the dark wood entry hall and walking up a flight of not entirely safe dark wooden stairs, I enter the elevator and say hello to the elevator operator. He is a diminutive man, perhaps five feet tall, who prides himself on how many cups of *chai* he can consume. I don't know how he does it. I would be running to be bathroom every five minutes, but he is always at his appointed place in the elevator.

He brings me up to the third floor and opens the gates for me. I exit and turn left.

Here in the light, plants grow in a combination of terra cotta pots and cutout plastic soda or water bottles. Despite buildings on both sides and the hutment below, the effect is of airy greenery. The houseboys greet me and one of them escorts me in, usually past Gopal who is ensconced at his own duty station: his computer. There are books all around, quite ordered. Wherever Gopal is, a book is somehow near to hand. Although his career was primarily with UNICEF, he is a film scholar and festival organizer of some national renown and greatly respected by film critics and others. Whenever we talk film, which is often, I marvel particularly at his ability to observe and explain the interaction of the technical, narrative, and emotional aspects of a film. I am very fond of him.

Asha calls out that I should come out to the balcony, although I'm not sure that's the right word. It is a room appended to the main room used for eating, resting, and entertaining. The balcony is all open windows and retains its comfort despite the heat and the occasional intrusion of a stray pigeon. Bombay has five seasons: hot, very hot, unbearably hot, "forget-about-it," and monsoon. Asha and Gopal's flat, with its high ceiling fans, remains comfortable.

The large central room, off of which are two bedrooms and two bathrooms, is a tranquil space of white walls, one of which is book-covered, carefully selected art and photographs, patterned fabric framed in glass and lit from above so that it seems to float, and a large Masai shield. There are two tables that can each seat six for dinner parties, and a large sitting area with an L-shaped, cushion-filled sofa, and three chairs, all upholstered in Asha's much-loved soft blue and blue-green solids or soft textures. Blue draperies and short white window shutters create a soothing effect: unassuming elegance created with great care. There is a roof terrace above, high enough to give a vista of the tops of nineteenth century buildings, mosques, birds in flight, and the full sky otherwise so elusive in Bombay.

We meet in the flat for planning and de-briefing, and often Lin and I are invited to a dinner party hosted by Gopal and Asha. More often, I am there for lunch. But first, over tea, we get to work. What went well at school number one? What could be handled differently, more creatively, more sensitively, more effectively in subsequent schools? And what are we going to do about teacher training?

We spend several hours puzzling our way through this, arriving at new approaches with the children, and preparing a day-long teacher workshop that will focus on blowing the dust of the nineteenth century out of the classroom while hopefully encouraging and being uncritical of the teachers. They, for the most part, try to do their best. They commute long hours for short pay. They do what they have been taught. It is unfair to find fault and yet in important ways the teachers are ineffective. The children do poorly in English, math, symbolic reasoning, and other academic areas, but the teachers have not been taught new ways of teaching. India's lower educational system stays where it has been while other countries pass it by, and yet it has a sophisticated and successful approach to higher education. Neither Asha nor I see much creativity from the *Learning and Eating Together* teachers, but they do see teaching the children, and knowing who the children are, as their duty. They are not without their own frustrations.

Asha and I are clear that the best we can do is try to open new windows for the teachers and at least suggest possibilities that go against the nineteenth century grain of rote memorization, lack of concern for reading comprehension, and over-worry about discipline, much too broadly defined. Ongoing teacher training is necessary, coupled with rigorous and monitored follow-through. That is beyond our scope and so we must plan small and trust that one bit of hopefully useful fresh air will enter. It saddens me to see such willing children being served by willing teachers who have not been given the equipment to do their duty as well as they might.

TAKING CARE OF FAMILY

We are working at a different school, talking with the children about what their lives are like, what their wishes are, and what causes tension in their hearts. Asha's mobile phone rings. She excuses herself and uncharacteristically takes the call. She must have been expecting something.

She comes back to the circle of children on the floor and whispers to me: "My mother has just died. I must leave now and quickly go to my family for the cremation and ceremonies. I'll be gone five days. You carry on." Asha needed to be present not only for the cremation, but for stepping into the river with her family to cast her mother's ashes upon it. The river, most likely the holy *Ganga* (Ganges), purifies the soul and hopefully leads to a good rebirth.

I continue with the group as if nothing has happened. While working with the children, my mind, on double-track, is thinking: How am I getting home? Asha has my return train ticket.

How will I handle the next several days? Then I remember that there is staff from *Learning and Eating Together* present. They know the situation and they know that this is the one year that my wife was unable to accompany me. She is in America taking care of her seriously ill elderly mother. But I remind myself that I am in India, with people who know me. Hospitality and problem solving are indigenous to India. By the time I am finished talking with this group of children and before the next group arrives, I am sure staff will have figured out several options for me.

Indeed, a *Learning and Eating Together* staff member comes over and talks with me before it is time to see the next group of children. "We have three possibilities. You can stay with the math teacher until Asha returns or you can stay with the English teacher. On the other hand, you might feel most comfortable being in your hotel, in which case you'll need someone to teach you how to ride the Bombay Commuter Railway and find the right stops for the other places you need to be. We can send someone back to your hotel with you who will show you where the other railway stops are and which trains you should take."

What seemed to the Westerner an outpouring of generosity is, here in India, simply a problem to be solved. Generosity is assumed. Something had come up and needed a solution. The hospitality was incorporated into their thinking and therefore not given a thought, certainly not perceived as a burden. Of course they would make sure their guest would be taken care of and be comfortable. This is a manifestation of the healing properties of India.

I preferred to stay in my hotel, with access to fresh clothes, toiletries, my planning notes, and the friendly faces of the staff at the

Colaba Guest House, who would wonder where I was if I were gone without explanation for days. I continued the work of the day. I asked the staff members present to help with translation in Asha's absence and to keep me in "cultural check," i.e., to be sure that I was speaking relevantly to the parents, my next group. Given the respect for hierarchy, I had to give explicit permission for someone to interrupt me and provide a correction if I should veer culturally off-course.

Fifteen parents, representing twenty students, missed part of a day's work to meet with me and learn about their children. None of them speaks English; everything happens in translated Marathi and Hindi. Since all their jobs are no-work/no-pay, they gave up income to hear about their children. However, what these parents really want to do is talk about how hard their lives are and to share some of their history. They speak of their work, their long hours, and the mothers' attempts to be home when their children return from school. Primarily, however, they want to share their histories. I wonder if they wanted to be understood by their children's teachers, rather than be blamed when homework isn't done. I think, "They want to be seen."

"I have nine children. My mother-in-law made me. My first child was a girl. She told my husband I had to keep having children until I had a boy. My next three children were also girls. I begged my husband for the operation but his mother said, 'No,' I had to keep having children until I had a boy." She starts to cry. "I had four more children, all girls. I was desperate and then I had a boy. My husband asked his mother if I could have the operation now and she said 'Yes.' My husband left me two years ago. My mother-in-law threw me and all nine children out in the street; that was when we moved into this slum. I am raising nine children by myself and working as much as I can. I need the oldest girls to work as soon as they finish school." She stands up proudly while weeping. "I have made sure that every one of my children goes to school. I won't let them be like me, uneducated, and so I have to take bad jobs and not much money for my work." She sits, having regained her composure. The parents listening to this tale offer spontaneous applause as a show of support for such courage.

An outpouring of words from a father with few pauses: "I brought my family here from the village because I heard we could live better here. But no, we live in one room and there are six of us me my wife our son our daughter my brother who couldn't find work in the village and my wife's sister whose husband left her and she had nowhere to go. I work in construction. They don't follow the safety rules. Some of my friends at work have died in accidents at the factory or when making a building. I am lucky I only had this muscle torn" (pointing to his leg), "that's why I limp but my job uses my strong chest and arms so I still have my job my wife grinds corn you can see her in the lane over there then she sells it. My brother works where I do and my wife's sister who is a good person can't work anymore because acid was spilled in her face at her job and she can't see much. It is not better here except my two children can go to school longer than in the village and we will live in our room until they finish school and get jobs then we will see if the rest of us can go back to the village. Or they can come back with us and maybe get a better job because they can read and write. I feel sad when I can't help them with their homework I don't read or write I couldn't go to school I won't let that happen to my children."

The parents have other tales to tell and want advice on how to help their children's behavior. They ask the teachers what their children are learning in school. The teachers try to explain but without visual aids or examples of the children's work at hand, these unschooled parents don't fully comprehend. At the end of the session they want their picture taken as a group and ask if it can be hung in the classroom. This is the closest they will come to an education for themselves. The fathers ask me to sit with them, one putting his hand over my shoulder.

Now that the long workday is over, it is time to head back to my guesthouse. A teacher has been assigned to give me a lesson in riding the Bombay Commuter Railway. Asha and I have been doing it, but I've been paying attention to negotiating the crowds and keeping an eye on Asha, who is riding with me, rather than in the Ladies Only compartment. I have not kept track of which train we were getting on or how many stops until we reached a destination. I knew how to handle the crush but not which train went where. Vedh comes with me and, being a teacher, gives me an ongoing narration of where we got on and the names of all stops (which he writes down). Once we are at the Chatrapati Shivaji Terminus, the last stop at the end of the day and the place to begin my journey in the morning, Vedh shows me the various listings of trains, timetables, and names of stops, written in English.

We walk a couple of miles together. This is a part of the route we share on our journeys to our respective homes. Vedh tells me he never takes a public bus as long as he can take "Bus Number Eleven." He points to his two feet, lined up next to each other. "This way I can stop in at the art gallery." This is his break. He still has two hours until he reaches his home. He tells me about his upcoming marriage and invites me to his wedding.

When I arrive at my guesthouse, I have a message to call Gopal. Asha, even in her rush to get to her family and her mother's cremation, has made tentative arrangements for a car and driver for

me for the next five days. I tell Gopal that I would like to decline.
I would prefer not to be the white Westerner coming to these remote slum schools in the comfort of a private car. I feel it is more
respectful if I ride the Bombay Commuter Railway, Second Class.
Like Vedh.

A DEATH IN THE FAMILY

*S*ilver Spring, MD and Queens, NY. December 2007. *My father has died. He lingered for six months after his stroke. He lingered long enough, six months longer than predicted, that his comatose state and shrunken appearance had become part of him. My picture of the robust man perpetually on the verge of a diet is merged with a wraith weighing less than one hundred pounds with sunken cheeks, eerily smooth, slightly yellowed skin, eyes always closed.*

I had seen him a few days before and knew he was at last dying. However, he lingered. He was looking for permission or some form of information or perhaps a promise. I decided it was a promise: he was worried about my mother. I told my mother that he needed her permission to go and his assurance that she was being looked after and would be all right. She turned on me and venomously spat out: "I won't do it. It's murder, and you promise me that you won't do it either." Lying, I promised in order to calm her down. She said, "You can go. Now!"

I left her; unable to talk with her about how she was feeling and what her immediate and long-term worries were. I wished she had shown some sign of mourning; perhaps her behavior toward me was just that.

Breaking my promise, I returned to the nursing home and my father. I sat down on his bed and stroked his hair. I told him that he didn't have to worry about Rosie because Ron and I would take care of her. We would make sure she has everything she needs and she will be all right. His breathing seemed to slow some. He could hear me. I assured him that he had been a wonderful father and that I loved him very much and was going to miss him. I kissed him on the yellow hollow of his smooth cheek and said, "And now I'm going to say goodbye, dad. I love you very much." I stroked his hair and touched his cheek for the last time, gave him one more kiss and left. He died twenty-four hours later, to the minute.

The nursing home informed my mother before I could. When I called she said, **"So he's dead. What's being done about the funeral?"** *I assured her that all the plans were in place, and that in fact dad was already at the funeral home. The funeral would be delayed a few days because Christmas was tomorrow and the cemetery was closed so its Christian employees could have their holiday with their families.* **"Families…I don't give a damn about families except my own…my mother and father and all my brothers. You're not going to put him in a plain pine box, are you? Don't you dare because then that's what you would do to me and you can't do that to me."**

"No, mom. No plain pine box but I did keep it simple. Dad's wishes were for me to plan a funeral and pick a coffin that would suit my level of observance. That's what we're having and I promise no plain pine box. Not for him and not for you."

"I hope you're not lying just to shut me up."

"You'll see at the funeral. It's going to be on Thursday. I hired a limo to get us to New York. The hearse will get there a little before we do."

"Is your brother coming?"

I told her "Yes, and Lin and Gabriel."

"I don't know if I'm going. I hate that place and I'll have to see the graves of my parents and all seven of my brothers and all of their wives except Miriam."

"Mom, it's going to be hard, I know. But this is Dad. You need to go."

*She ended the visit with, "**I'll think about it.**" When I called her later to see how she was doing and to tell her what time the limo would pick us up for the trip to Queens and back, she docilely said, "I'll be ready."*

Our son Gabriel, my brother Ron, Lin and I made four in a limousine made to accommodate six. We drove over to my mother's place. She was downstairs and ready. She didn't speak and turned her face when I tried to kiss her. I helped her into the car. On the five-hour drive she said not a word, while the other four of us were talking and telling stories, alternately somber and funny.

As we pulled in to the cemetery, with its narrow lanes designed pre-automobile, we stopped at the main building so I could speak with the rabbi about my father. I wanted this kind rent-a-rabbi in another city to be able to personalize his words about my father. The hearse was waiting and I asked the attendants to open the upper portion of the coffin. The shrunken, yellowed, comatose man, now gone, looked the same. I removed the part of the shroud covering his head, stroked his hair one last time and said "Goodbye, Dad." The shroud was replaced over his head, the coffin lid reclosed (not a plain pine box but nevertheless simple and made only of wood), and we in the limo followed the hearse to the family gravesites where my father would join my mother's family.

My mother refused to get out of the car. She was angry and adamant but after ten minutes with the rabbi she emerged and he helped her join the rest of us already standing in place. I walked over and stood next to her. She did not acknowledge me. She was welcoming to my cousins, the children of her many brothers, who loved her for her alter-ego charming, warm, hospitable, self. Her public self.

*She bitterly spoke her first words of the day on the ride home: "**Now my social security check will be six hundred dollars less.**" Gabriel looked at me; this was not the grandmother, his "Momo," whom he knew. She was silent until she was hungry on the New Jersey Turnpike and asked to stop. She looked at her food and said, "**I can't eat this shit; let's go.**" The rest of us did eat. We hadn't had anything since morning except what Lin, thinking of all of us, had brought for the ride.*

*As we rode, I reminded my mother that we had talked about the Jewish mourning ritual of shiva being observed at our home, and that this had been her choice. What time would she like me to pick her up tomorrow? "**I'm not coming,**" said in such a way that there would be no discussion. She had made up her mind. And indeed my mother was not present at the shiva observance for her husband of sixty-seven years.*

THE BOMBAY COMMUTER
RAILWAY

The Bombay Commuter Railway, starting at Chatrapati Shivaji Terminus, were it a territory rather than a means of transportation, would be one of earth's most crowded areas. Intended for nine-car trains and close to two thousand people, the six second class carriages are so laden with crushed humanity that often six thousand people are aboard, each body touching each other body, everyone surrounded on all sides.

Narrow benches that in America hold three, in Bombay hold four or five. The windows have bars but no glass. There are no doors, just large openings for getting on and off. People like to ride leaning out of the doorways, where the air is. There are not enough handles for everyone who cannot find a seat, which is almost everybody, and from a standing position there is a certain beauty in seeing thousands of outstretched arms and hands of many colors clutching too few handles.

Marc Nemiroff

When the train is less full, the handles are necessary. When on a packed train, the handles are unnecessary. No one can move, thus no one will fall. I have a friend who passed out on the Bombay Commuter Railway from the heat of so many bodies in such close space and insufficient air. He awoke twenty minutes later in exactly the same position as when he fainted. One day I was riding with my hand in my pocket. I needed to remove my hand in order to reach a handle. Impossible. My hand had become a sardine canned by the masses of people.

Time to alight. Utter chaos. Those waiting to get on push their way forward while those waiting to get off must push through them. The train will not wait for this doorway dance to resolve itself. It is scheduled to leave in two minutes and leave it will.

I love the Bombay Commuter Railway. Somehow, in the crowd there is kindness. Asha was routinely offered a seat even if she had to cross a sea of bodies to get there. Those who noticed that Asha and I were traveling together—not always discernible as we easily got separated in the churning mass—made space for me next to her if I could only get there. I like the crowds; I like the speed of movement of the people; I love the diversity of colors and languages and occupations and ages. It is the Indian urban landscape squeezed into a tapestry woven with the finest of fabrics to portray the greatest amount of life's details. I even like the train stop mayhem; I take it as a challenge and it brings out the New Yorker in me. I felt exhilarated when I had to run and jump onto a train as it was slowly leaving the station (Asha had already gotten on), with a dozen hands reaching out to give me room where there was no room.

Standing so near the door I have to be careful to avoid becoming a statistic, one of the thousands of people killed annually by being extruded from the train. I inch back a foot or two. That is enough.

When lucky, we find the cargo car where men and women carrying thrashing fish in basins on their heads, enormous cartons of toilet paper and other dry goods, put down their burdens, squat (no seats) and talk. On one trip while Asha was away, I got into a dual-language "conversation" with a cargo man about how in the world he carries so much on his head. We were each speaking our own language that the other could not. The cargo man asked if I wanted to try—witness the power of gesture in a country of gesture. I couldn't pass up this opportunity and so the carton carrier and several of his friends put a towel "cushion" on my head and four of them hoisted an enormous carton of toilet paper, softly supporting it so I could feel what it was like but that I wouldn't be hurt. I laughed. They laughed too, lowered the carton, and slapped me on the shoulder. I almost missed my stop.

"SIR, YOU ARE A VERY GOOD ACTOR."

With Asha still away, I handle our agenda alone, with the help of a teacher for translation and the watchful eye of someone I requested from *Learning and Eating Together* to double-check my cultural attunement with the children.

In a group of twenty-seven mixed Eighth and Ninth Standard thirteen- to fifteen-year- olds, we work on the importance of education in general and for girls in particular. Girls deserve an education as much as boys do, are as valuable as boys are, and should not be married off young by their parents—nominally illegal but who is watching? Who would care? Who would know except those directly involved? The children understand but have only partially internalized the concept of educational equality.

Again I have a slight shiver of pleasure at how enthusiastic and engaged Indian kids are in acting things out. We design a set, using their small iron and wood floor-desks to create a mini-*bustee*, and moving the floor mats to the other side of the room to represent a classroom. I am the mother who wants her fourteen-year-old daughter to go to school but can't afford to keep her at home anymore. Thus I have arranged an engagement and pending marriage. A fourteen-year-old girl is eager to "be" my daughter. The rest of the children go into the hall and decide together how they will handle the problem. They have no idea how I am going to behave. These youngsters compose something that evolves into a three-act play. We have a Marathi and English-speaking teacher doing translation, but sometimes we find we don't need the translation; somehow we understand each other. The proficiency of the translation allows our play to proceed with much flair.

Act One, Scene One: At School. The teacher stands at the head of the class with the students on the floor, has finished her lesson for the day, and is checking the homework, student by student. She dismisses them and all rush to their homes to start their chores.

Act One, Scene Two: At Home. I, the mother, am inside waiting for my daughter to arrive. When she comes in, I gently ask her to sit down. I have something important to tell her. I tell her, trying not to cry, that I had to arrange a marriage for her and that she has to stop going to school once she is married and move in with her twenty-five-year-old husband's family. I explain agitatedly that I wish I didn't have to do it, but because there are three children and Daddy doesn't work because he drinks, I can't make enough money to feed everyone. She is the oldest girl and so I have no choice. I tell her how sad this makes me. (Despite the need for translation, what is occurring is compelling enough that the fourteen-year-old student's eyes start to well up before the translation ended. The children have been expecting an ogre mother and I am a kind and sad mother doing something I wish I didn't have to do.) My "daughter" explains how she really wants to go to school. I apologize and tell her I wish she could but it isn't possible.

Act Two, Scene One: At School. In class, my daughter sits apart from everyone else while the teacher leads a lesson. Sad, unresponsive (and very convincing), she weeps. The teacher goes over to her and asks what is the matter. My daughter explains through her tears. Other children begin to gather around. They decide as a group that the teacher will go to her home and talk to me about *Learning and Eating Together.*

Act Two, Scene Two: At Home. The teacher accompanies my daughter and tells me that she understands the problem and asks if I know about *Learning and Eating Together.* I don't, and I ask for information. The teacher explains to me that my daughter doesn't have to be one more mouth to feed. Lunch is provided at school through this special program. My daughter, energized, urgently pleads that she will go without dinner every day at home in order to stay in school. I tell the teacher and my daughter that that still won't be enough help. I need more money than that to feed the family and provide for their daily needs. My daughter will have to go. I pretend to be near tears myself. (The youngsters are not expecting this response in the role-play.) The teacher becomes angry with me and tells me that she will report me to the police for marrying off my daughter when she is under age. I matter-of-factly state that the police won't care or do anything. They all know that this is likely the truth.

Act Three, Scene One: At School. The teacher joins her students in a discussion of what else can be done to help my daughter stay in school. This has now become a community problem, replicating one facet of the social structure of the *bustee.* They all understand that I am not trying to be mean, that I don't *want* to discontinue my daughter's education; nor do I want to send her away to be married at fourteen. I just don't know what else to do because of the money. All the youngsters start whispering, looking over at me to be sure that I am staying in role, cleaning up and cooking in my home. They are intent on my not hearing them.

Act Three, Scene Two: At Home. The entire class, along with the teacher, accompanies my daughter home from school. The teacher tells me that everyone has figured out a way for my daughter to stay in school and not have an arranged marriage at age fourteen. Each student will get a small job. Just an hour or two, a few days a week. Each week, they will put all their earnings together and bring the money to me so I can buy food and have enough to take care of my family. I, as the mother, moved by their kindness and by their now-"claimed" commitment to education for this girl, stand still and quietly think. "It's the only way your daughter can better herself and have a job that pays more money. It will help everybody." I nod my head, thank them tearfully, tell my daughter she can now stay with our family and go to school. I tell the still play-acting students that they are very generous. The role-play is over.

I am overwhelmed by the generosity shown in the children's three-act opus. These are youngsters who have almost nothing material, who live in slums. Who I have before me are twenty-seven teenage *Mahatmas*, Great Souls.

A boy and a girl come very close to me, touch my arm and say, "learning is important and marrying girls away so young is a bad thing." I am deeply moved; the message has gotten through. Several of the kids come over and touch my back. They say in Marathi, quickly translated: "Sir, you are a very good actor."

SON AND FATHER

Asha has returned and we go to another city slum school. Eighth Standard students file in. We are going to do the same exercises—we call them "lessons" to keep school authorities happy—as we have done at three other schools.

These youngsters have a better command of English in general and there is less need for translation. One soulful boy comes up to me at the end of our time together and says, "Sir, there is something I want to tell you." I ask him about it; I want to convey how truly interested I am. He says, "I am most proud because I am my father's teacher. I have taught him how to read and write, which I learned through *Learning and Eating Together*. He can read and he can write and every night I teach him what I learned that day. It's not easy because it's noisy and there are a lot of people and the television is on. Now people don't cheat him. They know he can read the signs and he knows how much things cost. They give him the right amount of rupees back. He likes to learn. I wish he could have gone to school like me."

As we have done in each school, we are holding a parent meeting to discuss their children's progress in school, and to explain what their children are learning and why going to school is important. Most of the parents have received minimal or no schooling themselves and don't fully understand what goes on in a classroom.

The parents listen politely; I do not believe that they fully understand. How can a parent make sense of the importance of her child's reading when she doesn't know herself what an alphabet is? Of what use is learning the principal commodities and rivers of Ghana? Sending their children to school, although it is the law, is often a hardship. The parents have, however, taken in the general concept and concrete idea that the only way their children can become something more and live better is through education. Some of them just have trouble linking it to specifics.

These meetings often focus on parents' questions about getting their kids to do their homework, a nearly impossible task in slum conditions and not always easy in much better conditions because thirteen year olds are more interested in music, sports, and movies than in homework. "Homework" is the American term for what in Bombay is referred to as "Review," i.e., nothing new is learned. Some parents ask child development questions. Usually only the mothers attend. Occasionally there is a father or two or an uncle. The parents are often moved because we have treated them with respect. I suspect this may be because in many schools teachers typically contact them only when there are complaints about their children. It would be easy for teachers to confuse parents' lack of knowledge about education with lack of commitment to their children's schoolwork.

As this parent group is breaking up, a few parents hang back with questions specific to their own children. One beaming father comes up to me and says, in English not quite as good as his son's: "Do you know why I am so proud of my son? First, he is smart. But I am most proud that he is my teacher. He teaches me to read and write. I can stand up for myself in a store and get the right change because I can read the signs. I try to learn everything he is learning and my son is very proud of me. I want my son to be proud of me." He puts his arm on my shoulder before offering a parting *Namaste.*

TWO DAYS IN A TRIBAL VILLAGE: SCHOOL CONFLICT REGARDING UNTOUCHABLES

Learning and Eating Together has made inroads in two tribal village schools. Asha and I have been asked to spend two full days in one of them. We are to travel by train several hours to reach the village and stay overnight in a nearby home.

The village, in the shadow of a hill station, has perhaps thirty homes, but the school pulls students in from farther away, too. The homes, square and mostly built of brick and sturdy woven plant leaves, sit close together. Most have two rooms, a bedroom for parents and a general room that serves as bedroom at night for the others in the family, kitchen and gathering area for eating and watching television. A few houses have a low brick walled interior area that functions as a latrine. No plumbing. Water generally comes from a shared public source.

The village population is composed of two tribal groups, Adivasi, who are Untouchables, and Agri, who are low-caste. The two have managed to achieve a functional peace over time. However, the Fifth and Sixth Standard (10-12 year old) children have lately erupted into caste-Untouchable conflict. This is the reason Asha and I have been requested. When first asked if I would be willing, I thought "Well, there are several thousand years of failure behind us; what have we got to lose? We'll certainly join good company if we can't accomplish anything." I expected to work hard and intensely, with little gain.

Together, Asha and I work with the *Learning and Eating Together* teacher in the school, but not academically. We meet with the local *panchayat* (elected village leader and political representative), the teachers, and many of the parents in their homes over the course of these two days. We are the overnight guests of the founding patron of the school program (and have running water and an interior bathroom).   I believe that the people in this village have never seen a white person before.

Although the students wear the same school uniforms, we can generally tell Agri and Adivasi apart from their level of cleanliness, presence or absence of ringworm, and whether they wear shoes or go barefoot. Agri children tend to wear cleaner clothes and shoes, and comb their hair with some care. I only see two children with ringworm on their scalps. Both are Adivasi. Adivasi girls enjoy dressing up in what look like bright colored Western style birthday dresses that seem out of place in this outpost.

The children group themselves by tribal membership when playing in the dusty yard. Light brown dust permeates the air, has settled on all surfaces (I think including our lungs). The village is flypaper to swirling brown sandy particles, attracting the dust away from the green trees just beyond. All families wash their clothes and hang them up to dry in the dusty hot air: khaki and white school uniforms; Adivasi bright pink, green, turquoise, and red taffeta; Agri saffron, orange, and red saris hang on clotheslines or rest in branches of trees or drape over dusty shrubs.

Asha and I, with the teacher, enter the small school and meet with the assembled and tribally mixed Agri and Adivasi school children, perhaps twenty-five in all. I tell them the story of my grandmother the cleaning lady—always an icebreaker that seems to remove some of my strange Westerner whiteness. We need the children split into two groups. The teacher says, "You'll never get them to mix voluntarily." We ask them to form two groups by themselves. Indeed, along tribal lines. Then we have them count out "one" or "two" in order. Once we have all the "Ones" and all the "Twos" in groups, we have managed to create the tribally mixed groups. I believe that the curiosity about my skin color overrode the usual animosity toward each other.

For the first day, we work with putting on a "play" from one of India's two great epics, the *Ramayana*. This tells the tale of Lord Rama, an incarnation of Vishnu. The main story has to do with Lord Rama's pursuit of his consort Sita, who has been stolen away. There are numerous side tales that present moral teachings. In one, Shabari the Bhil, an Adivasi most likely from central India, wants to offer the god, Lord Rama, some fruit as a token of honor, humility, and generosity. Lord Rama is sitting with his less wise brother, Lakshman. Shabari has the "temerity" to taste the fruit, making sure that it is worthy of Lord Rama. Thus, an Untouchable is offering partially eaten fruit to the god. She approaches Lakshman first, who will not accept her gesture and reviles her. Undeterred, she moves slowly toward Lord Rama, bows and offers the fruit with teeth marks on it to him. He understands her gesture and its genesis in honoring him and accepts her offering. Her Untouchability as an Adivasi is irrelevant. Her worship of him and her wish to give him the best of what she has, are what register.

We then have each group of children act out this three-person story. Since they are now Untouchable/Non-Untouchable mixed groups, these enactments require Untouchables sometimes to take the part of a god and children of a casted group to offer something to him (sometimes played by a her). Adivasi and Agri have to touch each other and break the otherwise immutable caste/ Untouchable (out-caste) hierarchy.

The children become engaged, each group of three trying to find a new way to present the same scenario. Some mime picking the fruit offering off of student drawings of trees on the wall. Others imitate the biting of the fruit. A variety of harsh or mean or ignorant Lakshmans refuse the offerings. Kind, obligatory, desultory, and generous Lords Rama accept the fruit. It takes the children awhile to realize that they have interacted with each other across caste and tribal lines. They are having fun with a story they know well.

We visit the younger children, with much ado about my white skin and the hair on my arms. I make a point of touching each child and ignoring tribal origin when playing or putting someone in my lap. After seeing the young ones, we make our way around the village, stopping in many houses with an emphasis on the Untouchable homes. Children of all persuasions follow us. Asha refers to me as the Pied Piper, although I'm not sure I've done anything to promote this other than be a human novelty.

We are invited into one Adivasi home where both parents receive us and offer their money to buy soft drinks for us...another example of people with so little offering their hospitality. Many people follow us in. The father is overwhelmed. There are nineteen people in his small, dark, all-purpose room with a tiny window, and ninety-five degrees of heat oozing its way in.

Agri and Adivasi, adults and children, dark and white skin all coming into an Untouchable's home. The father is deeply moved and close to tears. He takes out his harmonium to sing two songs of his happiness as an offering to the people who have come to visit. Black, white, and a spectrum of brown skins, heat, dust, insects, nineteen people in the shadowed interior, and the full-throated sounds of musical gratitude issuing from this man's throat create a time-stopping scene.

Asha, the teacher, and I walk from the village, children in tow, to the home where we will be spending the night. This belongs to the teacher's mother, a gracious woman concerned about the education of these children. She is greatly respected from areas near and not so near, and the greater community voluntarily brings all her meals to her from their own homes. She is in her mid-eighties, living alone, although with help inside and out. Her main worry is whether she will be a good enough hostess to her overnight guests. We spend the early evening talking in Marathi and English. Then it is time for dinner and bed. I have a room to myself, as the only man present. The three women share a room. I shower in what I took at first to be a clean bathroom by my own standards. I step into the shower, turn on the trickle of tepid water, and pick up the soap that turns black when I rub it. I keep scrubbing until it is white again, and use it on my body.

When I enter my room I discover that the mosquitos have staged a coup and taken over its governance. I quickly find the mosquito coil and light it, chasing the enemy away, at least for the one night that I will be in that room. There are no chairs or a table or dresser and so I lay down my suitcase (closed against insect encroachment) with the next day's clothes on top. Realizing that I have to keep the window shut all night against the attacking mosquitos, and determined not to get between any sheets or covers, I sleep on top of the bed until morning. Standards of cleanliness are different and I understand that our elderly host has done her best to make the bathroom and bedroom as acceptable as possible in order for her guests. I thank her honestly for her attentiveness and generosity in opening up her home to strangers. She then takes us around to look at the flowering plants.

Returning to the village, we find the children already assembled and waiting for us, eager to have a new activity and seemingly unconcerned about the caste breaches of the day before. They easily return to their same groups, mixed by tribe/caste and by gender. For the second day, Asha and I have devised an exercise. Group One is going to mime what makes a bad village and Group Two will mime what makes a good village. We are trying to promote discussion, non-verbal interaction, and literal touching of Untouchables. I find it interesting how alive the caste system and Untouchability are the farther I move outside the more educated large cities, despite the fact that it was abolished in the Indian Constitution, adopted in 1950, itself written by a distinguished and highly educated Untouchable.

The children's teacher believes that the children don't have the capacity to think in terms of "good" and "bad" village and wants to tell them what to do. I ask her to please trust the children. Asha takes the Good Village Group and facilitates their discussions.

The teacher facilitates the "Bad Village Group. I stand over this group so I can remind the teacher not to offer suggestions but to leave the children alone.

Animated talking fills the room. I think this is for four reasons: the children are having fun with an unusual activity; they are being asked to think for themselves; they are not being told what to do by anyone other than the general large task; they can be active.

When the hubbub dies down, the mimed presentations begin. The Bad Village group decides to present first. They have elected a spokesman/narrator, a most appealing undersized boy who likes announcing things. This group enacts through movement and touch, the evils of alcohol, harassment of women, kidnapping, loud arguing, people not getting along.

The Good Village presents itself. Its approach is to have everyone guess what they are doing and to forego an announcer. Three girls, of mixed tribal origin, stand up and place themselves with their backs touching and arms down. They looked around the room to see if anyone can guess yet. No takers.

Slowly, ever so slowly, ever so gracefully, they raise their six arms in unison. They pause. They move their outstretched arms, ballet-like, so that each girl eventually forms a "Y." Then they open their fingers fully extended, intertwine them and smile. A most beautiful, gently unfolding tree appears.

The group enact an easily recognizable market scene with people milling about looking at imaginary merchandise, potential purchasers bargaining with potential sellers, boys walking down a dusty street arm in arm. During the discussion period, three boys have been busy bending their hands and trying out different ways to turn. Neither Asha nor I can figure out what they are doing. It is now their turn. They come forward, enjoying having everyone's eyes upon them. One of them whispers "one, two, three...GO" (in Marathi). Six legs, six arms, and thirty fingers twist very quickly and wondrously create a three-wheel auto rickshaw with engine, three wheels and two benches. Pure magic. All the children gasp and applaud and then Asha and I have all the children applaud each other and themselves.

After lunch, we visit more of the village, trying to pay a call on every home.   Our retinue of mixed children and mixed adults, many talking at once and wanting to show us things along the way, prevents us from dropping in on every home.

The afternoon wears on. Asha and I have something planned for the Fifth and Sixth Standard children before we leave. However, when we exit the building after having lunch with the teachers, who told stories of trying to manage their own families and the alcoholism of some of their husbands, we discover that we have to change our plans. I think of this as "India taking over." No matter how fully I plan for something in India, something else will probably happen, planfully or accidentally, perhaps a result of miscommunication or just plain spontaneity. But all too often, what I think is going to happen, what I planned on happening, isn't what happens. This makes India the place where serendipity happily flourishes.

We walk outside and the children of many ages play two parallel games of Frisbee. The seemingly uncrossable line is tribally based. It is hot. It is dusty. We are tired. Asha and I both join the game being played by the Adivasis. She eventually drops out. Tired as I am, this seems too good an opportunity to let pass. One boy throws the Frisbee to me. I throw it back. A number of Agri children now want to be included. Once they get the Frisbee, they keep throwing it either to me or to someone else of their own tribe and caste. I begin to direct the game: "You! Try throwing it to him. Now you throw it him. OK, I'm ready if someone wants to throw it to me. The game enlarges and the second game shrinks to just the very young children while everyone else is involved in this larger game. I think it will last a few minutes. After a few minutes I think it will last half-and hour. After half an hour, I realize I am in for about an hour. In the dust. In ninety-five degree heat. And, in fact, the game ends after fifty-five minutes.

Dripping wet, shirttails out, sweating, I look like a middle-school kid just getting out of P.E. As I am trying to put myself in order before heading to the train station, the pint-sized announcer of the Bad Village Group comes running after me. He pulls my shirttail out of my trousers by tugging on it until he can get a good hold and stops me. With irresistible earnestness he says, "You come back next week? We get along better when you here."

Two years later, their teacher sent Asha and me an e-mail. The children have been asking when we will be coming back to help them get along. I ask myself: was this a successful, or simply naïve, endeavor? I don't know. But if at least a small handful of children can hold the memory of amity, I am satisfied.

MY MOTHER'S LAST WORDS
TO ME

Silver Spring, Maryland. Late September. My mother, recently turned ninety, is currently in a nursing rehabilitation unit recovering from a fall that fractured her pelvis. She is making good physical progress and will soon transfer to an assisted-living apartment. She has fairly mild dementia, but her paranoia is now more pronounced. I have had to take over her finances, at first over her fierce accusations, when I found her checkbook in chaos and discovered several unpaid bills in her apartment's freezer. "I hid them there. You know damned well that they are coded with information about me, and those people can spy on me. But not if they're in a dark freezer." She is referring to a three-month-old telephone bill.

*I now pay the bills and send her, as she has requested, monthly overviews of her finances. After awhile, she has stopped asking for them but she eyes me suspiciously. Occasionally, she calls at various times of day and night to scream at me, "**What are you doing with my money?!?**" She has called in the middle of the night demanding that I divorce Lin, whom actually she* *loves, and relinquish my career **"to take care of your mother; that's what any son with human feeling would do."** She ignores my attempts to limit her 1:30 a.m. phone calls and so we do not answer the phone.*

My mother is even bitterer than she used to be and visiting her regularly has become increasingly toxic. I am developing insomnia and other symptoms of severe stress. I now see her less frequently, and always take Lin with me because my mother will not speak to me angrily in public. She has always saved the venom for when we are alone. Lin drives over by herself in between. Our visits are filled with my mother's angry complaints, her distrust of nursing staff, warnings about stairways where "they" are waiting to kill us, and how everything is now miserable and has always been miserable. Her face naturally falls into an expression of sour fire.

On a golden late September day, Lin and I have come to visit. We help my mother walk down the hall to a visitors' alcove that is relatively private and has a large window looking out on the early autumn sun-dappled trees. My mother doesn't see them. "Oh life's just a bitch. Here I am. No one comes to see me." (A friend had left minutes before we arrived and another arrives while we are there. She stays for a while and leaves.) "Nobody cares. Life's a bitch. I never thought it would come to this."

She continues for an hour. We sit and listen, noticing the sun outside. "So, what's new?" my mother asks. We tell her an abridged version of our activities. "How's Gabriel and what's-her-name?" referring to his wife, her granddaughter-in-law whose name she really does know. Although her litany of grievances (many justifiable—being ninety, widowed, and limited in mobility is indeed a bitch) continues, she appears temporarily emotionally milder. Lin takes the opportunity to use the restroom.

My mother watches her carefully with crocodile eyes, planfully. Once she sees the rest room door close, she turns on me. Her eyebrows knit together as she scowls and transforms her face demonically. She spits out the words she has been waiting to say. **"You dirty son of a bitch. You put me here"** *(forgetting her fall, hospitalization, and broken pelvis)* **"just to get rid of me. You have always hated me and tried to get rid of me. AND NOW YOU ARE STEALING MY MONEY FROM ME. YOU DIRTY BASTARD."**

"Mom, this visit is over," and when Lin returns we leave. I stopped visiting and calling my mother after that day, as I had been advised to do for years by friends and professionals. And so, **"You dirty bastard"** *were my mother's last words to me. Not new, but no longer endurable.*

Rose Nemiroff died in her sleep on June 27, 2009.

BACK TO BOMBAY AND BACK TO SCHOOL

Asha and I had developed a warm working relationship with *"Learning and Eating Together,"* and worked over several years with the children, their parents, the special *Learning and Eating Together* teachers, and the staff. Our next project was to help the children and teachers approach the teaching of English in new, hopefully more effective, ways.

English is now necessary in Bombay to get most respectable jobs. Ancient textbooks redolent of the Raj handicap the children of the *bustees* educated in the city schools. For discipline, in a number of classrooms the ruler tends to rule. A long wooden pointer makes a good substitute. Reading selections are from nineteenth century English literature and sometimes also make reference to long-dead popular American figures who have no meaning to these youngsters (nor to most of today's American kids): the

London Eccentrics Club of the 18th century, the American comedian from the 1930s to the 1950s, Groucho Marx.

The most galling English textbook chapter for me is from Dickens' *Oliver Twist*, in which a hungry little boy in a London workhouse dares to ask for more to eat and is taken out and sold. And this is used with often-hungry slum children who are in a special program that feeds them at school.

Conversational English is generally ignored in the regular curriculum as near as I can tell. Teachers I speak with confirm this. Certainly, conversational English as a class subject is hard to find. Thus, these children will be recognized as undesirables from the slum as soon as they speak three words in public. They will not be hired for any position requiring proper English. Even a courier has to be able to say "Sir, I have a package for Mr. X; might that be you?" Educators tell me that other cities, Delhi for one, have much more advanced curricula.

Nevertheless, Asha and I, just like the children, must work with these textbooks as well as weave a therapeutic component into what we are doing. We work with one Eighth Standard and one Ninth Standard class for close to a week. The children have been taught to read by the rote method, so they can accurately read and speak the words of a selection in a staccato, unemphasized, flat manner betraying complete lack of understanding of both vocabulary and meaning.

"I AM ASHAMED TO SPEAK ENGLISH"

Dharavi, Bombay. 2011. Dharavi is the largest slum in Asia. It houses 1.3 million people in narrow quarters. One city school serving the area is just on the edge of one of the many entryways into the dark alleyways of this slum, filled with multiple *bustees* containing countless *guhlees*.

The school is old and in disrepair, its walls the witnesses of many failures. It is home to future alcoholics, wife-beaters, laborers, men desperate to support their families, hard-working mothers, and a few children who will make it out and become lawyers, engineers, and doctors. It is, for many, a house of lost dreams. Not so for the *Learning and Eating Together* children. They eagerly gather in the hot sun in front of the dull building in the treeless dirt, waiting for school to open.

All the children are clean, bathed—they use the delightful verb "to refresh," to refer to a bucket bath or shower in the public bathhouse—and ready for school in their navy pants and blue-and-white striped shirt uniforms. The boys are quickly putting on their clip-on neckties. The girls are in similarly colored jumpers and blouses, with frayed ribbons carefully arranged in their hair.

School opens and this crew in blue makes its way up the old stairs, sticky railings, ignoring the walls that have witnessed failure. They talk loudly; the girls giggle; the boys noisily push each other around. They look much like the fourteen-to-sixteen year olds they are, Eighth and Ninth Standard students happy to be at school. Although this is a "new" school for Asha and me, it is a replica of the uncaring, uncared-for schools we have already been in. The *Learning and Eating Together* classroom is cleaner, but it is still basic, with little color in the room other than what a few outdated, unattractive posters can provide. It is eerie to go from school to school and find ourselves in the same classroom.

I have learned from the previous year to rid myself of American assumptions linking poverty with lack of motivation. *Learning and Eating Together* has asked Asha and me to work with the children on their English lessons, their biggest burdens. Somehow these youngsters are supposed to acquire English as a third language from grossly antiquated textbooks that reek of colonialism and condescension and are full of archaic or irrelevant vocabulary. Children of the slum need daily English to become competitive when looking for work. The only time they read or hear the language is at school. No one at home speaks it. Many of their teachers may not speak it.

They have been taught how to read English through the use of rote learning. The result is that they can read the words, without any expression because they do not know what they mean, and they cannot speak a single proper English sentence. The Bombay school curriculum fails them. *Learning and Eating Together* provides its own English teachers, who are troubled by the lack of progress of their students. The teachers have been trained in the same out-moded methods of teaching.

Asha and I have been given lessons from the textbooks to use, one for each Standard. I am appalled when I see them. "Asha, I can't teach this. It's mostly irrelevant material with no appeal. The vocabulary will not help the children; it is full of words they don't need. We will be contributors to the irrelevant drudgery of learning English." Asha, accustomed to such textbooks, at first doesn't see what I am talking about. I show her many examples and she is shocked that she couldn't discern the problem. "I've become so used to seeing material like this that I missed what you're pointing out altogether. I've got it now."

After this many years of working together and observing my interactions with the many different people we have worked with, after noting my comfort when in slums, after our long discussions of my sharing my observations, Asha has asked me to "be up front." She wants me to do most of the talking and interacting with people and she will put herself in the background as a resource, for translation and cultural correction should I veer off course. I am game to try almost anything.

I re-write one of the lessons we are to teach, keeping the content but changing the vocabulary. We use it with the Eighth Standard children on our first of four days in their school. It is a failure. I structured the lesson too much like what they are accustomed to and so they revert to rote reading and non-comprehension. We put the textbooks away and begin a conversation instead. This works a little better, however the children are still reticent. We add role-plays, which livens the classrooms. It is difficult to watch the children working so hard to understand the English and failing. No, it is heartbreaking. They so want to learn.

On the last day, I notice after ten minutes a quiet sadness in the classroom. It is evident on everyone's face, but there are only a few youngsters who will speak up. I turn to one of them, lean forward with interest and concern, and gently ask, "How do you feel when you speak English?"

"Sir, I am ashamed to speak English." Despite the irony of this being a fine English sentence, these few words free the other children to begin speaking. Some try in their verb-less English, others speak in Marathi, their first language, still others in Hindi, the more general (but by no means universal) Indian language. Asha translates Hindi-to-English and back. She is working hard. The children are speaking quickly. The cork has been removed from the bottle. I gather all of us into a tighter circle on the classroom floor. "Let's talk about being ashamed."

"If we speak English people know we are from the *bustee* and they look at us differently." "They try to take advantage of us because they know we can't read the signs saying how much things cost." "Once they know we can't speak, they are mean." "My face turns red once I try to say something in English, even in school." "I have no one to help me with English except in school; I am all alone and it is hard."

The discussion continues for forty minutes. Asha whispers to me, "Marc, you're going to have to come up with an activity to follow up on this." I whisper back, "I know, and as soon as I think of one, we'll do it!" I think I hear Asha stifle a small laugh.

At last it occurs to me. I get up and write a simple sentence on the board, one that I know will evoke a very Indian response from these children.

<u>I am upset when my son is sick.</u>

I explain that this is a sentence in English. The game is that everyone has to take a turn changing one word to make it a different sentence. The Indian response I anticipated comes first and fast. Speaking in Hindi, one youngster says, "Sir, it upsets me when your son is sick. I want to change it." Asha is translating. I give him the chalk and go with him to the board, carrying an eraser, and say "In English." Asha does not translate. He asks me in Hindi, but Asha doesn't translate, to erase the word "son." I understand what he wants. He then starts to write "pet." I help him with the spelling.

The other children undertake the exercise, at first shyly. After five of the fifteen children take a turn, their learning furnace has ignited, and they are excited, lining up to change words, morphing the sentence into dozens of permutations. They don't want to stop...so it is time to up the ante.

Now they have to change a word and read the sentence out loud. Their enthusiasm remains. I mistakenly had thought it would abate, that they would revert to shame. They don't. Reading their sentences is difficult, but because these are *their* sentences and not in a book, they are willing. They are more than willing. They are fueled.

It is time to up the ante again, to what they are most afraid of: speaking without reading. I change the task. They have to change the sentence, read it while looking at it, and then face away from the blackboard and say their sentence to all of us without peeking back. They are a little frightened but the tone in the classroom has been transformed from shame to delight to pleasure in learning something that has always been so difficult. A few of the youngsters need support. No one needs coaxing. This is an act of academic courage in reading and remembering, of publically doing what is most difficult. Every child accomplishes the task, gradually. They glow with pride.

It is time to stop, and to say goodbye. All the children put themselves in formation around me for Asha to take a picture of us together. They want her in the picture, too. I offer to leave the formation and take a picture. As in other schools, an excited class of kids escorts Asha and me down the stairs. They point out where a step is cracked so we will be careful. On a landing that has some sunshine, a group of boys from the class gently, laughingly, push me against a wall. "One more picture." I start to laugh and put my arms around them. A few are my height. I say, "You are wonderful." They smile and one boy says, "We are *EXCELLENT!*" His face briefly clouds over and then, realizing what he has done, he beams and says, "I made my own sentence!!"

I have heard too often, and never want to hear again, that children who live in poverty are uninterested in learning.

A LETTER TO THE MINISTER

Asha and I switch to the Ninth Standard. The textbooks are as abysmal, as outrageously outdated and as depressing as the Eighth Standard's. We decide to go through one cursory reading of the written lesson—duty fulfilled—and then do away with it. The kids smile; pleased that we are as aware as they of the fourth-rate academic material they have been given.

My personal feeling about the books that the city schools provide for those who should be considered as "their children," is an act of immoral disregard for the learning needs and futures of these children. It is as if the city does not claim these youngsters. It is a betrayal of the children, who most decidedly are capable of learning and willing to learn. What the students cannot do is review at home. They haven't the time. They have too many chores and other responsibilities. They must be concerned for their safety or the safety of their youngster brothers and sisters or of their mothers. They haven't the room. They live in tiny spaces with many people. Yes, if they can steal a few moments for a quick game of football or cricket, they will take it. They are teenagers. But motivation is not a problem.

Same school, same classroom, but because this is Ninth standard, they have practiced English one year more than the ashamed students in the Eighth standard. Their errors in speaking are the same but they are less ashamed. They have that wonderful bit of swagger of the fourteen or fifteen year old. We have dispensed with the reading of the textbook, to everyone's relief. We spend our time talking about the lesson's content: pollution and the interrelatedness of the scarcity of birds, the air that the *Mumbaikars* (Bombayites) must breathe, the quality of grain grown with dirty water, and the dearth of trees. The children, with help, understand these concepts as we go verbally over them one by one in Hindi and English. Some of them demonstrate true concern.

Nevertheless, there is a sense that they feel unimportant. They talk a little about how they feel comfortable in their slum neighborhood because "everyone is like us." They also relate how differently they feel "outside." They are at risk for their poverty to push them into the ground, to bury them or break them down. I suppose this is the derivation of the overused term "grinding poverty" that, in its overuse, diminishes the abuse done to the poor by being poor.

Asha and I decide to use this as an opportunity to tie the lesson on pollution to the children's sense of alienation within their own larger city in their own very large country. We decide that we will have the children write, in English, a letter to the Indian equivalent of the American Secretary of the Interior regarding pollution.

"We're not important enough to write a letter to the Minister."

"This is why you learn English, to write letters like this. And yes, you are important enough to write this letter. Everyone is important enough, but some powerful people haven't figure that out yet." The concept is alienating in its strangeness, perhaps in its American blunt outspokenness about social injustice, but it is also a little thrilling.

The kids worry, however, that this will become a tedious endeavor and entail homework. Asha and I explain that we will all do it together the next day and we will do it all in the classroom. Then they become excited. A letter from a slum school to a Minister! From schoolchildren! As the children bustle about, I am reminded why sending a letter to a Minister would seem so extraordinary. The people in the *bustees* have no addresses. They receive no mail as many, or most, of the parents and grandparents are illiterate. They also, having so little, do not want to be identified by corrupt tax collectors. If they have an address on record, they can be tracked. So families pay their sometimes cheap, often exorbitant rent, exist in their undersized spaces, live, have babies, argue, love, raise their families, do the laundry, wash, cook, get sick, and die without any address, visible proof that they have ever existed.

Letter-writing day. The youngsters arrive early to their *Learning and Eating Together* classroom. We all gather around a table. The children are anxious that they will have to put English to paper themselves. Anticipating this potential roadblock to a much larger lesson, Asha and I have planned for both of us to help the children formulate sentences for the Minister. We teach them the proper salutation to a Minister of the Government. There is a collective tingle in the room. With help, they begin to put together sentences about pollution and what they see happening in their neighborhood, information about air quality and tainted food sources. They voice their worry. They ask the Minister to consider this as an important problem and add a few ending sentences. "We will do our best, too, in our neighborhoods by watering trees and being careful with the garbage. We will do our part, too." The sense of communal responsibility in fourteen and fifteen year olds causes me to share their tingle.

Asha has been the scribe. It is time to sign the letter. The children gather around the table and grab a pen. I stop them. "No. In this room, you are all important people. When important people write a letter to a Minister, they sit down to sign their names. I remove the small table and place the teacher's desk in the middle of the classroom. I take a large chair and put it at the desk. "Now, each person takes a seat and carefully signs the letter." The students become serious. Something solemnly important is happening for them. They spontaneously form a queue and, one-by-one, slowly sit down at the teacher's desk in the teacher's chair, and carefully put their signature to paper. They stand around and silently watch as each youngster signs the letter.

It is done. Now Asha addresses the envelope, narrating the address and putting the return address so it will be clear to the Minister that this letter came from Dharavi children. The next step is to place the stamp on the letter. It is likely that some of these children have never seen an addressed, stamped, envelope before. Now we have a Folding-of-the-Letter ceremony. All the children put their hands on mine as I crease the letter in thirds and place it in the envelope. One youngster is chosen to lick the envelope. The hands of fifteen children lower the moistened flap and seal the letter. They hold it up for a photo with great pride. All go down to the street letterbox, place it in the slot, and come upstairs and report that they have mailed it together.

Asha and I burst into a shared smile and applaud them and they break into applause for themselves. I believe, I hope, that for these moments the children did, indeed, feel important.

Following school, Asha and I, along with *Learning and Eating Together* staff, visit some of the children's homes in Dharavi. We also wander the different neighborhoods within the city-sized slum and stop into random homes in some of the lanes.

DHARAVI, 2010

Dharavi. The name slides so beautifully off the tongue, almost poetic.

Dharavi. The place is the shocking repository for over one million impoverished people. Long and narrow, placed between the two major railway lines, it is a convenient place to live if you have little money and need to get to work. Rents can be cheap and second-class train fare is minimal. Rents can also be shockingly high, up to fifty percent of a family's monthly earnings.

Dharavi. The city-within-a-city where many of the students live. Dharavi is so large and dense that there are many neighborhoods, *bustees*, within it. Even narrower lanes, *guhlees*, feed long narrow footpaths. Dharavi comprises a crazy-quilt maze of multiple *bustees* fed by innumerable *guhlees*. The children come out of the sunshine and into Dharavi's darkness. Asha and I are going home with several of the children to meet whichever parent is there.

Our guide is Anand. He is a *Learning and Eating Together* graduate who completed Tenth Standard last year. He meets us at the top of a stairway flanked by orange flags of the local political party waving in the soft breeze. Anand has a winsome, gentle face; smooth black hair carefully combed, accenting his large brown eyes. His expression hovers between an open smile and a furtive tear. He wears ripped jeans and a light green sweatshirt over a t-shirt whose logo I cannot make out. On his feet are knock-offs of American shoes popular with the local teenagers.

Anand sees his role as more than a guide. He is our host. He waits for us at the top of the stairs, takes our hands and leads us down into Dharavi's darkness. Large black woven mesh storage bags, outside each upstairs railing, overhang the narrow street below on both sides and add to Dharavi's darkness. These hanging nylon trash holders contain the family's garbage until there is notification that trash will be picked up. Since this is an erratic occurrence, they are full and close to overflowing. They look like long black, bloated tumors, so fat that they almost touch each other across the footpaths below, blocking the sun. It is three o'clock outside where it is bright. In Dharavi's streets and lanes, it may as well be nighttime.

Anand shows us his home. His mother isn't there quite yet and so we visit several other homes. Usually the mother is home from her jobs. If the father works, he is still out. Otherwise, he is in a drunken torpor, lying either on the floor or in a bed, depending on the size of the room. In several homes, I have to lean up against the oblivious father. His wife invites me to do this, as there is no place else for me to be. He doesn't move.

One mother tells us, while her husband is out working, how proud she is that she managed to get him to stop drinking. She announced that she would leave if he came home drunk one more time, or hit her again, or harshly touched either of their children. She had a place to go, that she would not tell her husband. He moved to strike her across the face. She moved closer to him and repeated herself. "Touch me and I am gone and so are the children. You will not know where we are. The drinking stops or we leave." Her husband, himself somehow empowered by her forcefulness, in fact stopped drinking and got an industrial job which he has kept for three years. He has not had any alcohol, treats his wife differently—almost with gratitude—and does not mistreat the children. The mother is enormously proud of herself. The multiple people who have crowded into her house, following us around out of curiosity, applaud her. She blushes. She is demure. But she knows she is strong.

In another house, a different mother tells us of her attempts to stop her husband's drinking and her failure. Nevertheless, she always places herself between her husband and her children and never leaves them alone when he is home. She wears her bruises as badges that she is her children's protectress. She is a goddess whose picture belongs on a tree, marking the living space of the street children.

Rats abound in the streets and *guhlees*. Since vehicles cannot enter—the "streets" are too narrow—Dharavi is alive outdoors. It throbs with over one million heartbeats. Children run in the lanes of each separate *bustee* area. The houses are long blocks of concrete with doors for access and a lip to step over. This may be intended as a rat deterrent but it is inadequate. Even a short-legged rat can handle this barrier. They don't enter, however. The rats keep to the black lanes. Those unlucky enough to have foolishly entered a home are brutally swept out and sent flying against the concrete houses across the narrow *guhlees*. Rats are smart. They don't want to be thrown against a wall a second time.

The interiors of Dharavi's homes, much like Machimar's and other slums', are very small. A six by ten foot room for four people is almost luxurious. On the ground level there are almost no windows. Too dangerous. The upper level dwellings, reached by narrow ladders placed at almost 90-degree angles to save street space, might have a barred window with an inside shutter. The residents of Dharavi lock themselves inside their cells at night. This protects them from mosquitoes, prowlers, rapists, rats, bandicoots, and husbands returning home late, drunk and ready to pummel a mother or child who crosses him. Vessels with the night's human waste are emptied in the public toilets in the morning. Dharavi is hot; it smells of the street urine of rats and the vomit of drunks.

And yet, each morning the mothers will sweep their enclosures—their homes. The entire family will bathe and brush their teeth. They will carefully comb their hair and then ready the day's laundry for when the water taps are turned on. What food is available will become some bit of breakfast even if it is just a cup of tea. The children will put their school uniforms on, mothers will get ready for work cleaning wealthier people's houses, grinding wheat or corn, sweeping streets, or collecting vegetables to sell. Some fathers will also get ready for work, usually manual labor, sometimes driving a cab. Other fathers will spend the day sleeping off their night of drinking after cuffing someone in the house. Children may turn on the television briefly, to catch the latest video being shown to advertise a new movie. They will study the dance moves and quickly pick up the melody. These youngsters will collect their friends and make their way to school. They will hop over thick concrete slabs, lain down like tectonic plates over what otherwise would be an open sewer. They are careful how they walk and always alert to any shifts in the plates. The brown water slowly ripples underneath its concrete tombstones. The youngsters' movements, in the morning darkness, have the grace of the movie video dancers.

Once enough children are together, older ones looking after younger ones, they run almost without care through the streets and lanes, laughing, on their way to school. Some teachers, who see their collective beauty, will welcome them into the sunlight and the school with big, open smiles. Others, who are more interested in their paychecks than the children, will curtly say good morning and then complain about unfinished homework. The children, however, have unabated energy and verve.

ANAND'S STORY

Sixteen-year-old Anand now realizes that his mother has re-turned home. He wants us to meet her. He is her only child. Their living space is four feet wide by eight feet deep, including the cooking area. Anand looks at his mother with pride in the knowledge that she has done all she could to take care of him. He is gently, almost delicately, playful with her as well. She is dressed in a worn green sari whose trimming is by now so threadbare that it cannot be repaired. She reciprocates his pride in her. He is her hope and her treasure.

They live alone, the two of them. It wasn't always so. Until just a few years ago, her husband was murderously alive. A chronic and violent alcoholic, he often went out drinking with his friends, coming home late. He took particular pleasure in beating his wife with rocks that he carried with him. Sometimes Anand's mother had advance warning that he was coming, delivered through the ever-present slum grapevine. Then she would take nine year old Anand and leave, staying with neighbor families, both Hindu and

Muslim. Her husband would enter the home, look for someone to beat, and find no one. He would try to rage against the house itself, except it had no belongings other than a few articles of clothing and kitchen pots. Anand's mother knew he was home when she heard her lovingly cleaned pots being thrown against the walls of her cubicle. Then he stuporously fell to the floor and slept. She would return home, negotiate her way around him, retrieve Anand's school uniform, and leave. Later she returned. When not drunk, her husband was mean-spirited, occasionally contrite, but physically harmless. Anand would safely go off to school.

Once, Anand's mother got word that her husband was coming after her with rocks in the morning. Anand's teacher was visiting. She had brought tea and two biscuits because she knew that otherwise Anand and his mother would have no breakfast. Hearing the loud ranting of Anand's father from far away, she quickly gathered up both mother and son, took them to the school and hid them until he had time to pass out.

Often, Anand was at home sleeping when his father returned. His mother hid him behind the kitchen pots and lay down as if she were sleeping. Sometimes, not often, her husband would leave her alone if she were sleeping. This night, one of many, he awakened her by kicking her in the back. He carried two large sharp stones, one in each hand. He raised each hand in turn and forcefully dragged the jagged rock across her body. And again. And again. Anand's mother stayed silent. Any word might provoke her husband and intensify the beating.

After his father collapsed, Anand came out of hiding. He saw his mother lying still, breathing rapidly. He saw blotches of red on her nightclothes, blood seeping through where his father had scraped the rocks against her. He saw blood oozing through the material covering his mother's breasts; her nipples were bleeding still.

Anand took a water pot and ran to the tap, hurrying home. He gently pressed a cool wet cloth against the angry red rips in his mother's clothing. Almost a caress of healing, but he knew not to be too tender. She was the mother and he was the son. She turned to him, saw that he was unharmed, and smiled. "Get your uniform on and go to school." "Mummy, what will happen to you?" "I will be all right. This has happened before, remember? And I've always been all right. Now go to school so you can learn."

Anand returned from school and his mother was back home from her two jobs. His father was out. He and his mother spent that night at a different neighbor's house. There is no dearth of neighbors in Dharavi.

Some months later, Anand's father was found dead in the gutter, knifed in the stomach and heart during a street fight. Anand was confused that his mother followed the Hindu cremation rites for this man who treated who so cruelly. She explained that she was doing her duty but she was glad he was gone and couldn't come back to hurt her or frighten Anand. All of eleven by then, he looked up at her with tears in his eyes.

Anand introduces us to his mother. She is sweetly diffident, clearly strong-willed, and looks at her son with love in her deep brown eyes. Anand starts to tell us his current story. He graduated from Tenth Standard last year and wants to go to engineering college, in many ways equivalent to eleventh and twelfth grade trade school, so he can become a draughtsman. He is not there now because it costs more money than he or his mother has been able to make and save. He has worked two jobs for almost a year and has saved the equivalent of $25.00. School costs $325.00. He was sure he would never be able to go.

Anand's mother secretly took a third job. She only told her son that her employers wanted more time from her. She didn't want to promise him something she might not be able to earn enough to pay for. She also wanted to surprise him. He leans against the wall of his home as he tells us that for his birthday she gave him the $300.00. He could now enroll for the next semester of engineering college.

As he tells us this story, Anand begins to shake. He looks at his mother. He looks at his former teacher who has accompanied us. And he falls to the ground, weeping as he buries his face in his teacher's sari. We all bend down and comfort him…and weep. It becomes so extraordinarily clear to me never to confuse degrading circumstances with the people who must live in them.

Anand gathers himself together without shame, and leads us to meet other families. He puts his hand around my shoulder or holds my hand. He is sure to help everyone cross the concrete slabs thrown over the moving sewage. He would like us to meet a Muslim friend of his.

A PARAKEET IN DHARAVI

Many developers have had their eyes on Dharavi. They would like to demolish it, or as much of it as possible, and resettle the residents of this massive horizontal area, spread out over many hectares, in spare high-rise apartments nearby. They want to claim the land that over a million people call home and that has become a community, and exploit its proximity to the airport by building hotels and high-rent apartments. Splendor and squalor do not live far from each other in Bombay.

Anand's Muslim friend Hassan and his family live in a high rise. Although their quarters are cramped, there is a separate kitchen. The elevator may or may not work. Although many resettled families move back to the horizontal community of Dharavi, Hassan's mother, father, grandmother, grandfather, sister and he are happy here. We enter to sparsely furnished apartment, one bed and a plastic chair the only furniture.

Anand looks at us, his once tear-filled eyes now twinkling. He whispers something to Hassan. Hassan disappears and returns with a beautiful, well-tended, green parakeet in its cage. He takes it out, shows it to us. There are at least ten people, from grandfather to young children from down the hall, piled into the one apartment room, admiring this bird. Hassan hands the bird to Anand who strokes it and talks to it. He then makes his way through all the people to me and just so sweetly places the bird on my wrist. Hassan smiles that beautiful Indian white-toothed smile and watches to see if I will pet the bird. I do, and I talk to it, which evokes some friendly laughter. The bird is passed around and is accommodatingly docile. Hassan then takes it and returns it to its cage, carefully setting it on its resting place. The whole family is smiling. They ask for their picture to be taken, with me in the center. (Again I am uncomfortable, but I am misreading the situation. The family is not fawning over the white man in a colonial fashion. It is honoring its guest. I accept the honor.)

After leaving Hassan's family and his bird, Anand takes us on a small tour of his section of Dharavi and points out the vegetable *wallahs* (sellers), the *chai wallah*, and the tailor. He takes us up the steps where orange flags still fly, beckoning for the slum dwellers' votes in the next election. He shows us the public toilet and mentions that there is always someone working to keep it clean. He poses for a picture with me, arm around my waist, smiles, shakes my hand Western style, and we leave. It is late in the afternoon and we have a commuter train to catch. The sun is starting to go down. It will not be noticed inside Dharavi.

However, it is Anand's mother's love for him, and their story of horror, tenderness, sacrifice, and gratitude, that lingers in my mind

"PLEASE REST"

*Q*ueens, NY. June 30, 2009. *Today is the day of my mother's funeral. Lin, Ron, Gabriel, and I ride up to the cemetery in the same limousine with the same driver as we did for my father's funeral eighteen months ago. We feel unburdened yet somber during the five-hour journey.*

My mother's space, now a six-foot by three-foot hole in the earth, is waiting to receive her. This city of the dead, incongruously green between tombstones packed so closely that it is hard to walk between them, is perhaps the last place where the name of the Eastern European town of Rosulner still lives. The Nazis destroyed the town, long after my grandfather and grandmother, David and Nettie Schwager, left. This plot of land is for the descendants of the original emigrants. David and Nettie are here. All seven of my mother's brothers are here, waiting for her, the last of their generation, their only sister, to join them.

The cemetery is densely populated with the dead whose spirits have long ago ceased to hover over their own graves. From knee height the cemetery resembles a large city landscape. Its backdrop is the real landscape of

Manhattan. There are no plaques. All tombstones; of all heights. Some in Hebrew; some in English.

Not a peaceful place, it is where so many bodies must find rest. My generation is the last that is gradually being buried here. Then there will be no more room. This is where I am supposed to go.

The incongruous disquiet of the place disturbs me. This is where the secrets of my mother's misery are buried, never to be known. This is where my older cousin Norm, a teenager, threw himself into his mother's grave, hugging her coffin and screaming for her. My enigmatic cousin Harold is here. He spoke with the remnants of a Yiddish accent although he was born in New York. He always seemed like an empty person to me. My Uncle Max, dead in his mid-thirties of heart disease, is over there. I am named for him.

What of my mother's secret? Her father David, my grandfather, whom I never liked being near? Any of his sons? Someone else? No one? I will never know. I will also never know if her mother, my grandmother Nettie, knew.

But I know the secrets are here. The story of what made my mother a monster to me lies in this ground, along with her conviction that men were part of a conspiracy of evil. The reasons I continued to love her, even after I stopped speaking to her near the end, are not buried here. They will never be buried here. I will not be buried with these people. I do not want to turn to dust in the earth of this cemetery, with the people of Rosulner, with the family of David and Nettie. Lin and I have arranged it otherwise.

The hearse arrives with the casket. It is identical to my father's. My mother will not enter the ground in the plain pine box that so frightened her. She will be more shielded from the earth. However, it will take longer for that earth to reclaim her, to take her back. Dust to dust.

I ask the attendants to open the coffin so I can see my mother and speak to her alone one last time. Unlike my father, who looked peaceful in death, my mother looks as angry and sour and she did with me in life. I am shocked by her expression. I had hoped that death would bring her some relief. She died in her sleep and this is how she looked. Her skin is that dreadful yellow that sets in soon after death and since Jews don't embalm (or embalm as little as each State will allow), there is no hiding that lurid color. She is in a shroud, as my father was, draped and knotted for burial in an Orthodox cemetery.

I approach her and ask the attendants to expose her face. Her eyes are covered with clay shards. I touch her cheek. Cold. Very cold. Even in late June. I stroke it. We are alone together for the last time. I speak to her aloud.

"Mom. I am so sorry you had such a difficult life. I wish it had been easier. I wish you could have been happier. I wish you did not hurt. But it is over now and you can rest. Please rest. Goodbye, Mom." I touch her face one last time and ask that she be recovered with the shroud.

The funeral is rather reserved. A few tears. The last of the eight children raised by David and Nettie Schwager, their second youngest, their only girl, joins the family she always wanted to be with, the family that eerily never spoke of anything negative, that always sought the absence of conflict, the family that would not speak of my mother's mental illness or of the child—or perhaps two children—whom she was abusing.

When my mother's tombstone is unveiled in eleven months, it will say "Rose Schwager Nemiroff." It will be the only family tombstone with a maiden name. When strangers walk by, they will know that she belongs there, that she is with her own. My father's tombstone matches hers. In death they are companions.

Have I forgiven her? I think not yet. I have, however, come to accept her.

MIDWIVES TO A MAP

Bombay, 2012. Even the Bombay air is bright and warm. Gulls circle around college buildings and minarets. Its people continue to fill its streets with their selling and laughing and gossiping and hawkers' cries. The black and yellow cabs now share the street with more privately owned cars. Lin and I are once again surrounded by and part of Bombay's warm life.

Asha and I are continuing to work with *Learning and Eating Together.* An article appeared in The Times of India citing an international study of educational levels of success in ninety-four countries. India scored as having the second worst educational results in the world. Does this bother the Bombay Board of Education? I don't know, but I haven't heard of any change in curriculum or teaching methods to suggest that the anonymous "they" care one bit.

The area of symbolic reasoning, the ability to think in symbols such as letters, numbers, maps, is a notable failure of the Indian educational system. Reading, reading comprehension, math ("Maths" in India), and non-verbal representation (maps, graphs) are all problem areas. With little discernible change coming from outside, the eager and bright children of slums continue to be denied the opportunity to learn. How clear it is that they do not matter. It is a shame. It is a crime. It is unforgiveable on such a large social scale. And it is terribly, painfully sad.

Asha and I have offered to spend the month in multiple schools working on map reading as the entry to symbolic reasoning. *Learning and Eating Together* has given us carte blanche in the classrooms. Knowing the reality of the children's lives, as Asha has for many years and as I have come to know, we realize that we must start our days of work in each school using the students' direct experience.

However, there is little that the children see as symbolic in their daily lives. There are chores—cleaning, cooking, washing and hanging laundry, managing rodents—bathing, eating, shitting, and, if possible, a few minutes respite in music or sports. However, the children also come from religious homes, Hindu and Muslim, and their worldview and spiritual teaching are decidedly symbolic, however concretely it may be expressed. So Asha and I know they are capable of learning what we have come to teach. We will be observed by their teachers in each of the schools and will work with the teachers in their own training.

We know we have to begin in academically backwards order, leading up to looking at a map rather than starting from a real map and explaining it. A map must first emerge from the children. We will be midwives to the birth of a map in each class in each school. We are working with Ninth Standard, fourteen- and fifteen-year-old children.

As we always do, we ask the children to remove the desks from the room and to sit in a large circle on the floor, which we join. One girl notices after an hour or so that I am moving around a bit, obviously sore at the hips. She quietly gets up and gives me a small desk to sit on, blushes, and goes back to her place in the circle. A small act of kindness from a girl to a male helper she sees as benign, in a society that so devalues women and girls, a gesture so easily overlooked, yet it comes with such open, quiet generosity that it seems a tiny miracle.

We begin by drawing the international symbols for Female and Male. The children are likely to have been exposed to some variation of these symbols from public restrooms and bathing facilities. I draw them on the board. Asha and I give the children large pieces of paper on which to draw a female symbol and a male symbol, and scissors to cut them out. They do this in groups, taking turns with the markers and the scissors so that everyone has had a hand in producing these cutouts. They animatedly consult each other. What is the best way to do this task?

We tape the symbols to the wall, enjoying the fact that we are breaking a classroom rule. The kids love it. I ask an impish boy to stand in front of the symbolic male and shy girl to stand in front of the symbolic female, to help bring her into the learning process. Pointing to the male cutout I ask, "Is this a real boy?" **"NO!!!"** "What is it then?" They are silent. I give them the Hindi word for "symbol," *chinhh*. (Thank you, Asha.) We repeat the process for the girl.

"How are the real girl and boy and the *chinhh* the same? Concrete answers reflecting ground-zero life follow. "They both have two arms." "The girl and the *chinhh* both have hair and are wearing skirts." "They all have heads."

Now it is time to push them farther. "What else makes this a real boy?" What I hoped would happen, occurs. I call it slum poetry and the children start speaking it. "He can dream." "She has hopes for a better life." "He can dance to the music." "He can kick the football." "He wishes that his father will not be upset tonight if there isn't enough money for lentils." "He knows how hard his mother works." "He thinks of how to study hard and make a better life for his whole family." "She does her home duties even if she thinks of the night stars."

"Can a *chinhh* hope and dream and wish?" **"NO!!!!!!!"** "Can we look at these cutouts, these *chinhh*, and think about real people hoping and dreaming?" **"YES!!!!"**

We move on to the next step, taping a large, blank sheet of poster paper onto the blackboard; another rule delightfully down the drain. "What is this?" "It is a piece of paper." This is an example of *bustee* concreteness. "Yes. What shape is it?" "It is a rectangle." "No, it is a square." I take out a ruler. "Let's measure the sides."

I raise the ruler intending to give it to a student to measure. Several children flinch. I say, "This is a ruler. As long as Asha and I are here, a ruler is for measuring. A ruler is not for hitting. No one will be hit." They relax and someone volunteers to measure. "I didn't know that is what a ruler is really for," he says, sheepishly joking. He reports the length and width of the rectangles four sides.

We determine that we have a rectangle. We then split the class into three groups. I fold an identical white paper into three equal horizontal pieces and have the students cut along the folds. We have three just-as-long-but-skinny rectangles. The children define them. They are intrigued but do not yet understand what is happening. Asha hands out two colored markers, orange for one group, green for another. I hold an unused blue marker in my hand. The third group waits. Their skinny rectangle will, to their disappointment, stay white.

Several of the children and I tape the skinny orange rectangle at the top of the poster paper already on the board. The white goes in the middle and the bottom is the green. They get it. "It's the flag!!" I say, "Almost, but something is missing." "The chakra wheel! We need blue." Mutual smiles as I produce the blue marker. They arrange a system for taking turns to place all the blue spokes of the chakra wheel onto the flag, attached to the blue center circle. "Now it's the flag," they say. I ask, "Is it a real flag? Can we raise it up a flagpole?" "NO!"

I respond, "Well, if it's not a real flag, it's a..." and the class screams out "**It's a *chinhh*!!!**" "What would you do if it were real?" We see them begin to think symbolically as they spontaneously stand up and do what one is supposed to do when the flag is presented. They sing the national anthem. I encourage them to become louder: "Let them hear *Jai Hind* (the last words) all over the school!" Everyone smiles and screams out ***Jai Hind*** ("Victory to India") and starts to laugh. I'm not sure they've realized that they are learning something. They are having fun and feel safe.

It is time to end for the day. No one wants to leave. They've been having too much fun. Asha and I tell them we'll continue tomorrow. "More about *chinhh*?" "Oh yes, we promise." "Good."

On the next day, we pull out twenty-six large sheets of paper and several rolls of cellophane tape. With the floor cleared, we tell the children that their job is to make a very long row of paper thirteen sheets long and two sheets wide. This fills the classroom. We announce that we are going to make a map. "I can't read maps." "You will when you make your own," I reply.

But first we must teach directions, a purely abstract concept. Asha has brought a compass. She places it in her hand and shows it to everyone, explaining how it works. The youngsters understand the words North, East, South and West, but they have no relevance. "Let's find North." They all gather around the compass and point to which of their classroom walls faces north. We look north together and describe everything to be seen on the north side of the room. Despite the paucity of objects, the kids see many things. This in itself is symbolic: they live with so little and see so much. Then we go to the windows and look outside, describing everything we can see out the northern walls. "Every map has north at the top. Who would like to write an "N" at the top of the map?" Many hands go up but only one is needed for the single letter.

We repeat this, with the children's increasing ability to observe matching their enthusiasm. This is not like any school lesson they have had before. Two boys in particular are entranced. As we look in each direction, inside the room and out the windows on the west (the only other windows), the students add the correct letter for directionality to the map. Asha and I make up a game. The children close their eyes and we name something that is only to be found in a single direction. They remember what they have seen and correctly identify what they saw in each direction.

The atmosphere in the room is becoming exhilarating, for all of us. But we have been at work for a full hour. The students are accustomed to classes of forty minutes and we have been given two-and-a-half hours each day. We ask them if they would like to take a break. **"NO! More map. What next?"** Following their lead, we continue.

We have all the children gather closely around the long thirteen sheets by two sheets of taped paper. It is blank except for N, S, E, and W in their appropriate places. We ask the kids each to draw his house. They are about to start when we stop them. There is a catch. They have to decide together on a symbol, a *chinhh*, for a house, because on a map symbols are used, and so all of the same things look the same. (We don't bother with the fact that real street maps don't have houses on them.) They are a little lost and so I draw a house that resembles a *bustee* house. One girl gets up, erases what I have put on the blackboard, and draws a Western style house with pointed roof, something rarely seen in India and certainly not in Bombay. Everyone agrees that this will be the *chinhh* for "house." Everyone, without being asked, sits down, grabs a marker from the bunch in the middle of the soon-to-be-map, and draws a house that hugs the paper's edges.

I draw a circle near the middle and say that is the *chinhh* for school. The circle is their school. I next draw a large square in the bottom right of the map and say that this is the Key to the map. It explains what the symbols are. We put the house and the circle inside the Key. Asha and I then ask them to draw a street to get them to school and to remember that streets run into each other and no one lives on a street that goes directly from his front door to the school. They start thinking about this and someone speaks up. "Wait, first we need a *chinhh* for street." (This is going so smoothly that it is hard to believe that it is happening through translation. The only universally shared word is *chinhh*.) After more discussion, the symbol for street is placed inside the Key box and all the children are drawing connecting roads.

"Now, we need symbols for all the things you pass and see on your way to school so you can put them on the map." Lightning strikes. It feels to Asha and me like spontaneous combustion.

These excited students jump up and start grabbing chalk to write symbols on the blackboard before committing them to the map's Key. Twenty-some hands are reaching for chalk, yelling out places or things they see on the way to school, inventing a *chinhh* for each one. The observing teacher seems concerned that matters are getting out of hand. She speaks English and I explain that it really is the opposite. The students have all grasped the concept of visual symbolization and they are excited. This is the goal, hardly a problem. They are so thrilled that they understand and are having so much fun that they are generating enough heat to burn the paper! Asha and I glance at each other; we each have tears in our eyes.

The youngsters settle down as soon as I say, "OK, enough *chinhh*. Now draw them." And all over the map crop up Outpatient Clinics, police stations, markets, trash, railroad tracks, temples, mosques, hospitals, and more. The map is now bursting with symbolized information. It has entered the world through the students' learning. The kids ask their teacher to sit down with them, draw her house and a road joining the other roads. She has to get to school too, so she can be their teacher.

Our time is up for the day again. A very fast two-and-a-half hours for all of us. Everyone, including the teacher, is excited. We tell them that we will see them tomorrow and that we have two more days together. The two serious boys look sad. Three eager youngsters come up to Asha and me after class and announce—the deal is done—"We are bringing you home to meet our mothers now. They don't know you are coming. You are our gift to them. We will show you the way." All the kids walk and run down the stairs after having their food, accompanying us out of the school. The three hosts take our hands (we have a Marathi translator with us), and show us the way to where they live.

INTERLUDE---SION SLUM

School is over and children ages six through sixteen come streaming out the doors, a parade of blue and white uniforms now more wrinkled from a day's activity. Boys with their shirttails out, girls' ribbons less carefully placed in their braids. They laugh and chatter, sounding like a buzzing whirlwind of bees. They are quickly making their way home despite being loaded down with canvas backpacks of books and papers, pencils and erasers, and the inexplicable miscellany of odds and ends that children collect.

Our young hosts lead the way across the street, into the train station and through it to the side where the tracks are unused. They help Asha and me, and the *Learning and Eating Together* staff member who will serve as translator. The children politely hold out their hands to help us jump off the platform onto the gravel and continue to hold our hands to help us maintain our footing over the now unused tracks. The rats and bandicoots are easy to spot. They keep to themselves. One boy says to me, "There many more at night. Don't be here." I imagine an undulating carpet of quivering rat fur in the moonlight, scavenging like all of us to stay alive with whatever resources we are able to muster.

We reach the concrete plates covering the light brown river of shit and piss, weaving across the pavement of the *bustee,* itself crisscrossed with water pipes. The kids know exactly where to place their feet and make sure we do too. As we enter Sion slum, I am stopped by a tall, dark-skinned, barrel-chested man in slacks and sleeveless undershirt. He reminds me of a *bustee* Stanley Kowalski. He has what looks to me like a scowl but I don't experience him as menacing. Clearly, though, he must be taken seriously. Stanley Kowalski is standing, observing three of his friends playing cards while sitting on their haunches. They use an upturned fruit crate as a table. He struts over to me and gestures as if to ask, or demand, what am I doing here. Everyone else has gone ahead. I point to the group in the distance and indicate that I belong with them. Stanley points to my arm, puts his arm over mine indicating the difference in skin color. What is a white man doing here? "Why here?" he says. I answer, "The children brought us home with them." Stanley is transformed. His rigid body softens; his stiff posture relaxes. He smiles, shakes my hand Western style and says, "Welcome to my neighborhood." I smile in return, thank him, and catch up with everyone else. One youngster has hung back waiting for my entrance examination to be over. He walks in front of me, indicates that I should look down to watch my footing, and together we catch up with the others.

We have entered the dark bowels of Sion. The standard-issue one room concrete housing is two stories high. The upstairs walkway overhangs the doors of the lower floor. There is so little light, so few places for it to enter, that it appears twilight on a dark grey rainy afternoon, rather than a bright sunny day at one o'clock.

The ladders for reaching the second story of homes, to take up less precious ground space, are narrower and more steeply pitched than in the other *bustees* we have visited. The *guhlees* are shockingly small, perhaps two feet across. They measure twelve inches wide where the access ladders to upstairs are placed.

We enter a particularly narrow *guhlee* and are welcomed into one of the children's homes. The doorway faces a solid concrete wall. It is ninety degrees outside. Inside it is hotter as the family is saving money on electricity (theirs is legally installed) and the hanging fan that reduces ceiling height to five feet is off. The floor space is twelve feet square, relatively large. Fourteen people live here: Jaskaran, our student, his school-age sister, both of his parents, his mother's sister's two infant girls from the village, father's younger brother blinded in an industrial accident and unable to work, father's mother and father, his grandmother's sister, and four other relatives also from the village. Everyone who can works or takes care of the home and the two young children.

There is no window in this house. It is on ground level and windows are dangerous. The door is locked at night. A makeshift loft that precariously holds two adults hovers creakily over the center of the floor. Access to the loft is from the single bed. Jaskaran's parents and the two babies sleep in the single bed. In the middle of the night, two village relatives step over them to enter the loft. Jaskaran and his sister sleep underneath the bed. The grandparents have a special corner with a thicker mat. The blind uncle sleeps on the floor along with the three remaining relatives. There is no room to move. There is no air. Nighttime toileting must be done by squatting in place over a bowl. Some people train themselves to go all night without need of a toilet.

Jaskaran's teacher knows where he lives and is careful not to ask him why he did not do his homework. When he gets home from school, his mother is usually back from work. His father is still out working. All able-bodied adults have jobs. Still, his grandparents are old. The babies must be watched. Water must be fetched. Laundry must be done and dinner for fourteen must be cooked and dishes washed. Bread must be made, if there is enough money for the flour. And the house must be swept. The house is dark but not dirty. I can't tell what color the walls have been painted since it must have last happened so many years ago that the original color is gone. It is simply grey. Perhaps it is the grey concrete showing through the small bits of flaking paint.

At one o'clock, Jaskaran's mother has just returned from work. She gets up very early each morning, somehow manages to leave for her job, and the other women of the house take over the chores necessary to get everybody off to school and work. Jaskaran introduces us and his mother, harried but pleased, invites us in. I have to duck to avoid decapitation by the fan blades hanging so low. We are all invited to sit and she makes a move to send one of the children out to buy a soft drink for us as an act of hospitality. Asha is quickly on this and thanks mother but asks her not to buy us anything, we have just eaten. She does it in just such a way that mother will not lose face. We have not declined her hospitality. Asha has graciously pre-empted it.

Jaskaran's mother is pleased to introduce us to everyone in the family who is currently home. She describes what each of the adults does for a living, i.e., the sources of money. The family has lived here for a number of years. Their rent is reasonable, although still twenty-five per cent of the total family income. There is usually enough money to buy grain for bread, lentils for *dal*, and even a vegetable now and then. Water is undrinkable unless boiled and the stove is kept going for long periods. Fourteen people consume much water. She tells us how proud she is of her children and gives her son a soft smile, in which he discreetly basks. She mentions, as so many mothers do, that life is very hard in Bombay, but it is here that her children have a better chance of getting educated and having a better life. Yet again, as if the idea cannot leave me, I am overwhelmed with admiration for the people of the slums. They give truth to the idea that living in degrading circumstances does not make people themselves degraded. I have just witnessed a functioning community of fourteen people in one small over-heated home, showing hospitality, generosity, love, pride, dignity, and respect.

Jaskaran, smiling all the while, tells his mother about the school meeting in his classroom in two days. She says she will work longer tomorrow so she can come to school the day after. He asks that Asha take a picture of everybody and wants all of us in the picture. Managing a single photo with so many people, not even everyone who lives here, is such a difficult task that I can only imagine the logistics when the house is full. Our visit is over and Jaskaran and his waiting friends take us on to the next home.

Talika's home is the next stop on our route. She lives with her mother and grandmother, both widowed. Their space is small-er and has no bed. Talika's father was run over by a truck while drunkenly weaving in the streets at night. The family's income did not shrink, as he didn't work. In fact, the family's income in-creased because he wasn't around to steal Talika's mother's money for whiskey. Nevertheless, in case Talika's mother had days when she couldn't work, grandmother took to grinding corn on the street for back-up income. She can often be seen on the outskirts of Sion slum, sitting on the gravel, under the sky where the sun shines and the mosquito repellent trucks have room to drive by and spray. She grinds the corn between two twelve-inch stones by hand, selling the cornmeal as she continues to grind. The grinding method looks no different than the stones on display in museums of Indian life a millennium ago.

Talika's mother tells us how proud she is of her very bright daughter. She just wishes Talika had time to do her homework. But this is a small household and the chores must be shared among fewer people, one of them old and not very strong. Mother is sure to shut the television when it is time for "review" of schoolwork. However, this family's house is surrounded on two sides by arguing families, drunk and abusive husbands, and the sounds of street toughs trying to find people to impress with their manhood. Talika tries but she cannot concentrate. Grandmother and mother are illiterate and cannot help her. She is motivated and tries to meet a friend before school starts to help her with her review.

While we are sitting inside and talking, two of Talika's friends stop by, curious about this strange mélange of visitors. They, too, have returned from school but are not in Talika's class. They enter the conversation. Mother smiles as if she knows what is coming. The three girls whisper and giggle and ask if we would like to see them dance to the latest Bollywood film song. We, of course, would be delighted. They turn on a small radio and search for the ubiquitous song. Once they find it, they start to dance, skillfully, and lose themselves in their pleasure. When the long song ends, they realize that they have forgotten that we were watching and start to titter quietly and then laugh at themselves with both pride and a hint of timorousness despite their wish to perform.

All three grab us by the hand and take us running through the streets and lanes of the *bustee* to meet Sudip's mother. He has patiently been waiting, holding his backpack. We dodge low-hanging concrete to which the kids point upwards as we run. I wonder why we are running. It is not simply for fun. We are running through the most disagreeable parts of Sion and the children don't want us to linger here. We negotiate the parts of the street where the concrete plates have cracked or are missing. We run through dark concrete tunnels with sticky green water coating their sides. We pass an impressive colony of rats and mice. Sections are almost completely black. We rush through congregating groups of men drinking from a bottle and we emerge at another section of the *bustee*.

Sudip takes us up the slimy ladder to his home. The other children slip away, rather than stay or come in. I think this is out of respect and so as not to embarrass Sudip. There is no room in Sudip's house for so many people, even standing. He and his mother live alone. Neither will speak of the father. Their space is barely five feet by four feet. It is upstairs and is an end unit. Therefore it has a window. Light comes in and reveals this un-painted cubicle of a living space. There is room for a narrow short bed and a table with cooking pots, plus a burner plate. Sudip, his mother, and one other person can stand in this space. Sparse spare clothing is folded, clean, and wedged between the bed and the wall. There is no place else to put them. Sudip is proud of his mother but he is a prankster and likes to tease. "Take our picture; no, only mine. She is too old." She looks at him a little embarrassed but actually she is enjoying his playfulness. She asks us to step out and wait, shutting the door.

The door opens and she has put on her best sari and refreshed the *bindi* on her forehead. "Now you can take our picture." She turns herself impishly to him and says, "*Now* am I too old?" He nods his head. She laughs. He laughs back. Their pleasure in each other fleetingly softens the extreme harshness of their living conditions. We take the picture and show them. Both are pleased. We inquire of mother if she will come to the meeting at school in two days. She says she has already arranged with her employer to do so. As we say goodbye, my hand is the last on the door. Sudip touches it and smiles at me. "She still too old."

We think we have finished our visit to Sion and start heading out to the railroad platform, but are stopped. A *chai wallah* asks us to sit down. He only knows us as visitors who have been surrounded by laughing kids. He offers us both a glass of Indian spiced tea with milk. It is, as *chai* always is, wonderfully refreshing, even though it is a very hot drink on a very hot day. The *wallah* refuses to take money. Actually, I suspect I insulted his hospitality. I apologize to him and he offers a large, bright-toothed smile. We pass the laundry man doing his ironing on the street. He smiles at us.

As we make our way out to the sky, another youngster with whom we work stops us. He says, "Please come to my home, too." We can't say no to this near-exhortation. I do wonder what is behind it. At school, this is a very earnest child. He takes us to his home, also a small, dark space. He lives here with his older brother, his father who is out working, his older brother, and his remarkable mother. He introduces us.

His brother has a dirty bandage on his leg, oozing blood. He has been hurt while working. He should be going to school but his father, he tells us, had an accident and became unable to work for several months. Father is still not at full strength and so, although he is back at work, his pay is less.

Mother takes over the story. She is a woman of dignified carriage, erect posture, red-patterned sari, dark hair pulled severely back and parted in the middle so the vermillion paste of a married woman will show, one hand held softly in the other. Since her husband's accident, the older brother decided to leave school and go to work. He wanted to be sure that his younger brother (the one we know) would not be deprived of his education. He is an earnest, soft-featured young man who belongs in Tenth Standard or perhaps now in college. His father's accident has been calamitous for the family income. They are all committed to the younger brother continuing in school. He is one of the two boys who try to hide their tears when we mention our next day departure from his school.

Mother goes on. She discusses the difficulties with food, her gratitude to *Learning and Eating Together* for feeding her son, her sadness that her oldest boy has had to stop school. She hopes he will be able to go back once her husband is fully well.

I think the boy wants us to understand him better by meeting his remarkable family. As we sit and talk, the older brother notices that I am carrying my papers for working with the children on maps, as well as my water bottle. He hobbles over to the bed we are sitting on and tries to find a plastic bag tucked between the bed and the wall. He is successful and gently takes my things and puts them in one bag. "You do ladder easy now."

We ask for a photo, which we take inside the home. But mother says she would like the picture taken outside, too. We all go down the ladder and find an area with sunlight. Mother does not want to be remembered on film that is based in her home. She wants a picture taken outside, where her full pride, and near-tears-worry, can be seen in their fullness.

Now it is time to say goodbye. The older brother helps us down the ladder. We have an entourage of children who help us find our way through the *bustee* safely to the late afternoon sun and the gravel and train track maze leading to the railway platform. We climb up onto the platform and the kids wave goodbye, some saying in Marathi, "See you tomorrow." We take the train, always second-class, home.

A REAL MAP: DO PARENTS CARE?

Today, Asha and I will know if our methods for teaching visual symbolic reasoning are successful. Have the children held on to yesterday's flash mob realization of what symbols are? Or have their daily lives at home intercepted their ability to take the concepts in?

As before, when we enter the school grounds the kids are waiting. They rush over to shake hands, say "good morning" in English, and accompany us up the stairs, lighting the way as ever with their enthusiasm. That buzz of bees is in this classroom; the children are talkative and excited. Asha and I take down the enormous map that the children have been working on. It is rolled open with an excited solemnity, as if it were a sacred scroll. Their eyes wide, realizing what they have made, they spontaneously identify the four directions, the key to the map's symbols, and point out their own houses and the way to school.

We ask if the youngsters would now like to see a real map. They all move in close as we carefully unfold a street map of Bombay. Asha whispers to me, "We have to be careful; I borrowed this from a friend!" All eyes stare intently at the map. It looks different from their map. It has much more detail and all the roads are named, in English. We put a small yellow sticky-note where their school is. They look hard. I am surprised the map doesn't catch fire from the heat of their concentration. They are having trouble in part because their own streets are not on the map. Slum streets are not named, nor houses numbered. It is as if the children's homes, so grounded in daily reality, aren't real at all. Such a social statement, expressed on a map, is disorienting.

We try to help. "We've found your school. Now, where is the nearest O.C. (Outpatient Clinic)?" They find it, quickly. "Can you find your temple or mosque?" They can. "How would you get from school to the OC?" They trace the route. "What is the name of the street?" "When you get to the end of that street, which way do you turn? What is the name of the street?" Two girls cry out, "Oh, this shows us how to get places! If you know where you are and you know where you want to go, the map shows you. There are *chinhh* all over the map."

Now begins an excited tour of Mumbai. All the youngsters are pointing to places they know and showing how to get there from school. Then we ask them to find places farther away. They take up their own tour, widening its boundaries. "Here's Chowpatty Beach." "This is the zoo. You follow this street and then there is a train station; see the railroad tracks? Sir, that's a *chinhh*, right?" "Completely correct!!" They shiver with the ease with which they understood how an actual map works. Everyone applauds for themselves and each other.

Asha and I remind all the children that today will be our last day with them. The two particularly sensitive boys, who have been having so much fun, hide their faces as tears start to drop. I don't want to embarrass them and so I wait until they look forward, after they have dried their faces. I sit between them, put one arm around each one, and continue talking to the class. One boy leans his head on my shoulder. "And today is when your parents are coming to school. Whose parents are coming?" Almost everyone's hand goes up. This would be a remarkable showing. "You know what we're going to do? You are going to be your parents' teachers. You will teach them how maps work."

This is new. Usually parents are seen separately from their children, or, if seen together, the children are quiet while the teachers speak at the parents. Not today, however. They start to talk among themselves, about maps, about what to say to their parents, about music. What is most important is how alive the room is. The rest will simply follow. The map is rolled up so that it can be presented later.

The parents begin coming in. They enter in twos and threes; latecomers enter singly. Most of the parents are mothers. There are a few fathers and one uncle. We greet each of them with a personal *Namaste*, which they reciprocate. Asha speaks more now in Hindi, as few if any of the parents understand English and we want to minimize translation. We introduce ourselves and thank them for taking time off work (no work/no pay) to come to this meeting. We appreciate their commitment to their children's education. We tell them that their children are going to explain what they have been learning. The children will take charge now.

And indeed they do. One spokesperson—I have no idea when or how she was chosen—stands up and explains how important maps are and that learning about maps helps in other subjects, too.

Maps help you know where you are and help you get where you want
to go if you don't know the way. She announces that the class has
made its own map. Two boys hold the large rolled map that the class
has made. They carefully place it on the floor at the far end of the
room. They start to unroll it and children on both sides of the map
carefully unroll it slowly, as if an expensive Indian hand-woven rug
were being displayed. In some way it is precious stuff.

Most of the parents' eyes almost bulge with awe. The size of
it! All the color! What does it mean? Each child then takes a parent's hand and they approach the map. Speaking in Marathi, they
show their own house, the school, how to get to school following the
roads. "This isn't a real road. This is a symbol." Their parents, the
mothers in their best, worn, saris, offer wide smiles and their faces
shift from looking worn to looking in wonder at what their children
have created. Unschooled themselves, their children's reading and
writing are ephemeral and perhaps unknowable. But this! This immense scroll that the children made, whose meaning they can actually see! And they can see their children's excitement at learning.
This brings them more concretely closer to understanding what
school is for. Their pride in their children needs no translation.
Their children's pleasure in their parents' pride speaks for itself.

We spend a few minutes just chatting with the parents who have
some questions for the American doctor. They mistake me for a physician and I make the correction: I am a psychologist. Some concerns
then emerge about learning and finding a way to help their children
do their homework (they mean find the time to do it). We talk and
then the parents wander out in the same twos and threes.

We have some time with the children before saying goodbye.
They roll the map up and decide that it will live in their classroom
on top of a big cabinet. "We can take it out and remember you."

Having accomplished this, they would like to dance and demonstrate their prowess. Many of them take turns doing variations of Bollywood dancing. Then they want the adults to dance. Since men and women do not dance together in public, Asha, the *Learning and Eating Together* staff member, and the teacher, do a gentle dance. The children, however, want me to dance like Bollywood. They have no idea of the impossibility of this. However, I get up and start shaking rhythmically, thrusting my pelvis a bit, and waving my arms. They are delighted and join me in the arm movements. We sit on the floor again. One boy begins to move his legs in a rhythmic pattern. I start to imitate him, badly. The kids love it and applaud, not my skill but my willingness to try.

It is time to say goodbye. It is hard to believe that this has only been four days out of a month and we will be repeating it in three other schools, as well as teaching the teachers in yet other schools the methods we have been using. The children become somber. They all walk us down those damned dark steps and into the bright light of the schoolyard. They shake hands goodbye and say thank you. Many times. A few want hugs. Asha and I leave the schoolyard and they are all there, waving goodbye.

We enter a three-wheeler auto rickshaw that will take us to where we can pick up a four-wheeled cab and head home. I don't hear the noise of the road, the honking of the cars, the street noises. At first I don't even hear Asha speaking to me.

All I hear is the children's excitement. All I see is their unfettered spirit while learning. No wonder I cannot find my way to these far-flung slums by myself, which, unknown to either Asha or me yet, will be my next year's task.

FLYING SOLO

Bombay, 2013. I knew several months in advance that I would be performing on my own. Asha had told me that family commitments would render her unavailable for this last year of my work in India. She e-mailed suggesting that I consider canceling, adding that the alternative would be to work with an "open schedule." That is, *Learning and Eating Together* and I would figure out ourselves how they wanted to use me and meld that with my observations of what the children most needed. After a week of mulling this over, I decided to cancel.

Within days, I received a second e-mail from Asha: would I reconsider and come to work? She perceived the changed circumstances as an opportunity and a fitting ending to our work. We began nine years ago with my being a bit in the background until I got my Arabian Sea legs. I would end by managing the entire endeavor on my own. Asha mentioned that I would then have come full circle. I corrected her: "No, full circle is going back to the beginning. This would be a straight line from second fiddle to soloist.

I agreed with her that this would indeed be a fitting ending.

Asha and I would be in contact about my work throughout my time in Mumbai. We would socialize together as two couples as always, but her commitments would not permit her to participate in the various activities, nor the labyrinthine negotiations regarding what I would be doing. I find Indian communication to be often oblique. "No" really does often mean "No," unless it means, "Let me think about it." "Yes" may mean, "Yes," or it may mean "No." "Let me think about it," may mean "I need some time to digest your idea," or it might indicate, "I need some time to devise something completely different." Even after sending an organization a written prospectus of activities and receiving agreement, I am not surprised to hear upon arrival, "I never saw that prospectus; this is what we would like you to do."

I've learned to expect this and so I have arrived for several years with the presumably agreed-upon plan, plus my best-guess Plan B for what I actually will be asked to do. Once in a while I am surprised when presented with a Plan C by the organization we are attached to. Yet, as with most interpersonal matters in India, in the end things work out. Most fortunately, the staff at *Learning and Eating Together* and I have a history, and we have a mutual respect and fondness for each other.

We have developed a plan, partly successfully negotiated in advance, partly a change in what we had mutually agreed upon. (This one I anticipated and was prepared for.) I will do a two-day training for staff from CEO down, and a two-day training for teachers integrating the children's reality with how to reach them educationally in the classroom, as well as a discussion of discipline. I will then spend several days in two schools with classroom teachers and students, demonstrating techniques for teaching conversational English, the most important skill the students need and the one that is generally absent from the curriculum. The classroom teachers will serve as translators. Judith, the new School Coordinator, will observe everything and she will instruct all other teachers of English in the methods I have used for reaching these children from backgrounds of poverty. The CEO will attend an English class.

This is not simply a pedagogical task; it is a psychological one, due to the children's shame. There are many methods for teaching conversational English. They seem, at the least the ones I have been exposed to, variations of the typical "sit still and listen, repeat after me, now say a few words" format used in Bombay and irrelevant to the ways the children think.

Their thinking is based on the ground reality of their lives. It is immediate; it is Now. It is quick. It is reactive a lot of the time, rather than contemplative. Who has time for contemplation when drunken strangers and potential rapists may cross your path at any moment? Who has time to think about formal conjugations and verb forms when the laundry must be done, the baby tended, the rats fended off, and the water cans filled at the tap before it is shut off? One aspect of the exhilaration of being with these children is their aliveness, their "Now-ness." On the other hand, long-term planning is a real problem, dictated by their circumstances. How can a teacher use this reality while instilling proper spoken English inside those fertile brains?

The tasks are set. *Learning and Eating Together* and I are now in full agreement about what is expected. I am comfortable working on my own, with a translator who hopefully will become less and less important as the English lessons proceed. But I have one nagging concern: transportation. Even when traveling the year before with Asha to some of the same places, the cabbie and we would get lost. Asha would need to ask directions several times to get us where we needed to be. The city is vast and there are few true landmarks once beyond CST (Chatrapati Shivaji Terminus), the World Heritage train station site in South Bombay. Fewer people speak English the farther out one goes. I am worried about getting where I need to be, and returning back to the Colaba Family Association Guest House each day. Everything else I know I will manage in one way or another.

Asha and, independently, the staff of *Learning and Eating Together* assure me that this will be taken care of. Lin and I step off the plane, this year unmet by Asha, and find a suitable taxi. He needs only a little direction as we near the Guest House. This part of town I know and I can give the cabbie directions. We check in, I give Asha a call that we have arrived. Indian hospitality takes over. Asha has found a reliable driver (and a very nice man) to pick me up each morning and get me where I need to go. She will join me each time there is a change of venue to be sure the cabbie knows his way. Otherwise he will come on his own. I call *Learning and Eating Together*, partly as a courtesy to let them know I have arrived. The remarkable founder and the new CEO inform me that all my mid-day meals and rides home have been arranged. "Marc, you are not to worry," Janya tells me sternly and then with a laugh. "Everything is arranged." And indeed it is. There is nothing oblique in this communication. It is clear and affectionate.

I start work the day after we arrive. I am not one for sitting still and I am sure this has much to do with my pleasure walking the crowded streets of this über-city. Asha and the cabbie drive up right on time. We are both most happy to see each other. We catch up quickly while Asha is keeping an eye out for where we are. She drops me off and I enter the staff offices of *Learning and Eating Together.* I know everyone and we are all glad to see each other. The exception is the new CEO, whom I have not met in person. She and I like each other immediately. This is one of those occasions when I meet someone with no foreknowledge of his or her background, interests, personal life, have no idea of what we may have in common, and I like her enormously. It is instant and it is reciprocated. She remarks on it. Within minutes we are in serious collaborative discussion of the work to be done. At first I am not sure she is a woman, despite her first name. In fact, she is a "woman who dresses like a man," in Indian terminology. What I am sure of is how much I like her.

We discuss some of the staff problems and the difficulties facing an NGO that is undergoing a transfer of power from a revered founder to a new leader. The great risk is that the organization will lose its focus and shift from its reason for being: educating children beyond what the city schools will do, while making sure that no child goes hungry. Hunger and education cannot coexist. With the gradual retirement of it charismatic Prime Generator, will *Learning and Eating Together* become yet one more organization that shifts its mission to mere survival, leaving the children, the original reason for its existence, in the background? This needs to be avoided. We spend two days of training working to help the organization plan on maintaining its integrity.

The teachers are next. Their task is formidable, as monumental as their commute to work. We discuss conversational English. They are concerned that they don't have time to teach this; it is not prominent in the curriculum. I demonstrate that it can permeate every subject if done with patience, playfulness, and ingenuity.

Some teachers are more engaged than others. One in particular is intrigued. She wants to see the children tackle conversational English before believing they can do it.

I pull out a ruler and ask what this is good for. "Discipline—that's what the children understand." I challenge this teacher. "If you use a ruler to control hitting, you are teaching them that hitting is a good thing. After all, what are you doing with them? Teaching them not to hit by hitting them? What will that teach them? Does that make sense?" After a bit of harrumphing, she becomes curious. "What else is there to do? They can get so wild." This comment always interests me since in all our work in schools, both therapeutic and teaching, Asha and I have never had a discipline problem. We have had children who are getting tired and needing to release some steam, but they are not wild and they do not need herding with a ruler.

I mention that using meditation will calm the students down if they truly need it. I also humbly comment on the irony that I am here in India, where meditation was born, teaching its use to Indians. The teachers feel complimented. They are both rapt and skeptical. I walk them through how it seems to me, as a non-Indian, that meditation can be brought into the classroom and describe how Asha and I have done it before, in some of the same schools where these teachers work. Still some disbelief but that is all right. The idea has been planted. It's the best I can do.

Now I move on to the schools, a few days in each. These are Seventh Standard students, young twelve and thirteen year olds whose conversational English is poor. They know individual words and can string perhaps two or three together, minus the verb. They find speaking English tedious, as would I if I were lined up in a row having to repeat over and over by rote the same stale sentences daily. I would become a discipline problem myself.

Once again, instead of fifteen students for forty minutes, I have twenty-five students for two hours. This is a lot of twelve- to thirteen-year-old attention spans and energy to engage for two hours. And the teacher/translator, School Coordinator, CEO, and a visitor from a private group that has been hired to teach conversational English are observing me. The private group appears not to be achieving great success.

As a solo flyer, I feel as if I am in "The Spirit of Saint Louis," and not at all sure I will successfully complete my flight. This is only a fleeting thought; I remember that all I have to do is rely on the children's eagerness to learn and the importance of being hospitable and helpful to the adults. As long as I show energy, the rest should follow. (Repeat to myself: "the rest will follow.")

Where to begin? It must be with the very basics. These youngsters know individual simple English words but not how to connect them. They tend to drop verbs. They do not know conjugation. I only have a few days with them. The most useful thing I can do is to provide a working model for the teachers to carry on with. Judith and the teacher have commandeered a large room with soft mats. No desks. I introduce myself to the children, translated into Marathi by the teacher, and announce, "No textbooks." They smile and a few boys applaud while some girls giggle.

The youngsters are in a circle; I stand in the middle. I repeat, without translation, "My name is Marc," with a slightly rolled "r," as the American "r" sound does not exist in Hindi or Marathi. "What is my name?" They repeat, "Marc." "Good. Now say 'your name is Marc.'" They do. I pretend I can't hear. "Louder." They get shyly louder. "More loud. Wake up the birds!!" **"Your name is Marc."** They are more relaxed now. I walk around the room. "What is *her* name?" "Her name Sabeena." I correct him, with a hand around his shoulder. "Her name <u>is</u> Sabeena." He repeats correctly and we all applaud. We go around the room with this exercise. I insert the word "is" almost every time. After all the children have put their names into the room, I ask them all to say their names at the same time, in the proper sentence "My name is _____." I again ask for a lot of noise. Twenty-five voices scream out correctly **"My name is _____."**

I ask them to quiz me. "What is <u>my</u> name?" I remember some of their names, and then purposely start making silly mistakes, calling a girl by a boy's name. They know I am playing and I ask them to teach me. I am sitting in the middle of the circle and each child has to come up to me and speak loudly to me. (I am trying to cut through their shame about speaking English and to eliminate the usual mumbling.) They do it and most of them are now using proper sentence structure, however simple.

I draw railroad tracks in chalk on the mats, making a large circle; the train of students has a "Start" place written down, and an "End" place. Their task is to take turns asking each other a question: "What <u>do</u> you <u>like</u>…?" "What *is* your favorite…?" "Do you <u>have</u> _____?" For each correctly asked and answered question, the train moves ahead one section until we are back at the beginning. I make sure that everyone gets it right by whispering to each child who has made an error so she can correct it herself out loud. The additional rule is that they must ask someone who is all the way across the room, speaking loudly. Although they are tentative at first, this catches on and these children are speaking loudly and with more humor: "What is your favorite mobile (cell phone) color?" "Can you ride an elephant?" They are disappointed when the train reaches its destination. The observers are surprised at the enthusiasm and that there has been almost no translation.

I suggest a break. An hour has gone by, quickly. "No break. More English." After the observers remove their jaws from the floor, and I recover from my delight at the children's eagerness to learn something they usually dread, I try a new idea. Partly I am flying by the seat of my pants, as I cannot know in advance how the youngsters will respond and when I will need to come up with something new. "The Spirit of Saint Louis" has not yet arrived, but the children are happy, engaged, and completely involved. All the observers are waiting for the discipline problems that are not happening.

It occurs to me that more physical movement might usefully be added. My thought is that the students might respond even more to English if they could not only see the letters and pronounce them, but also could *become* them, embody them. I pick three boys, as I want to be respectful about touching the girls. Two stand on either side of me and I pick up the smallest one and hold him horizontally between the two other boys. I ask, "What letter is this?" The kids are having difficulty with this, I think because of the three-dimensionality. They cannot see the "H." The boy I'm holding, the crossbar, says in Marathi, "Hurry up, Sir is getting tired!" as he notices my shaking arms. I laugh, which allows everyone to laugh, and put him down.

The boys have a better idea that becomes the template for our exercise. They lie down on the mat in the shape of an H. All the students get it immediately. "You're an H!" I then ask everyone who knows an English word with H to raise his or her hand and tell it to me, speaking clearly. They do so with a degree of decorum.

The kids want more. I ask for four girls and whisper "M" to them. They arrange themselves into the letter and again ask for words beginning with M. Less decorum and more interrupting as more words come to the kids' minds. As we work our way, in random order, through the alphabet, I make the task more difficult. "Once you guess the letter, make up a sentence that has a word with the letter in it." I am surprised, although perhaps I shouldn't be, that they get it.

The next letter is "Y." As the three Y children on the floor lie there, the room erupts. Decorum gone. They are jumping up and down and screaming: "I like **Y**ellow." "My mother **Y**ells me when I don't uniform off." (This needs some correction from me, but she is attempting a complex sentence.) "**Y**ou are my friend."

It is time to stop. Two hours have flown by. "The Spirit of Saint Louis" appears to have landed. The kids are excited and happy. They don't want to leave. They don't want me to leave. They ask for assurances that I'll return tomorrow. Fortunately, I will. They file out to get to their lunch and their regular, non-*Learning and Eating Together* class. The observers are themselves a bit breathless. Judith is so happy that she has a little trouble speaking. The teacher, a lovely benign woman, tells me that she can't believe what she just saw and that there were no discipline problems.

I take a deep, energized but tired breath and am simply relieved that I was somehow able to reach the children, and, best of all, alleviate some of their shame in speaking English. I regret that there is so much that must be accomplished for them to manage conversational English and all I can do is this small introduction and then go home. Judith, in her empathic way, picks up my wordless wonderings and says to me quietly, "Sir, I will follow up with this approach with the children and inform all the other English teachers. Don't worry." I look at her gratefully.

As we head out of the room, a teacher stops us. The students with whom Asha and I worked on maps last year heard I was in the school and want me to stop in their classroom and say hello. And so we wend our way through the dark halls to last year's symbolic reasoning students (who were also the dancers).

I remove my shoes before entering and as I come in everyone stands up, smiling, and shouts, "Good morning, Sir." I say "Good morning" back, offer a *Namaste* gesture and indicate for them all to sit. Their teacher graciously turns the class over to me for a few minutes. I ask them if they remember my name. They do, but more significantly, "Sir, we have given you a different name. You are Dr. *Chinhh*. (They've retained some of what they learned.) I ask if they remember what we did. **"A MAP WITH LOTS OF CHINHH ON IT. WE MADE IT OURSELVES AND WE COULD READ A REAL MAP THEN!!"**

I ask individual kids how they are doing, what they are learning. The teacher tells me that they have been practicing dancing like I did last year. The most gregarious of the boys, the one who loved to show off his dancing, comes forward and tries to teach me new dance steps. He sees my awkwardness, but also my willingness, and sensitively shifts his lesson to new rhythmic hand, back, and head movements, that I can do! We move together and the class applauds. "Sir, did you remember us?" "Yes, I did. In fact, I will never forget you." One of the two boys, who tried to hide his tears when we were leaving last year, looks sad now and turns his face away. I go over, stepping over multiple students, tousle his hair, and put my hand on his shoulder. He looks up at me, directly in my eyes, smiles, and touches my hand.

We all wave goodbye to each other as I leave. I am struck by how sad I feel that I will never see these children again. This is my last year of my nine-years of work.

Postscript. Three weeks after I return home, I receive an e-mail from Judith. "Sir, I have been using your methods with more children in another school. They are so excited. They said they never knew that learning English could be so much fun. They now speak English out loud and push to take turns reading and talking. The students you worked with when you were here asked me to tell you that they love you. I hope I can write and ask you for more ideas for helping the children."

GOODBYES FOR NOW

The time to leave has come. Asha and Gopal and Lin and I will surely see each other again. Lin and I will be back in India, seeing more of this glorious country. We will route ourselves through Bombay. Asha and Gopal will be in America to visit their daughter and route themselves through the Washington DC area to see old friends and us.

This is an ending, nonetheless. Asha and I will not be working together, as we did not during this final year, although I kept her informed. We are no longer a working team. We remain warm, good friends. The people we have worked with cascade through my memory: the elderly blind; Meenakshi; the workers at the orphanage/adoption agency; the street children still living and those who have died; Manoj; the parents of such sick children in hospital; Shakti; Mumtaz; the Railway Saint; Janya.

And especially all the children and their mothers. Hundreds of children. In their street homes, in their *bustees*, on the footpath and in their schools.

Asha and Gopal's friends, their relatives, and the homemade marmalade that Gopal's cousin sent to the guesthouse for us. The dance and music concerts the four of us went to, the restaurants and cafes, the movies we saw together. The art galleries Asha took us to. How wonderfully both Asha and Gopal shared their love of their city.

And farewell to Bombay itself, in all its density, its extremes and contradictions. So maddening to some, how caressing to me despite the vigilance necessary to be safe. It's very air is dangerous yet healing; its reverence for life both wondrous and damaged. What I will particularly miss is the verve on overdrive, the street crowds, and how Mumbai is the place where all that is good and all that is evil, all that is generous and all that is greedy, all that is refined and all that is vulgar meet in one massive cauldron of humanity. Bombay represents all of us, a caravan of contradictions. And how I will miss it.

The cabbie, who had been carrying me from place to place, had been hired by Asha to take us to the airport. He arrived, as always, on time and with a smile. He loaded a month's worth of bags into and onto his taxi. Guesthouse staff came out to say goodbye, as they always did. On the way to the airport we stopped, as usual, at Asha and Gopal's place. Usually Asha would come downstairs to say goodbye, give a hug and a *Namaste*.

This year, Gopal and their houseboys came down with Asha. As we said goodbye, Asha performed the Hindu ceremony for safe travels. From a tray, she dipped her finger into vermilion paste and placed a stripe on Lin's and my foreheads. Then she tapped two kernels of dry rice into place on the wet vermilion stripe. Last, she put a tiny leaf, much like a myrtle, on the red stripe and one in our mouths for us to chew and swallow. Red strings were tied around our right wrists, to be worn for two days, to complete the ceremony.

She handed Lin a gift, a pashmina shawl, with a note:

To Lin,
For enabling
Marc's pursuit of
Happiness.
With many thanks,
Asha

January 2013
Bombay

Asha and Lin and I all hugged goodbye. Gopal and I shook hands. The houseboys and I offered mutual *Namaste*s. One last *Namaste* between Asha and me and we got into the cab and drove away.

The cabbie indicated that he wanted to offer us something: a glass of *chai* as a goodbye gesture because he liked us. Driving through Dharavi, not too far from the airport, he pulled over, got out of the cab, and gave us each a small glass of very hot spiced tea with milk. He assured us that the water was boiled. He watched as we enjoyed the *chai* and his gentle gesture, and then off we all went to finish the trip to the airport.

Once there, he helped us with our baggage, shaking off the airport fleet of official and unofficial baggage handlers swarming like human ants with tags around their necks. He loaded our carts and indicated that he would be leaving. I paid him, which he did not look at, but rather simply pocketed. I said to him, "I like you. You are a good man." He looked embarrassed at first, said "no-no-no," and then faced me, man to man, equals, and offered his hand for a Western handshake. We said goodbye and entered the airport...with its own chaos.

EPILOGUE

INDIAN EPIPHANY:
("I FEEL SAD WHEN THE CAT CHASES THE RAT.")

Bombay, 2012. I was riding the Bombay Commuter Railway early in the morning, heading toward Day Three at one of the Ghatkopar area schools with the Eighth and Ninth Standard children, when I internally gasped. A full-body *frisson* rippled through all of me. A minute or so later, I understood. "Oh my God, I'm beginning to forgive my mother. I'm beginning to forgive the unforgiveable."

My mother had not been on my mind. She rarely is anymore, except as my memories of her live inside me, as do the portraits of all our dead. I was not thinking of abuse, of torture, of malevolence, of any of the sadnesses and cruelties of her relationship with me. The awareness of "I'm beginning to forgive my mother" simply went through me like a quick jolt of electricity.

Where had this come from? What was the source of this gift?

The day before, Asha and I had finished our day with the children and were about to head out to visit their homes. I overheard a conversation she was having, "What makes you sad?" Twelve-year-old Sunil said, "I feel sad when the cat chases the rat." Indian children often speak more deeply than their actual words and since his statement was so striking, I wondered what his layered meaning might be.

Sunil knew well that the rats in his *bustee* were disease-ridden; that if given the chance they would gnaw into the precious canvas bags of rice and steal food from whatever unlucky family harbored them. He knew that all families worked hard to keep rats out of their living spaces and restricted to the *guhlees.* He knew that rats could chew shoes and render them unusable, and he knew that rats make people sick. And yet he was sad when the cat chased the rat.

Sunil's reference was spiritual: all life is to be revered because all life is interconnected, and the forms life takes change throughout everyone's sojourn. Hurting a rat, undesirable as a rat may be, was equivalent to hurting anyone and therefore hurting everyone. Sunil, the unknowing representative of Mother India, was offering his ground's eye philosophical formulation of the importance of embracing the interconnectedness of all living things.

My mother was unable to embrace, other than in fear. She had tried to murder me by asphyxiation. She tortured me with repeated near-suffocations, always carefully stopping short of killing me. When I was older she tied me up with a rope. She tied me in a chair. She drove nails into the wall and tied my hands and arms to them. She tied me to the doorknob. She hit me, beat me in the face, and kicked me. She endlessly repeated how unworthy I was. She referred to me as a monster and as inhuman, undeserving of having been born. When I was angry, particularly with her, she perceived me as Evil.

And yet I loved her. When I was very young, I loved her because infants understand that they must mollify the person who is responsible for keeping them alive. Once I was four and my father turned her over to my care, I loved her so that she would not hurt my baby brother Ron or me. I sought to soothe her. At seven, I endured her sneaking up on me when I was quietly reading and suddenly screaming my worthlessness.

When she was no longer a literal threat to my survival, I continued to love her not for my safety but for hers. I wanted her to feel better, to be less miserable, to be less crazy, to smile at least a little, to feel that she belonged, a job designed for failure. I cared about her and for her.

I continued for decades to listen to her long rants and obsessive meanderings on the telephone and when she entered a near-hypnotic state repeating the incantatory list of what was wrong with the world.

She was clear with me since I was four that I was generally unwanted and "bad." What love she had for me was conditional. I believe that there were only four people she loved unconditionally: her adored younger brother Reuben; his wife Miriam; my father's younger sister Isabelle with whom she was close friends from adolescence and through whom she met my father; and my wife Lin, the daughter she had yearned for. All other relationships were ambivalent, shifting from good to bad, comfort to menace, safety to danger.

In her later life, her increased paranoid thinking made it necessary for me to take over her financial affairs. If the sum of a check number was an "evil number," she changed it and then recorded the amount on a different check stub with a "safe" number. I started finding overdue bills in the freezer, placed there so "they" couldn't find them or the information about her that had been secretly encoded. When I started to manage her finances, of course against her will, I became what she always knew me to be: part of the Evil Conspiracy of Men who wanted to ruin her. The last words she said to me, the last words that I permitted her to say to me, were: **"And now you're stealing my money, you bastard!"**

I discontinued contact with my mother nine months before she died and nine months after my father's death. Just as she had often refused to visit him while he was dying, she needed coaxing out of the car at his funeral. She did not attend mourning observances for him. Her only words were, bitterly: "Now my Social Security check will be six hundred dollars less." The drain on me was affecting my health as her vituperation became ever more vicious. This was not simply a matter of an old woman having difficulty adjusting to widowhood. It was an unbroken continuation of the person she had always been, but with fewer moments of calm.

Still wanting to fulfill my religious obligation to honor my mother, I continued to take care of her by dealing with bills, and talking with caregivers, nursing staff, nurse practitioners, and a geriatric social worker I had hired. However, I kept myself at a personal distance from her.

I had had to find a way to fulfill my dual duties: to care for my mother while assuring that I was not harming myself by continued contact with her toxicity. As Krishna tells Arjuna in *The Baghavad Gita*, by doing an action inherently true to himself, he fulfills his duty. Arjuna must fulfill his duty, in his case as a warrior, even though it will mean hurting his own family. I had the duty to place myself out of harm's way while still taking care of my dangerous mother.

As the Bombay Commuter Railway rocked back and forth, too many people in too small a space buffeted me. I was surrounded by the array of Indian life and its warmth that emerges in the most unlikely places, but ever emerges. I thought of my mother. She was, it is true, a bad mother most of the time. Her often-charming public persona was not the Fury I lived with growing up, nor the sour, vituperative, obsessional paranoid complainer of my adulthood. But she was my mother. I can neither simply explain away her destructiveness, nor make it evaporate into excuses and platitudes. I also cannot forget that there was a witty and charming part of her, mostly visible to others but occasionally available to me. She was monstrous but not a monster.

It upset Sunil when the cat chased the rat. I was beginning to become more fully aware that my mother, like Sunil's rat, had been a living being. She suffered throughout her life with only the shortest periods of peace. She rejected help. I don't know if I miss her. I do miss, in retrospect, what I wish might have been. I don't know what kind of life my mother earned for herself in the world to come. I do know that she was my mother, that she was very sick, that her life was sad, that she was a malevolent presence and a danger to me. I know that forgiveness is gradually coming.

It upset Sunil when the cat chased the rat. I believe, no, I am sure, that my process could not have begun in a different culture, a different spiritual climate, than India.

And so I wonder: Did I select India or did India select me?

THE NEXT BEGINNING

My nine-years of work in India over, while traveling in Africa I dreamed a long detailed narrative. Or perhaps I should call it a visitation. India had not been on my mind. Nevertheless, I awoke in the middle and the dream spoke to me out loud, while I was awake, saying that it would be the final chapter of this book, and I should return to sleep and submit to it. Wanting to be sure I understood, the "dream" repeated itself the next night, detail-for-detail.

A saffron and white silk tent the size of a four-story building sat in an indistinct background. Its shimmery cloth walls billowed slightly in a soft wind. A man, my assigned Guardian, was waiting for me at the entrance and greeted me with a gesture of *Namaste*. Other people my age, twenty-seven, entered as well, although the structure looked different to each of them: a chrome and glass and steel building in New York, an English country cottage, a Vermont brick-red covered bridge, an American suburban "town center" shopping area, a Spanish beach villa, a Navajo reservation. I recognized these people. They had been my classmates in graduate school and on internship many decades ago. We were our younger selves at the beginning of our professional and adult lives. Nobody spoke except the Guardians assigned to each of us.

We entered our shared-but-separate structure and, as we did, saw a grand hall again perceived differently by each of us. I saw the large temple at Ellora, a complex structure that was carved down from the top of a mountain until it was a free-standing, multi-tiered complex, every surface chiseled with figures from Hindu mythology/history. These reliefs emphasize the story of Lord Rama. Green parrots flew overhead; grey ibis with red feathers on the backs of their necks walked throughout the temple.

Each of us took our seat, carved into stone like a niche. In the middle of the room, we all saw the same thing: a larger than human-sized revolving and constantly changing figure, Adonai in a cloud of dust, Jesus, the crescent of Islam, Confucius, Buddha, Lao-Tzu, and others. One aspect of this ever-shifting image spoke to each of us, as the image halted before beginning to spin again. Our Guardians were standing next to us.

I spoke to the cloud of dust, praising it with a blessing. It talked to me in return. It told me, "It is time to say goodbye to me but you must remember that we are all one, in different forms." The cloud whirled quickly and Lord Shiva emerged from the dust, first his multiple arms with his trident in the lower right hand, then the crescent moon on his head, his face and his body. The River Ganges flowed from his matted hair and he was dancing on a turtle's back.

Lord Shiva started to speak. I asked, "Are you about to tell me how I am going to start over?" My Guardian intervened, "No, he will announce how you are going to *continue*."

Lord Shiva let me know that I was returning to India, to Mumbai, to start and direct a no-fee private school for slum children. Children from kindergarten through Standard Twelve would attend this school and be nurtured there. The school had enough money to pay teachers three times a typical teacher's salary. It would, for Standards Eleven and Twelve, qualify as a college in Indian terms. The school would involve parents in their children's learning. It would also train students in the higher Standards in the skills needed to maintain jobs beyond typical slum labor.

By making linkages with appropriate social-minded businesses, my school would begin to create an infrastructure to help release good students from the usual slum future. I would have to deal with resistance to this from the majority of businesses, legal and illegal, that depend on the cheap labor supply of poorly educated slum children.

As Lord Shiva was speaking, I recalled the great love and dedication between him and his wife, Parvati. I remembered being in a Shiva temple in Mysore at night when, in the dark, the statue of Parvati was carried to the statue of Shiva, as it was every night. Lord Shiva and Parvati would never spend a night apart. I began to panic. I thought of my wife. Until then, I had assumed she would be coming with me. Thin sheets of gold started to flutter throughout the temple. They were not carried by the wind; they moved of their own accord. I started to cry and asked, "Is Lin coming with me? Am I going to see her? Am I going alone? I want her."

My Guardian said, "It's not her time yet."

"Can I get a message to her? Please!"

One of the thin gold sheets gently placed itself in my Guardian's hand. "Yes, you can. Speak it."

"Please be sure that she knows that I told her...'Thank You.'"
The letters appeared on the gold sheet and it slowly flew away.

My Guardian indicated that it was time to start walking. We
entered a lit corridor. "The site of your school is in a part of the
suburbs midway between several of the slums that you have worked
in. That will allow access to more children. The building has been
selected and renovation has begun. You must involve yourself in
the details quickly. Oh, and all bribes have already been paid.
Don't let them tell you otherwise."

As we walked, a translucent figure in a Jewish shroud, hover-
ing about an inch above the ground, rushed toward me. It was
my mother, gone oh-so-many years. "Please, Marc, forgive me. I
treated you so badly and tried so hard to hurt you. I didn't know
what else to do. I was always so angry and scared."

I stopped and caught my breath. I wondered why this was happening. I recalled my experience in another life on the Bombay
Commuter Railway, that full shudder and the effect of one child's
words: "It upsets me when the cat chases the rat."

I remembered being a child and, despite the abuse, wanting
my mother to feel better. I remembered how much of a failure I
felt because I couldn't ease her pain. I remembered how angry
I got at her as an adolescent and I remembered loving her nonetheless. I had always wanted her to feel better. I became grateful. Here was my chance, decades after her death, to help her.

"Mom, I forgive you. And I understand why you did what you
did to me." She sighed and a single tear fell from her right eye.
I added, "Now can you at last rest?" She sighed again, kissed me

on the cheek with her still death-cold lips, and vanished. I didn't know if she felt any relief, but I felt lighter.

My Guardian and I continued down the corridor. "Marc, it is time for your next name. It is Vikram.

"Let me give you more details. You are being provided with enough money to support the school completely. That money is in two bank accounts with a company name so people will not associate it with you personally. There will always be money in those accounts. Whatever you take out will be replaced. This frees you to serve the children and avoid raising funds. Once you are settled, the renovators know to call you about the school. Two good contacts will also call you. Everyone has been waiting for you.

"Oh, Vikram, I haven't gotten to your living arrangements. We have refurbished a two-bedroom flat on the second floor of a three story apartment building in the neighborhood you like a few blocks behind the Taj Hotel. No, it is not the street where the Western businessmen have their sexual assignations with stolen ten-year-old boys. It is two blocks from there. It is fairly quiet, at least as quiet as Bombay can ever get, and has trees. We chose the second floor rather than the larger third floor so you wouldn't have to deal with roof damage from the monsoon. Your flat has a verandah and shutters that will close. You'll probably get some monsoon damage each year, but it should be minimal. Fixing it should be no problem, and remember, all bribes have been pre-paid. That means you won't be bothered with disruptions in phone service, hot water, electricity, and your mail won't get stolen. The police will leave you alone unless you ask them for help. And again, bribes have been pre-paid, so they will help you.

"Vikram, you also have two personal bank accounts, placed in different banks. Together they are plentiful. Individually they are middling and so will not draw any attention. They, too, will be replenished every time you take money out. First you'll need to furnish your place. Once we get there, you'll know where to shop. The same for clothing. Try to work with furnishing and clothing as quickly as possible; you have much work to do. The children are waiting."

We continued walking down the corridor. The artificial light yielded to a soothing but bright white light and the hallway became circular. I could see ahead that it was going to let out directly in front of my flat. I noticed my arms. They were becoming a golden, tawny brown and had more hair on them. My already black hair was getting a little longer and curlier. I was aware that I was starting to think in three languages, Indian English, Hindi, and Bombay Marathi. I had lost a few inches and was now standing five foot eight. My English would now sound accented in America. My slacks were medium grey and my shirt a small maroon and silver paisley that formed thin stripes on a grey background.

My Guardian told me, "Welcome Home, Vikram. And about your wife, for some time, you'll still be able to think backwards." He then told me that he wasn't leaving me altogether, that he lived nearby. I asked him, "Won't I be a burden?"

He responded, "Not at all."

My Guardian started to walk away, turned his head around, and said, "Don't forget. All bribes have been pre-paid!"

I thought: "And the children are waiting."

CANDLES ON THE RIVER

I cast my forgiveness
And the ashes of any bitterness
Into India's Great River of purification.

I pray that my written efforts have served as testimony to the strength, resilience, and beauty of the Indian people, particularly of the women and children who live in poverty. They are the enduring and unappreciated proof of India's greatness and the necessary human capital for its future, if India is to fulfill herself and be to the world the beacon so very much needed.

If these women and children, these blind adults and street families, these parents watching their children receive chemotherapy are remembered, if these people and slums have come alive for the reader, I will have succeeded.

I also offer my gratitude to a country of abiding wisdom
and healing.
Marc A. Nemiroff, 2015

In Memorium
Vasudha Kulkarni, Ph.D.
Psychologist

ACKNOWLEDGMENTS

Stepping Into the River: An American Psychologist in Mother India has had many midwives. The strangers, acquaintances, and friends; Hindus, Muslims, Sikhs, Parsees, and Christians; people dark-skinned and light, educated and illiterate, old and young, good and bad; the people of the Indian tapestry, are the first movers of this book. I hope I have done them justice.

Jonathan Kirsch served both as my publishing attorney and, as an established author himself, my official hand-holder. His unyielding assurance that what I had produced had merit was immeasurably helpful in my frequent times of doubt.

I independently networked the arrangement that made these nine years of work with the Indian poor possible. Although there were no umbrella agencies, nothing Indian happens without people and relationships. I am humbly indebted to Bapu Deolalikar for believing in my intentions, and finding me worthy of making the linkage to Asha Dutia and her husband, Gopal. Bapu set the top spinning.

Asha, I thank you with all humility for taking on this American stranger, for being open to working together, and for permitting this beautiful Indian/American relationship to flower. We worked hard, agreed and disagreed, argued, laughed, and thoroughly enjoyed our rich alliance. Thank you for being my Indian Gateway, my guru, my cultural guide, and, over time, a dear and close friend to both Lin and me. You are a model of sharp intelligence, graciousness, humour, taste, utter honesty, and warmth. Our shared passion for social justice (and for the arts), helped seal an inspiring and ongoing relationship. Thank you Gopal, for supporting our work, and adding your succinct wisdom to our often-long discussions of how we should try to be useful to the people we worked with. Thank you for being a gracious host, for our frequent conversations about film, for the films and performances the four of us attended, for the whiskey, and, with Asha, for sharing your friends and relatives with my wife and me. I mustn't forget: thank you, Gopal, for your wonderfully endearing laugh.

In terms of the writing of *Stepping Into the River*, I offer my warm gratitude to the New Directions writing program of The Washington Center for Psychoanalysis, in Washington, DC. New Directions taught me, and continues to teach me, how to enhance my writing, fitting form to function, writing the emotional truth whether in fiction or non-fiction. This is a unique writing community of warmth and support. Together, those of us in the various mental health fields produce memoir, creative non-fiction, poetry, and fiction, as well as professional work. New Directions is my writing's emotional safety net, as well as my teacher. Special thanks to Bo Winer, Ernie Wallwork, and Jeanne Lemkau, particular teachers who encouraged me to write *Stepping Into the River*, and to my fellow travelers Kate Wechsler and Lynne Harkless, for understanding what I was trying to do.

My dear friend, the poet E. Laura Golberg, helped me think through formal and structural problems that I confronted in the act of writing this book, and had such faith in its worth. The encouragement and support of my non-blood brother and sister, Howard and Barbara Gradet, is always in the background of every challenge I undertake. Thank you, as always and forever. Thanks to my brother, Ron, for being my brother. I am particularly grateful to my son, Gabriel, for his ongoing insistence that the material in this book be shared.

To my wonderful wife, Lin: nothing I accomplish in this life happens without you. I keep your enduring love and support with me at all times. Thank you for understanding and accepting my inexplicable passion for India and its people, for accompanying me and, indeed, embracing, the literal and symbolic journey that *Stepping Into the River* represents, for helping me think through the shaping of this work, and for the frankness of your editing. I so admire your quiet grace, and treasure the simple existence of your presence.

Lastly, I offer my adoring love to my grandson, Zev Nemiroff, my little New Mexico *lobo*. When you are older, I hope you will read this book, come to love India, understand the importance of social justice, and, maybe, learn a thing or two about your *Saba*.

ABOUT THE AUTHOR

Marc Nemiroff was born and raised in Brooklyn, NY. He earned his B.A. from The University of Maryland, in College Park, MD, and his Ph.D. in clinical psychology from The Catholic University of America in Washington, D.C. He served his internship with The National Institute of Mental Health, St. Elizabeths Hospital, Washington, DC.

Marc Nemiroff has devoted much of his career attending to under-served people in poverty, subsidizing this with his private practice. Nemiroff is the co-author of articles and a textbook pertaining to group psychotherapy with children, as well as eight children's books. He teaches and lectures widely on such topics as childhood and adult trauma, adoption, resilience, Asperger's Syndrome (high-functioning autism), and the philosophy and practice of cross-cultural mental health work.

During the Gulf War, Nemiroff represented the American Psychological Association to the electronic and print media on subjects relating to the effects of real-time televised violence on children. He has been cited in numerous national newspapers and appeared many times on local and national radio.

Marc Nemiroff is a member of the faculty of the Developmental Psychotherapy Program of The Washington School of Psychiatry and is affiliated with the Baltimore-Washington Psychoanalytic Center. He is a graduate of the New Directions writing program of The Washington Center for Psychoanalysis. He maintains a private practice for the treatment of adolescents and adults in Potomac, MD. He is currently at work on a book of linked short stories about the experiences of the first baby boomers.

Made in the USA
Middletown, DE
29 December 2015